Early Black American Leaders in Nursing

Architects for Integration and Equality

Althea T. Davis, Ed.D., R.N., C.S., C.N.P.

NATIONAL LEAGUE FOR NURSING SERIES

NLN
PRESS

Early Black American Leaders in Nursing

Architects for Integration and Equality

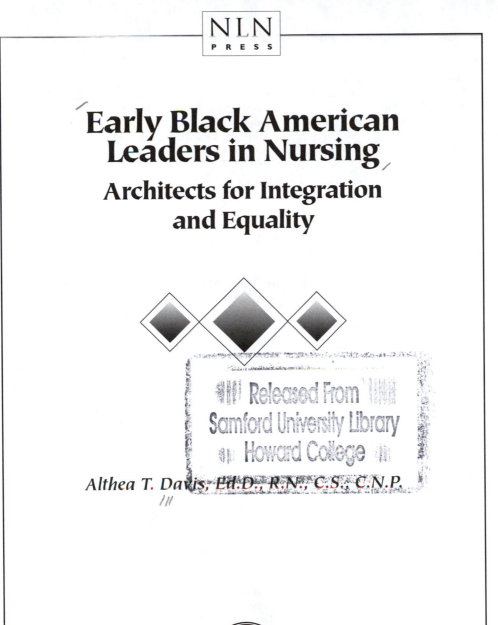

Althea T. Davis, Ed.D., R.N., C.S., C.N.P.

JONES AND BARTLETT PUBLISHERS

Sudbury, Massachusetts

BOSTON   TORONTO   LONDON   SINGAPORE

World Headquarters
Jones and Bartlett Publishers
40 Tall Pine Drive
Sudbury, MA 01776
978-443-5000
info@jbpub.com
www.jbpub.com

Jones and Bartlett Publishers Canada
2100 Bloor Street West
Suite 6-272
Toronto, ON M6S 5A5
CANADA

Jones and Bartlett Publishers International
Barb House, Barb Mews
London W6 7PA
UK

PRODUCTION CREDITS
ACQUISITIONS EDITOR   Greg Vis
PRODUCTION EDITOR   Linda S. DeBruyn
MANUFACTURING BUYER   Kristen Guevara
DESIGN   Argosy
EDITORIAL PRODUCTION SERVICE   Argosy
TYPESETTING   Argosy
COVER DESIGN   Stephanie Torta
PRINTING AND BINDING   Braun-Brumfield

Library of Congress Cataloging-in-Publication Data
Davis, Althea T.
    Early Black American leaders in nursing : architects for
integration and equality / Althea T. Davis.
        p.   cm.
    Includes bibliographical references and index.
    ISBN 0-7637-1009-1
    1. Afro-American nurses—United States—Biography. 2. Afro-
American nurses—United States—History. I. Title.
    [DNLM: 1. Nurses—United States biography. 2. Blacks—history—
United States biography. 3. Leadership. WZ 112.5.N8 D61e 1999]
RT83.5.D38   1999
610.73'092'273—dc21
[B]
DNLM/DLC
for Library of Congress   98-52865
                                                                    CIP

Printed in the United States of America
02 01 00 99   10 9 8 7 6 5 4 3 2 1

Dedicated to
my mother,
Althea Estella Cumberbatch Davis,

my sister,
Miriam E. Davis Williamson,
and my nieces,
Shaneese Williamson Carlton,
Ciara Diamond Carlton,
Nakisha Helen Davis

Preface

BY DR. ALTHEA T. DAVIS

Nursing history as presented in the past taught only selected aspects of nursing history while excluding Black nursing leaders and Black nurses' experience, evidenced in nursing history texts. On rare occasion these texts included fleeting attention to or inaccurate information about Black nurses. Nurse historians and historians have begun to fill the void.

The purpose of this book is to enlighten the reader, provide inclusive history about Black leaders in nursing and women's history, and interpret the history and nursing's past and future implications.

My interest in nursing history was ignited at Teachers College, Columbia University (Department of Nursing Education), a mecca for preparing nurse educators and nurse historians.

The outstanding resources of Teachers College have provided quality experience and an outstanding faculty in history and social studies to further this goal. The support of historical research as an important avenue for scholarly research in nursing by the department of Nursing Education has ensured a cadre of well prepared historiographers for the future (Fitzpatrick, 1977).

Specifically, I was amazed at Teachers College, Columbia University (Department of Nursing Education), when Dr. Patricia Sloan of Hampton University, presented research at the Annual Stewart Conference on Early Afro-American Schools of Nursing. I was fascinated and yet concerned. I was in graduate school, then at the masters level, and like so many nurses there, I had never heard this history. How is it that this history—the Black nurse's experience—had been carefully excluded and virtually buried? At that time my future research agenda was focused.

The value of knowing one's professional history, its context within American history, and the leaders that shaped the profession inclusively as it grew, instills a pride about the leaders who made it possible for Black women to have access to success. We did not merely arrive on our own.

The past is our present, nursing history is alive, our future bears heavily on what we retain of our history. Nursing history provides answers to the past—a revelation through interpretive studies, an understanding of the present—to contemporary problems and issues, and a clear vision for the future.

ACKNOWLEDGMENTS

Through my travels to collect data, I encountered many people who were not only interested in my study, but helpful in their direction and in providing information. In Richmond, Virginia, at the home of Adah Belle Samuels Thoms, I met librarians at the Richmond State Archives who were extremely helpful and courteous. At the home of Martha Franklin in Connecticut, I met many people who contributed to my successful acquisition of information on Martha Franklin. Special thanks to Mrs. Edna Carnegie, curator of the Connecticut Afro-American Society; her assistance and direction are indeed commendable. And thanks to Dr. Reverend Edwin Edmonds, Dr. William Massey, M.D., Mrs. Georgie Saunders, Mr. Leroy Pierce, and Mr. And Mrs. Williams.

At the home of Mary Eliza Mahoney in Boston, I met her relative, Mr. Frederick Saunders. I wish to express my sincere appreciation and special thanks to Mr. Saunders for his time and knowledge. Through his efforts, I visited the neighborhood where Mary Mahoney lived, her church, and the hospital where she trained to become a nurse.

I would like to thank Mrs. Mabel Staupers, nursing pioneer, now deceased, whose memories of Mary Mahoney, Martha Franklin, and Adah Belle Samuels Thoms provided me with personal knowledge; her vitality provided me with inspiration that I shall never forget.

Special thanks to all those involved in the production of this book, including Greg Vis, Linda DeBruyn, and Collin Tobin at Jones & Bartlett and Cecelia Musselman and David Dobmeyer at Argosy. And last but not least, my family. In memory of my father, Edward S. Davis, Sr., and my brother, Edward S. Davis, Jr., and the continual support of my mother, Althea Davis, Sr., my sister, Miriam Williamson, and my brother, Nathaniel Davis.

—A.T.D.

Contents

List of Illustrations

THE BUILDERS*

Henry Wadsworth Longfellow

All are Architects of fate,
    Working in these walls of time;
Some with massive deeds and great,
    Some with ornament of rhyme.

For the structure that we raise,
    Time is with materials filled;
Our todays and yesterdays
    Are the blocks with which we build.

Let us do our work as well,
    Both the unseen and the seen;
Make the house where God may dwell,
    Beautiful, entire, and clean.

Else our lives are incomplete,
    Standing in these walls of time,
Broken stairways, where the feet
    Stumble as they seek to climb.

---

*This poem was read by Adah Belle Samuels Thoms at the end of her presidential address to the National Association of Colored Graduate Nurses at the 1920 National Annual Meeting of the NACGN, held at the Tuskegee Institute, Alabama, August 17–21, 1920. (Presidential Address, *the Builders*, *JNMA*, 1920, p. 75).

Chapter 1

Historical Overview: Cultural Influences

> Opportunity follows struggle, effort, and hard work.
>
> *Shelby Steele*

Among the nursing pioneers posthumously admitted to nursing's Hall of Fame are three Black[1] women:

Mary Eliza Mahoney	1845–1926
Martha Minerva Franklin	1870–1968
Adah Belle Samuels Thoms	1870–1943

They were simultaneously admitted to the newly organized Hall of Fame in 1976. These three women were early leaders in the struggle for integration and equality within the nursing profession. Individually and in concert with each other, these three women worked to upgrade the quality of nursing education and all aspects of employment for practicing Black nurses, as well as much needed respect and dignity. Mahoney, Franklin, and Thoms were role models for the Black professional nurse. Like architects, they were individually and collectively the founders, organizers, builders, and cornerstones of a national movement. These architects sought integration and equality, which required a great deal of effort, hard work, time, and perseverance. And, these early Black nursing pioneers planned and contrived (as if they had blueprints) like architects to achieve their goals.

This book portrays and analyzes the professional endeavors of Mahoney, Franklin, and Thoms. Focusing primarily on their professional contributions to nursing, this book also reveals their families, personalities, and what these three nursing leaders were like as women.

It is apparent from the actual official minutes of the National Association of Colored Graduate Nurses (NACGN) that Mahoney, Franklin, and Thoms knew and respected each other and worked harmoniously together. These three women were also respected as leaders by their Black colleagues. Mahoney was the first Black professional nurse in America (*Minutes of the NACGN* 1911; *18th NEHWC Annual Report* 1879, p. 13). She was the first role model for and the matriarch of Black professional nurses. Franklin was the first nurse to actively campaign for racial equality in nursing. She was the founder, organizer, and first president of the NACGN (*Minutes of the NACGN* 1908, pp. 10–16; Thoms, 1929), and through this organization, a unified movement of national consequence emerged. Thoms challenged the U.S. Army and the American Red Cross regarding their refusal to accept Black nurses during World War I. In 1929, she wrote *Pathfinders*, the first classical text about the plight of Black nurses.

Conceptualizing these three women as the architects and cornerstones of change, they may be viewed as a prism through which illumination of the Black American nurses' struggles for integration and equality were waged during the early part of the twentieth century. As with all prisms, light shines through in three directions, thus providing an individual, collective, and continuous spectrum for analysis.

Viewed through a prism, we can analyze the forces and factors that shaped their lives, professional education and endeavors, collective work toward common goals, and relationship to one another. This book explores factors that provide insight into their emergence, the impetus for their leadership, their initial encounter with one another, and the subsequent professional bond and trusting friendship that spanned many years together. Their relationship, both inside and outside of nursing, had a profound effect upon the integration of the Black nurse into the mainstream of American nursing, and for the future Black nurse.

Mahoney, Franklin, and Thoms demonstrated their historical significance as role models through education, national networking and communication, raising the entry level of education for all nurses (high school diplomas), and improving the quality of nursing education for Black women. These three nursing leaders also organized to eradicate discrimination within the nursing profession, provided leadership, and produced leaders within the ranks of Black nurses. In addition, they fostered feminism, decision making, and choices for women by organizing family planning clinic demonstrations, encouraging Black women to vote, work, consider nursing as a career, continue their education, and seek higher education. These nursing leaders also improved health care for Black Americans through national networking and organization.

These architects were unique representations of Black women trying to enter what had been historically described as a White woman's world–the profession of trained nurses. The stories behind the professional endeavors of Mahoney, Franklin, and Thoms are not only exciting but an interesting and enlightening walk back into their time.

In order to envision the need for early Black American leaders in nursing, a review of the historic nature of American society prior to and following the Civil War is in order. In particular, it is important to note the specific aspects of American life germane to the emergence of Black leaders in nursing, which parallel the scenario in American society as it existed for the Black race, women, untrained nurses, and the advent of organized schools of nursing with training programs.

In the eighteenth and nineteenth centuries, many nurses, both African American and White, were untrained, in the modern sense of the word. They acted as midwives, administered folk remedies, and were called upon to care for the ill in the early days of the United States. Particularly in the South, many of these nurses were Black. When illness struck, it was sometimes the mistress of the slave-holding household who acted as nurse, but more often it was a slave, and most likely a house slave.[2] In most Southern cities, free Black women frequently served as midwives and nurses for both Blacks and Whites (Low & Cliff 1981, p. 652).

The household slave was taught such necessary skills as cooking, sewing, and nursing. Generations of nursing skills that were practiced prior to the advent of formal training programs were learned through cultural heritage and experience.

Cultural tradition and health care for African Americans were synonymous, and knowledge was transported from the mother country, Africa, by medicine men and women who were priest physicians to other slaves. Early distinction between the nurse and the doctor was not evident and this designated cultural healer provided all the care combined in one role. Holistic care, which encompassed physical, emotional, and spiritual health, was commonly practiced. Under the medicine man or woman's supervision, the family and the community were involved in providing health care. Today's concept of holistic care involving the family and the community actually has its roots in this not-so-primitive social health care system.

Tribal medicine, practiced for centuries, provided vast knowledge and experience with roots, minerals, and wild plants in treating illness. Birth control and caesarean section practices were known by slave midwives upon their arrival in the Western Hemisphere. This knowledge later caused suspicious slave owners to believe that the high rate of aborted babies was intentional. Financially, this was a problem, as some Southern plantations had designated breeding places, and breeding was forced to produce selected equalities. Trained midwives and wet nurses therefore were not only prevalent but a necessity because of the strategic breeding of slaves. Thus birth control, transported to America with slaves, formed the basis for today's present flourishing use of herbal medicines and home remedies.

The preparation of a person for this traditional healing role consisted of an apprenticeship along with practical training. The chosen healer was designated either by ancestry, community choice, or divine calling, and was taught by speech, storytelling, and observation. This was a rudimentary form of the teaching principle—demonstration and return demonstration. Therefore, the healer was also a trainer, skilled in practice, teaching, and guidance. Health care generally came from revered older slave men and women who had learned the practice of medicine as a means to survive.

Thus the medical practice that evolved in the slave community was a combination of herbal medicine and roots from Africa, observation of appropriate care of illness in the household when assigned as a domestic slave, and trial and error.

Common illnesses were taken care of by other slaves or overseers. Slave physician services were frequently loaned to other plantation owners during illness. Female nurse slaves were either servants from the big house or older field hands who were no longer able to do a full day's hard labor. They were most often available to care for the plantation owners' families. The slave nurse prepared and administered medicine along with the other care duties (Branch & Paxton 1976, p. 118).

For rare or extraordinary illness, in order to prevent death and to protect the owner's interest, a White physician was summoned to the slave quarters to provide care. Slave hospitals were established in Savannah, Georgia; Charleston, South Carolina; Montgomery, Alabama; and New Orleans, Louisiana.

Mental and emotional illnesses were underreported in the slave community and were directly related to slavery, excessive punishment, and family separation as slaves were sold for profit. Slave narratives reveal women becoming instantly insane—never to recover—when their children were torn from them and sold. These slaves were not institutionalized and were described as bondsmen on the owner's property list.

The nurturing role for Black female slaves was enforced while they still needed nurturing themselves. Slave girls were put to work earlier than little boys. By age four or five, they were assigned to take care of babies and were then sold at an early age to be nurses to White children. One slave girl described her day's work as nursing newborn babies for slave mothers, who returned to the field to cut cane until midnight, and caring for White children too (Sterling 1984, p. 7). In this instance, the nurse was actually a baby-sitter. However, these roles often evolved into identifiable nursing situations (see Illustration 1–1).

Large plantations had nurse houses that were actually primitive day-care centers, caring for up to 100 children that were one month to five years old. The nurse in this setting was usually an older slave woman who had one or two children to assist her. On smaller plantations, an older girl often acted as the baby-sitter.

Having a trained nurse-midwife was profitable for slave owners. Women slaves who trained to be midwives earned substantial sums of money for their owners. A slave woman recounted that her mistress sent her to work with a doctor because so many women in the plantation were having babies. After working with the doctor for five years, he soon began to allow the slave trainee to deliver the babies while "he sat down." "She made a lot of money for her mistress delivering babies, didn't sleep regular hours or have meals on time for four to five days at a time because she always went when called and delivered as many White babies as Black babies and never lost a case" (Sterling, 1984, p. 17). This midwife's account also revealed that she used referral as a mechanism of safety when she recognized a high risk of fetal demise. She explained she was able to determine if a delivery was complicated beyond her midwifery skills and would send for the doctor. If challenged to pursue the delivery, she would stand her ground and insist that they get the doctor (p. 17).

The domestic household nurse (Mammy), housemaid, laundress, cook, butler, and coachman were considered the elite (see Illustration 1–2). This group of household slaves had personal contact with the master and mistress and were fed and clothed better than the field slaves. This group of slaves was viewed as the Black aristocracy. They developed and performed their daily tasks with speech, manner, taste, and habits that set them apart from field hands. The privileged house servant and artisans were usually selected from among the

HEWLETT & BRIGHT.

SALE OF

VALUABLE

SLAVES,

(On account of departure)

The Owner of the following named and valuable Slaves, being on the eve of departure for Europe, will cause the same to be offered for sale, at the NEW EXCHANGE, corner of St. Louis and Chartres streets, on *Saturday,* May 16, at Twelve o'Clock, *viz.*

1. SARAH, a mulatress, aged 45 years, a good cook and accustomed to house work in general, is an excellent and faithful nurse for sick persons, and in every respect a first rate character.

2. DENNIS, her son, a mulatto, aged 24 years, a first rate cook and steward for a vessel, having been in that capacity for many years on board one of the Mobile packets; is strictly honest, temperate, and a first rate subject.

3. CHOLE, a mulatress, aged 36 years, she is, without exeception, one of the most competent servants in the country, a first rate washer and ironer, does up lace, a good cook, and for a bachelor who wishes a house-keeper she would be invaluable; she is also a good ladies' maid, having travelled to the North in that capacity.

4. FANNY, her daughter, a mulatress, aged 16 years, speaks French and English, is a superior hair-dresser, (pupil of Guilline,) a good seamstress and ladies' maid, is smart, intelligent, and a first rate character.

5. DANDRIDGE, a mulatoo, aged 26 years, a first rate dining-room servant, a good painter and rough carpenter, and has but few equals for honesty and sobriety.

6. NANCY, his wife, aged about 24 years, a confidential house servant, good seamstress, mantuamaker and tailoress, a good cook, washer and ironer, etc.

7. MARY ANN, her child, a creole, aged 7 years, speaks French and English, is smart, active and intelligent.

8. FANNY or FRANCES, a mulatress, aged 22 years, is a first rate washer and ironer, good cook and house servant, and has an excellent character.

9. EMMA, an orphan, aged 10 or 11 years, speaks French and English, has been in the country 7 years, has been accustomed to waiting on table, sewing etc.; is intelligent and active.

10. FRANK, a mulatto, aged about 32 years speaks French and English, is a first rate hostler and coachman, understands perfectly well the management of horses, and is, in every respect, a first rate character, with the exception that he will occasionally drink, though not an habitual drunkard.

☞ All the above named Slaves are acclimated and excellent subjects; they were purchased by their present vendor many years ago, and will, therefore, be severally warranted against all vices and maladies prescribed by law, save and except FRANK, who is fully guaranteed in every other respect but the one above mentioned.

TERMS:—One-half Cash, and the other half in notes at Six months, drawn and endorsed to the satisfaction of the Vendor, with special mortgage on the Slaves until final payment. The Acts of Sale to be passed before WILLIAM BOSWELL, Notary Public, at the expense of the Purchaser.

New-Orleans, May 13, 1835.

ILLUSTRATION 1–1
Sale of a Mulatto Nurse Who Was Also a Domestic House Slave and Functioning in a Combined Role.
Courtesy of Schomburg Center for Research in Black Culture, The New York Public Library, New York.

ILLUSTRATION 1–2
The Negro Nurses Stroll on the Sidewalks, Chattering in Quaint French to
a Little Child.
Courtesy of Schomburg Center for Research in Black Culture,
The New York Public Library, New York.

mulattos, thus giving rise to a caste system within the slave group that served to
divide and weaken the oppressed group.

One of the key figures in the socialization of White children was the Black
Mammy, who ran the household, interceded with their parents to protect them,
punished them for misbehavior, nursed them, rocked them to sleep with bed-
time stories, and was like a more attentive, second mother. The influence the
Mammy had on her White charges' thoughts, behavior, language, and personality is far-reaching. The child often formed a deep love for the Mammy and, as an
adult, would defer to her wishes. The early association with Black people, especially the Black Mammy, had a profound influence on the White Southerner.

The historical portrayal of the plump, well-fed, matronly slave with a Mammy rag tied around her head, suckling White babies, depicts a life of pre-ferred status in comparison to a field hand. However, the coveted position of nurse in the master's house was often accompanied with great sacrifice and unforeseen perils. Though the master owned all slaves (house and field), the close proximity of the slave nurse in the house provided ample opportunity for her to become his prey if he so chose, making her the object of the mistress's envy and rage.

Some conscientious slave owners applied the Victorian moral code to the quarters as well as to the big house, but the majority—and their sons, neigh-bors, and overseers—held to a double standard that coupled exultation for White womanhood with disrespect for Black. House servants were particularly susceptible to sexual exploitation. For female slaves, this personal contact with the master or males in his family often had an agenda beyond the scope of mere domestic household help. Sexual exploitation of Black women was so wide-spread as to be general. Some Black women made the best of an inescapable necessity and others tried to strike an advantageous bargain. And yet others tried daring escapes. Here is one such story.

Linda Brent (Harriet Brent Jacobs 1818–1896), born a slave in South Carolina, was a nurse. She came from a family of nurses and she wet-nursed her master's family. She was also mulatto; thus, Brent's future was a fait accompli.

Brent published her biography[3] in 1861—before the Civil War—to awaken the women of the North to the condition of two million women in the South, "still in bondage, suffering what I suffered, and most of them far worse." Brent described the harsh plight of her Aunt Nancy, a nurse in the master's house. Aunt Nancy was required to lie on the floor at the door of her mistress's bed-room. One night in labor, she had to leave and gave birth to a premature still-born baby. Two weeks later, she was required to resume her floor station as night nurse because her mistress's baby needed her services. One can only speculate about Aunt Nancy's frame of mind, the possible experience of post-partum depression, and her emotional stability. However, this initial stillbirth would be repeated throughout her nursing experience in the master's house. Working during the day and deprived of rest as her mistress's night nurse, Aunt Nancy gave birth to six stillborn babies and two more that died shortly after birth.

No doubt excessive work, lack of sleep, and inadequate nutrition contrib-uted to the stillbirths. Her poor health soon made it obvious that this valuable slave—the night nurse—would also die if her routine weren't changed. Thus, she was allowed to sleep in a bed except for when a family member was ill. "'Slavery," wrote Brent, "is terrible for men, but it is far more terrible for women. While all female slaves were subject to sexual abuse, mulattos in partic-ular were exploited" (Brent [Jacobs] 1973, p. ix).

Dr. Flint (as he is called in her true story), a respected community physician then in his forties and Brent's master, employed every imaginable opportunity to keep her within his physical presence in pursuit of a sexual encounter. He would not punish her or allow his wife to punish her. During the night in the big house, Brent slept with her aunt to prevent Dr. Flint from molesting her. She thought this physician, respected in the community, would be too ashamed to try anything in front of her old aunt who had been in his family for years.

As Brent approached her sixteenth birthday, the mistress, realizing Dr. Flint's ulterior motives, found Brent's presence intolerable and cursed her regularly. Frequent verbal altercations occurred between Dr. Flint and his wife over Brent. As the arguments escalated, he decided to take his youngest daughter, then four years old, and move to an apartment he owned. He decided the child needed a nurse and, of course, selected Brent. Struck by fear, Brent realized Flint's strategy to remove her from her aunt's safety net and away from the mistress. "The first night the doctor had the little child in his room alone. The next morning, I was ordered to take my station as nurse, the following night in his room."

Dr. Flint's plot was foiled when his wife somehow learned of his plan for Brent to sleep in his room and a storm ensued. This incident was followed by an interrogation by the mistress in which Brent revealed the prior attempts Dr. Flint had made to sexually exploit her. The mistress, struck with shame, vowed to protect her from Dr. Flint. However, this promise was a potpourri of envy, jealousy, rage, and shame and afforded her little protection. Dr. Flint never gave up his sexual pursuit of Brent and pursued her relentlessly.

In 1839, at the age of twenty-one, Brent escaped from slavery to avoid her master's sexual exploitation, and spent seven years hiding in the crawl space of her grandmother's house before escaping north. Public notices for her capture were posted and Dr. Flint personally went north on numerous occasions in pursuit of Brent. As a fugitive slave, she lived in constant fear of being recognized and recounted numerous hair-raising close calls and maneuvers to avoid capture. While living with this deep fear that was compounded by the fugitive slave laws enacted in 1850, Brent also faced the cruel discrimination as a nurse in the North, a manifestation she thought was everywhere.

Traveling to Albany from New York City on the steamboat *Knickerbocker*, Brent, employed as a nurse, feared discrimination. She advised her employer, Mrs. Bruce, that she would rather not go to supper; however, she was convinced to accompany her. Observing several White nurses go to the supper table with their ladies, Brent followed suit. Her fears were promptly realized when a "colored" waiter told her in a gruff voice, "Get up! You know you're not allowed to sit here!" and thereafter refused to serve her. Brent refused to move. Bruce gave Brent her cup of tea and she was served another cup. Brent was quite hurt over the incident and, although she knew the waiter was doing his employer's bidding, she felt surely he could have spoken in a different tone.

Brent later accompanied Mrs. Bruce to a seaside hotel in Rockaway, Queens, New York. There, thirty-four nurses, Black and White, were employed by vacationing families. Brent, joining the nurses when the bell rang for tea, was singled out, directed to a single chair, and told: "Will you please seat the little girl in the chair and stand behind it and feed her? After they have done, you will be shown to the kitchen where you will have a good supper." Brent described the disdain White nurses directed at her. "Women who were nurses, as I was, only one shade lighter in complexion, eyeing me with a defiant look as if my presence were a contamination."

In sympathy with Brent, this humiliation prompted her employer to order room service. However, this strategy invoked a dual outcry and more pain for Brent. The hotel waiters complained they were not hired to wait on "Negroes." And Black servants and nurses complained that Brent was being treated differently—no doubt they thought—as a result of her light complexion.

Another story involves Nancy Watson, the slave nurse of Henry Grimke and his family. Archibald, the son of Henry Grimke and Nancy Watson, recounted his mother's plight and his family's history. After the death of Grimke's wife (Miss Simons), "he took my mother who was his slave and his children's nurse; her name is Nancy Watson. By my mother he had three children [Archibald, Francis, and John]" (Lerner 1973, p. 52). Grimke willed that this extramarital family be treated as family. However, upon the death of Grimke, they were thrown out by his children from marriage, placed in servitude, and sold back into slavery. Archibald described the experience as emotionally and physically traumatizing.

Slave women were far less healthy than their mistresses, suffering from a host of gynecological and back problems and joint diseases. When Fanny Kemble married, she was unaware that her husband was co-owner of a large slave plantation. When Kemble visited her husband's Georgia plantation, she found every other slave woman with a prolapsed uterus or similar disorder. Female slaves, perhaps recognizing her sympathy, begged her to speak in their behalf for longer lying-in periods after childbirth (Sterling 1984, p. 39).

So many pregnancies ended in miscarriage that slave women were suspected of deliberately aborting. Considering the circumstances of forced breeding, it is conceivable that many tried combinations of roots and seeds either to prevent conception or to bring about abortion. Suspicions of deliberate abortion and accusations that female slaves were just careless persisted. Plantation owners, outwitted on some plantations and without adequate proof for years, discovered that planned breeding was not always successful nor financially beneficial.

In 1849, Dr. E. M. Pendeleton of Hancock County, Georgia, reported that abortion and miscarriage occurred much more frequently among slaves in comparison to White women. He theorized that the cause was either "slave labor (exposure and violent exercise)" or as the planters believe:

> The blacks are possessed of a secret by which they destroy the fetus at an early stage of gestation. All country practitioners are aware of the frequent complaints of planters about the unnatural tendency in the African female to destroy her offspring. Whole families of women fail to have any children (Gutman 1976, p. 80–81).

Dr. Pendeleton noted that there were several domestic remedies to produce an abortion but he was unsure if slave women knew them.

In "An Essay on the Causes of the Production of Abortion among Our Negro Population," a paper read before a Tennessee Medical Society in 1860, Dr. John S. Morgan of Murfreesboro, Tennessee, listed "tansy, rue, roots and seed of the cotton plant, penny royal, cedar berries, and camphor" either in gum or spirits as "remedies mostly used by the Negroes to produce abortion." Morgan and his colleagues agreed, however, that medicines alone would not effect an abortion in a healthy woman. Slaves miscarried because they were overworked and received poor care.

Although planters blamed careless mothers for the high rate of infant deaths, most babies died because of poor maternal nutrition, unsanitary conditions, and inadequate care. Tetanus from improperly dressed umbilical cords was frequent in the slave quarters but rarely seen in the White household.

Dr. Morgan's presentation generated much debate and further revelation of common experiences among planters. Blaming slaves for the high rate of abortion, an owner recounted how his human investment failed to multiply:

He kept between four and six slave women of "the proper age to breed" for twenty-five years and "only two children had been born on the place at full term." The white sold the suspect couple but that did not end the frequent abortions. Neither did the purchase of new slaves. Every new conception was aborted by the fourth month (Gutman 1976, p. 81–82).

This revelation clearly suggests that the couple taught other slaves to prepare the herbal medicine for an abortion. This transfer of knowledge was culturally traditional.

Another owner revealed that he knew of an "old Negro woman" who prepared and supplied the remedy to his slaves and had been instrumental in all the abortions on his place.

Slaves eventually admitted using herbal remedies to effect an abortion or to prevent pregnancy. The impetus to reveal their herbal remedies was not documented but can be imagined within context of the era. Finally acknowledging that they took herbal medicines, their owner was shown the plant that was the preferred and most commonly used remedy.

Dr. Morgan revealed that Tennessee slaves he described as "old women" found rue more effective than tansy. However, rue was not widely grown, whereas tansy was commonly cultivated in plantation gardens. Cotton plant roots were also effectively used by slaves for abortion. And, since slaves were used to pick cotton, it was easily accessible.

Dr. Morgan's colleagues (other physicians) advised him that cotton root was a "most excellent emmenagogue and used it in practice more than any other remedy." Morgan cast doubt on camphor as a stimulant to prevent conception or to produce abortion but quickly added, "from the extent it is employed it must effect something."

Herbal remedies for abortion were widespread among the rural Southern and some Northern White populations as well as among slaves. Current research lends merit to the wise "old woman" remedies who nursed in the quarter and the effects of selected herbs. The herbs known today as contraindicated during pregnancy that correlate with those used by "old women" to counter abusive breeding of Black women include the following:

barberry (uterine stimulant)
pennyroyal (emmenagogue)
rue (emmenagogue)
tansy (emmenagogue) (Romm 1997).

After short lying-in periods, mothers were obliged to leave their infants. On plantations that had no nurse house, slave women either took their infants to the field and left them under a tree, or left them home alone—which exacerbated the lack of care and nutrition they received (enforced neglect) (Sterling 1984, pp. 39–40).

During the Civil War, Black men were purchased from slave owners and placed in Black regiments to fight. Black women served in various military posts as nurses, laundresses, spies, and cooks. G.O. (General Order) No. 390, dated December 8, 1863, stated, "Officers of the Medical Department in Charge of Hospitals for Blacks are authorized to employ as cooks, or nurses, either males or females who will be paid by the Medical Purveyor or Storekeeper at the rate of $10.00 per month. In cases where White females are employed, they will received 40¢ per day. All such persons will also receive one ration per day" (Gladstone, 1993, p. 144).

White females were paid at a rate that provided $12 per month, $2 more than Black males or females. Thereafter, Order No. 390 was amended by order No. 23 to allow Black men and women to work inside U.S. general hospitals. "The employment of person of African descent, male or female, as cooks or nurses will be permitted in all U.S. General Hospitals" (dated January 16, 1864).

After the war, the newly emancipated Black population—free but without financial resources or employment—could not afford health care. Racial discrimination was prevalent and health care was generally inaccessible. The most readily available resources were self-medication and home remedies from those known to be successful healers, such as grandparents, family members, and others known in the community as nurses and midwives (Branch & Paxton 1976, p. 119).

In contrast, health care for White women in the nineteenth century who could afford health care was gender-biased, a result of collusion between her spouse and her doctor. It was politically designed to contain a woman in her proper place. Late in the nineteenth century, medical treatment for women bore very little connection to medicine, but it was undoubtedly effective at keeping certain women—those who could afford to be patients—in their place. Surgery was performed with the explicit goal of taming a high-strung woman and whether the surgery was effective, the very threat of it was probably enough to bring many women into line.

Prescribed bed rest was obviously little more than a kind of benign imprisonment—and the prescriptions prohibiting intellectual activity speak for themselves. In fact, the medical attention directed at these women amounted to what may have been a very effective surveillance system. Doctors were in a position to detect the very first signs of rebelliousness, and to interpret them as symptoms of a "disease" that had to be "cured."

The patent medicine industry also conspired with the physician and his gender bias. This industry preached that menstruation was a serious illness that required a daily dose of their compound. Women with special talents (who might consider themselves exceptional or extraordinary), as well as women in good physical health, were believed to be prone to the perils of femininity. For example, all women were thought to experience "the temporary insanity of her menstruation," and that fact alone should keep her at home (Rothman 1978, p. 24–25).

The issue of race complicated gender in the lives of Black women. Female slaves were not cloaked in traditional Western assumptions about feminine fragility and emotional delicacy, nor were they excused from work for monthly madness or physical weakness from menses. Moreover, when extra hands were required for heavy field work, female slaves were field hands without distinction as to gender.

After the Emancipation, the sexual exploitation of Black women continued in the North and South. "A myth was created that all Black women were eager for sexual exploits, voluntarily loose in their morals and, therefore, deserved none of the considerations and respect granted to White women" (Gerda 1993, p. 163). This myth was self-serving to perpetuate the status quo.

Black women had major hurdles to overcome regarding their image and respect. Particularly in the South, Black women were never addressed as Miss or Mrs., denying them equal respect accorded to White women. And the Black Mammy caricature[4] persisted into the twentieth century, giving cause for alarm at the manner Black women were portrayed in ads, public billboards, and magazines (Neverdon-Morton, p. 179).

The Emancipation Proclamation was signed by Abraham Lincoln on January 1, 1863. However, discrimination was prevalent in American society, and when formal nurses' training began after the Civil War, nursing was subjected to segregation and discrimination (Low & Cliff 1981, p. 652). Therefore, although the proclamation was signed, equality in its broader sense only exists when it is found in the attitudes of a society.

The problem of segregation and discrimination occurred in various forms, such as Black Codes and Jim Crow, escalating to a point where Whites took part in race riots and lynchings, killing numerous Blacks. According to Tuskegee Institute records, at the turn of the century, 115 Blacks were lynched in various communities (Hughes et al. 1983, p. 256). Some Blacks responded to these lynchings in a passive manner, and many felt they had no legal protection against violence. There were a few Black anti-lynching speakers who traveled and made public speeches.

Texas-born Jesse Daniel Ames, a White woman, was a suffragette, a social reformer, and an advocate of civil rights. Ames believed that women could organize and band together to bring about social and political reform. In 1924, Ames became the director of the Texas-based Commission on Interracial Cooperation (CIC) and, thereafter, the national director. African-American women in the CIC believed that if Southern women wanted lynchings to stop, they would have to speak out against the atrocity. In 1930, with the help of twenty-six colleagues, Ames organized the Association of Southern Women for the Prevention of Lynching (ASWPL). They campaigned locally and nationally against the dual atrocity of White men lynching Black men and the acceptance of White men sexually exploiting Black women.

Ames's work in this endeavor helped eradicate the cloak and veil, exposing the racism behind the lynching and thus drawing anger from local Southern groups. However, she gained the national support of influential women's organizations and is credited with a gradual decline in lynchings.[5] Ames had the support and alliance of Black women's groups who organized and campaigned against lynching Black men. In 1905, W. E. DuBois organized the Niagara Movement, which reflected the goals of political, economic, and educational equality for Blacks. In 1909, this movement provided a basis for the establishment of the National Association for the Advancement of Colored People (NAACP).

The economic threat of free Black Americans during the antebellum era cast the die and was a yardstick to measure the economic status of the Black population post–Civil War. Free Blacks, emancipated slaves, and fugitive runaway slaves heightened the anxiety of the White Northern populations regarding a competitive job market and were the subject of Northern legislators at constitutional conventions.

In 1834, a group of Connecticut petitioners rallied their economic causes, citing:

> Those who have just emerged from a state of barbarism or slavery have few artificial wants. Regardless of the decencies of life, and improvident of the future, the Black can afford his services at a lower price than the white man. The sons of Connecticut would soon be driven from the state by the great influx of Black porters, black truckmen, black sawyers, Black mechanics, and Black labourers of every kind (Morrow, 1970, p. 161).

Using the foregoing argument, petitioners urged the various state legislators to adopt appropriate entry restrictions. Fearing riots, virtually every antebellum Northern legislature and Constitutional Convention expressed fear about the Black population entering into occupations that were previously dominated by the White population. Emancipation posed a serious threat of thousands of free slaves arriving North to "undermine wages and worsen working conditions" (p. 161).

The gradual abolition of slavery in the North provided a perfect picture of the economic determinants of the system. In 1973, historian Edgar McManus (1973) analyzed this system:

> When white workers in Boston and New York City took over the jobs of Negro slaves, they also displaced blacks from skills and occupations they had long practiced under slavery. The bitter paradox of emancipation in the North is that it excluded blacks from economic opportunities needed to make a go of freedom. Even the physical presence of Negroes tended to be negated by census takers who underreported the black population. Emancipation in some ways strengthened the tyranny of race by imposing on blacks new forms of subordination that better served the economic interest of the whites (McManus 1973, pp. 196–197).

In 1904, forty-two years after the Emancipation, Fennie Barrier Williams wrote *A Northern Negro's Autobiography,* reflecting the Black women's continued plight following the Civil War and into the twentieth century, in which she stated:

> It is a significant and shameful fact that I am constantly in receipt of letters from the still unprotected colored women of the South, begging me to find employment for their daughters according to their ability as domestics or otherwise, to save them from going into the houses of the South as servants, as there is nothing to save them from dishonor and degradation. Their own mothers cannot protect them and white women will not, or do not. The colored woman deserves greater credit for what she has done and is doing than blame for what she cannot so soon overcome.
>
> Prejudice is everywhere, but it may not manifest itself so brutally as in the South. The chief interest in the North seems to be centered on business and where race prejudice shows itself the strongest.
>
> In the North, the white woman who will recognize and respect a colored woman of intelligence in the same club or church will probably not tolerate her as a fellow clerk in an office or shop.
>
> In the South, the chief interest is in social supremacy and emerges even in the most imaginary approach to social contact.
>
> In conclusion, whether I live North or South, I cannot be counted for my full value, be that much or little. I dare not cease to hope and aspire and believe in human love and justice, but progress is painful and my faith is often strained to the breaking point (Lerner 1973, pp. 165–166).

In 1931, Estelle Massey became the first Black nurse to earn a master's degree in nursing, which she completed at Teachers College, Columbia University. She compares and draws parallels between the history of Blacks in America and the history of nursing in America:

1. Both existed during periods when social order demanded extreme sacrifice.[6]
2. Both emerged from these respective periods with great expectations for future development, only to find they were dominated by caste systems that made it next to impossible to convince the public that either had anything above mediocrity to offer.
3. Both were victims of social ostracism and political exploitation, resulting in prolonged dark periods.
4. Both struggled against the influences of superstition and quackery.
5. Both labored under adverse conditions in order to survive (Massey 1934, pp. 806–810).

The Black nurse was trapped in the midst of two evolving processes of social order: racial and professional. The Black nurse belonged more to a race that was not considered equal to other races. Professionally, the Black nurse belonged to a group (nursing) that was also not fully recognized by society or professional groups as a profession (Massey 1934, pp. 806–810; Kalisch & Kalisch 1978, p. 554). The third issue that the Black nurse faced was her sex and the status of women at the turn of the century. The status of women compared to men was very low and they were barely, if at all, recognized.

Black schools of nursing were organized in response to the discrimination and segregation in American society that affected the nursing profession. The manifestation of this was that Black women in general were not accepted into White schools of nursing. The first four Black schools of nursing are well described in a doctoral dissertation entitled *A Commitment to Equality: Early Afro-American Schools of Nursing* by Dr. Patricia Sloan. These schools were Spellman in Atlanta, Georgia, which opened in 1886; Dixie in Virginia, which also opened in 1886; Provident in Chicago, which opened in 1891; and Tuskegee in Alabama, which opened in 1892. Dr. Sloan stated that most of the nursing faculty in these four schools were White and dedicated to educating Black nurses. In summary, Dr. Sloan stated that the graduates of these Black schools of nursing improved health care and health teaching in their local communities. Black schools of nursing provided the major avenue for many Black women seeking a career in nursing, since the exclusionist policies of White nursing schools precluded admission of Blacks. These exclusionist policies can be documented into the mid-twentieth century.

Women in American society were indeed second-class citizens. But women began to exert an influence on American society during the nineteenth century. Between 1830 and the 1840s, antislavery agitation and other social movements had obtained feminine support. It has been historically theorized that White women operated on two pioneering fronts: their goal or purpose, and as a group of women seeking social equality. However, the Black woman operated on three pioneering fronts: their goal or purpose, as a group of women, and as Black women (Loewenberg, Bogin et al. 1976, p. 20). Perceptive Black women of the nineteenth century were committed to the Black cause, and to the cause of women of any color. "First class citizenship is necessary for uniform opportunities in education, voting, and income. Such equality provides diversity in human and cultural development and the equal right of women to be themselves" (p. 2).

The road toward equality was overtly strewn with impediments. American culture and prejudices conspired to constrain and contain women in their proper place. Black women experienced all the impediments encountered by White women, and in addition, a deep-rooted bias in American society—race discrimination. This analysis is clearly aligned with the endeavors of Mary Mahoney, Martha Franklin, and Adah Belle Samuels Thoms. Their goal was to improve the quality of and access to education and nursing practice for Black nurses. They sought professional justice as a group of women—and as Black women. Indeed, as Black women, their race was the major barrier to professional access and success.

Historically, women were to be seen and not heard. During the nineteenth century, very few women dared to speak in public meetings. Moreover, and in particular, Black women were certainly not to speak. However, Black women who chose to speak publicly, abolitionists and suffragettes, were moved to find words that expressed problems common to the Black population, Black needs, and problems common to women and women's needs. Racial equality was the first order of business for Black women abolitionists, and the movement for women's rights was a close second. "All Black women abolitionists were feminist.[7] But when it came to a question of priorities, race for most of them came first" (Giddings, 1984, p. 55). And, for Black feminists, gender as a category of analysis cannot be understood independent of race and class (Brewster 1993, p. 221).

Many Black women were publicly defiant though action or speeches, displaying bravery in contrast with their proper place in American society. A woman who could and would articulate the cause in public provided an excellent role model for emulation. Black women who had the courage to speak publicly about the injustice of slavery and the inferior status of women gave heart, hope, and courage to other women of any race. Sojourner Truth and Harriet Tubman are representative of Black women who were untrained nurses. Both women became nationally known for their abolitionist and feminist endeavors. However, within the context of Black women in nursing, they represent the era of the untrained nurse who in addition to nursing, chose to become actively involved in eradicating the social injustices of slavery and the inequality of women in American society. The historic advent of formal training schools for nurses and the origins of professional nursing organizations provide the bridge that connects Sojourner Truth and Harriet Tubman with Mahoney, Franklin, and Thoms.

Sojourner Truth (1797–1881), a Civil War nurse, was born Isabella Baumfree, a slave in the village of Hurley, Ulster County, New York. Nursing was an early role for Truth and she was purchased by the Dumont family to be a nurse while still enslaved. Truth was freed by the 1827 Emancipation Act in New York and experienced a calling to travel (journey) and speak out against the injustices of slavery and women's equality (truth). A powerful orator with the gifts of voice and song and a commanding presence, she changed her name to Sojourner Truth. She is well known for her many famous speeches, one of which was at a women's equality convention, entitled "Ain't I a Woman."

Truth has the distinction of having met face-to-face with three U.S. presidents. On October 29, 1869, she met with President Lincoln who told her he heard of her before he became president. In the summer of 1865, she met with President Andrew Johnson concerning the free slaves on the Freedman's Village, but forgot to have him sign her Book of Life. And on May 31, 1870, she met with President Ulysses S. Grant to lobby for racial justice and farm land for Blacks in the western United States.

Shortly after meeting with President Johnson, the War Department assigned Truth to work at the Freedman's Hospital. Her responsibilities were to promote order, cleanliness, industry, and virtue among the patients. At the age of 70, Truth accepted this challenge to primarily promote cleanliness, working in the Washington, D.C., area.

Truth spent a great deal of time in Freedman's Village caring for patients in the hospital. Cleanliness was a major thrust of her work and she organized a group of women to clean Freedman's Hospital. Her philosophy was that the sick can never be made well in dirty surroundings. Truth's strong voice could be heard throughout the corridors: "Be clean! Be clean!"

Truth knew the value of a trained nurse and she urged Congress to provide funds to train nurses and doctors. A legend among early nurses prior to formalized programs in nursing, Truth was an abolitionist, suffragist, and humanitarian. Truth was honored by being the subject of a U.S. commemorative stamp for her contributions to Black history.

Harriet Tubman (circa 1820–1913), a Civil War nurse for the Union Army, was born a slave in Dorchester, Maryland. Fearful of being sold, Tubman escaped at the age of twenty-five and thereafter devoted her life to helping those left behind gain their freedom. Tubman gained a notable reputation as the Moses of her people. With a bounty on her head, she led more than 300 slaves across the Mason-Dixon line via the underground railroad.

A brave and daring scout and spy during the Civil War, Tubman actually was a compassionate nurse and wise healer with knowledge of herbal medicine. Tubman began her career as a Civil War nurse at a hospital set up for contrabands (escaped slaves) on Port Royal, an island off the coast of South Carolina. Here, she bathed soldiers, cleaned and dressed their wounds, and prepared medicinal brews, a skill she learned in the slave quarters.

Concerned over the daily loss of life due to the prevalence of dysentery among the soldiers, Tubman resorted to cultural remedies she knew had worked for generations. She went to the woods and picked tow plants, the root of the white flower that floats on the water, and crane's bill. Returning to the hospital, Tubman boiled the plants and prepared a bitter-tasting dark brew for the soldiers. The dysentery ceased as she nurtured soldiers back to health. Cited for outstanding nursing during the Civil War, a Union general urged Congress to award Tubman a pension. After the Civil War, Tubman financed and built a home for older homeless and Black Americans.

Harriet Tubman, well known for her underground railroad endeavors, was an abolitionist, a nurse during the Civil War, and a women's rights activist. Living near Seneca Falls where the women's movement originated, Tubman was a frequent and familiar face at suffrage meetings. In the 1880s, Tubman addressed a convention chaired by Susan B. Anthony. Ten years later, having maintained her concerns and interests, Tubman traveled to Boston for a party given in her honor by the New England Women's Suffrage Association. And like Truth, Tubman was also honored by being the subject of a U.S. commemorative stamp for her contributions to Black history.

Many other nurses were the forerunners of early trained Black nurses. Susi King Taylor (1848–1912), also born into slavery, worked as a volunteer nurse on the battlefield for more than four years during the Civil War, and volunteered to nurse the sick and wounded soldiers in Company E at a Union camp. King was also a teacher, and taught soldiers to read and write.

Loewenberg and Bogin (1976) surmised that Black women displayed four areas of self-expression: social reform, education, religion, and family life. Their aim was to ignite the American conscience and improve the national character. Black women experienced exclusion not only from professions such as nursing but also from employment in the few areas open to White women, except teaching in Black schools and doing menial work. The problems of race relations were overcome in part by some Black women through their own efforts. They learned responsibility, competence, and initiative in addition to generosity, self-discipline, and steadfastness in the face of adversity. These were among the many creative qualities Black women brought into their own lives and the lives of those around them who needed inspiration. Mahoney, Franklin, and Thoms characterized these areas of self-expression and personal qualities.

Many Black women lived out their lives silently, whereas other Black women responded to internal motivations that shaped and directed their actions, speeches, writings, deeds, and organizational endeavors, all of which revealed their individual leadership and collective interest.

> Black women of eminence took their place on the lecture platform and in the classroom. They joined as pioneers or pioneered social, civic, and educational reform. Black women addressed large influential audiences, traveled to Europe, and linked hands and hearts with others who found error and evil in the ways of society (Loewenberg, Bogin et al. 1976, p. 6).

As early as the eighteenth century, free Black women were involved in women's organizations. However, these organizations actually proliferated during the nineteenth century. "Religion was pivotal to black American life.

Womanhood in each of its phases was sanctioned by religious values. Religion suffused black thought and generated the dynamics for black action" (Frazier 1982).[8] In addition to church organizations, Black women organized around schools and at the community level. While these local groups continued, national Black women organizations began in the 1890s (Loewenberg, Bogin et al. 1976, p. 9).

The achievements of Black women's groups to uplift the race with social service and self-help programs were analyzed by Neverdon-Morton:

1. These women were able to identify clearly the problems affecting them and other Afro-Americans.
2. In spite of limited resources, they were able to create programs that were meaningful and enduring.
3. Their efforts to provide social service programs often served to unify Black communities.
4. The women were willing to work within the existing social order to effect changes, yet, if necessary, they would challenge the attitudes of the larger White society and the conditions favored by Whites.
5. The programs developed by these Black women won for them the approval and support of traditionally White organizations and individuals, and so furthered interracial understanding and cooperation (Neverdon-Morton 1989, p. 234).

Low and Cliff wrote that many Black women provided American history with a rich and proud legacy. Ida Barnett Wells, an author; Josephine St. Pierre Ruffin, who organized the First National Conference of Colored Women in Boston, Massachusetts, in 1895; Mary Margaret Washington of Tuskegee Institute who helped organize the National Federation of Afro-American Women; and Mary Church Terrel, who was leader of the National League of Colored Women all made major contributions. Many of these groups later affiliated with each other and formed the National Association of Colored Women (NACW) in 1896. This organization, which was an umbrella for many smaller groups, focused on the prevalent problems affecting Black Americans, including health, education, and the numerous lynchings. Thus, education and health care were identifiable factors that had an adverse impact on the Black population, and subsequently within professions, as in the nursing profession.

In 1924 through 1925, Ethel Johns, R.N., conducted a national survey of nursing education for Black women sponsored by the Rockefeller Foundation. The purpose of the survey was to ascertain from accredited schools of nursing their policy on admission of Black students. Three questions were asked in the survey:

1. Are colored students admitted to the school of nursing?
2. Are colored graduate nurses used in the hospital?
3. Are any graduate colored nurses serving in private duty in your hospital? (Johns 1924–1925)

Based upon the list of accredited nursing schools published by the American Nurses Association on January 1, 1922, there were 1,696 accredited nursing schools. Almost all, or 1,681 nursing schools responded to the survey, of which 1,588 stated that Black students were not admitted. Fifty-four responses stated that Black students were admitted. Among the schools of nursing reporting that they admitted Black students, twenty-five were connected with hospitals for Black patients, or departments or wings of hospitals for Black patients maintained by city institutions. The majority of the schools that admitted Black students were in the South. Nineteen of the schools that admitted Black students on the list of accredited schools had a capacity of fifty beds or less. The bed capacity reflects the limited experience to which the student was exposed.

From this study it was determined that twenty-seven states had no facilities for the education of Black nurses. These states were Arizona, Arkansas, Colorado, Connecticut, Delaware, Idaho, Iowa, Maine, Maryland, Michigan, Minnesota, Montana, Nebraska, New Hampshire, New Jersey, North Dakota, Ohio, Oklahoma, Oregon, Rhode Island, South Dakota, Texas, Utah, Vermont, Washington, Wisconsin, and Wyoming. There was no accredited nursing school at all in the state of New Mexico.

Twenty states reported having one or more schools of nursing for Black students: Alabama, California, District of Columbia, Florida, Georgia, Illinois, Indiana, Kansas, Kentucky, Louisiana, Massachusetts, Mississippi, Missouri, New York, North Carolina, Pennsylvania, South Carolina, Tennessee, Virginia, and West Virginia.

Black graduate nurses were employed by sixty-six of the institutions responding to the survey. Among these, seven stated Black nurses were employed only in private duty, two reported their use as supervisors, two said Black nurses were employed "on request," and one reported the use of a Black nurse in the "colored contagious ward." Of the sixty-six that reported using Black graduates as specials, eleven stated they were only utilized in caring for Black patients. Two replied that they employed Black nurses when requested and another replied that they were used only "with patient's consent." One hospital stated that they would employ Black nurses if and when they had Black patients.

In 1925, Johns conducted an additional study on the present status of the Negro women in nursing. She found that there were certain factors affecting the general situation:

There are certain definite disabilities arising directly out of racial conflict which bear heavily upon the Negro nurse throughout her training and afterward in the practice of her profession. The degree of difficulty varies, according to the part of the country she lives in, but there is no part where she is free to practice on a basis of absolute equality. No matter how high her personal and professional qualifications may be, certain doors remain closed to her (Johns 1925).

These surveys conducted by Johns impart the historical gravity of the Black nurses' plight, and the doors that were closed to Black women who wanted to enter nursing. Thus, it requires little effort to imagine what it was like for women who wanted to enter nursing or the status of the Black nurse at the turn of the century. It also requires very little effort to imagine what it was like just after the Civil War when formal training schools for nurses were being organized. Moreover, these surveys substantiate that the historic nature of American society produced the need, impetus, and mandate for early Black American leaders in nursing.

Henry Adams made an important historical announcement at the turn of the century. "New varieties of women," he proclaimed, "had been created since 1840; all were to show their meaning before 1940" (Loewenberg Bogin et al. 1976, p. 3). Mary Mahoney, Martha Franklin, and Adah Belle Samuels Thoms were all born after 1840, embodying the new variety of woman and professional nurse who did indeed show their meaning before 1940. The architects were the pathfinders, the builders, and the cornerstones of a movement that sought to improve the status of the Black professional nurse in all aspects. These early Black American leaders were inspired and consequently inspired others to reject futility. They chose to seek personal and professional development, and to realize themselves as full human beings despite the opinions of American society. It was evident that Black nurses needed role models, leaders, and an organization to meet their goals of integration into the mainstream of American nursing.

As in the case with any profession, nursing can be best understood and appreciated if we approach it from the viewpoint of history. Black women heroines are absent from historical literature or given fleeting attention. In general, there is a dearth of literature reflecting Black nurses' experiences. Therefore, many inspiring nurses, their ideas, and professional contributions and endeavors have been lost to history, except as they have been made known or effective in the work of those who followed (Thoms 129, p. 1). Biography takes on greater meaning when it can illuminate the struggles, effort, and hard work that bring about opportunity and change, related to great events, and evaluated as a representation of far-reaching developments.

Notes

1. Black is used throughout this book. Historically, through the present, and by definition of Carter G. Woodson, Black is interchangeable with African American, Afro-American, Negro, and colored. Varied terms have been found in historical documents and have been preserved.

2. Though all slaves were in bondage, their experiences differed. Slaves were real estate or chattel, and were categorized in three groups: *household slaves*, who worked in the master's house; *artisans*, who had a skill, such as carpentry; and *field hands*, who worked the land farming the master's crop.

3. All accounts were true; however, Brent used fictitious names to protect those individuals who facilitated her escape and continual evasion from capture.

4. Black women protested the erection of the "Mammy Statue"—a symbol of a plantation nurse—by sculptor George Julian Zolnay in Washington, D.C. The proposed statue was to commemorate the Mammy holding a White child, as her own Black child cried by her side, unconsoled. Mary Church Terrell, leader of the National League of Colored Women, voiced the concerns of Black women and the statue never came to fruition.

   An aggressive commemorative project reported in *The Baltimore Sun* was described as noble and worthy. Mrs. A. Moore, Jr., daughter of a former slave, donated a site in Berryville, Virginia, to erect a church in honor of Black Mammies.

5. In 1940, no reports of lynchings surfaced. And in 1942, World War II brought about dissolution of the American Southern Women to Prevent Lynching. This organization dissolved just as Black men would enter the Armed Services to defend a country in which life for them had been the threat of lynching (Lunardini 1994, p. 223).

6. This comparison by Massey reflects the monastic and dark ages when nurses had to practice extreme abnegation and work endless hours. In comparison, the Black race in slavery was denied personal interest, intellectual growth, and self-esteem. They also worked very long hours.

7. The definition of *abolitionist feminism* is one of the main theories of nineteenth-century feminism. This theory views that women's oppression and emancipation paralleled the struggle for Black liberation from slavery. And, the nineteenth-century movement to abolish slavery in the United States preceded, and provided strategies for, the development of feminism. For example, Sara Grimké based her feminist ideas on abolitionsist politics (Humm 1995, p. 1).

8. Franklin Frazier observed that the Black church sought to affirm the man as the authority figure in the family. This position would continue to render the wife subordinate to the husband and present a paradox.

Chapter 2

Mary Eliza Mahoney, 1845–1926

You are the architect of your personal experience.

Shirley MacLaine

Mary Eliza Mahoney was the first Black professional nurse in America (see Illustration 2-1). Her professional career was outstanding, which made her an example for nurses of all races. She gave more than forty years of expert nursing service to humanity in addition to her remarkable contributions to local and national organizations. Like an architect, she was the builder of a foundation and a pathway, inspiring Black women to seek a career in nursing. Mary Mahoney was not only a role model for the Black nurse but she also worked diligently for the acceptance of Black women in the nursing profession, and to improve the status of the Black professional nurse.

Mahoney created a path that made the way easier for the future Black nurse, allowing "students to catch a new vision of the heights they could ascend. And a sound builder for the future, a builder of foundation on which others to follow may safely tread" (Chayer 1954, pp. 2–3). Through Mary Mahoney's pioneering interest in the status of the Black nurse and her early support of the National Association of Colored Graduate Nurses (NACGN), she developed a professional bond with Martha Franklin, R.N., and Adah Belle

ILLUSTRATION 2–1.
Mary Eliza Mahoney, 1845–1926
Courtesy of Schomburg Center for Research in Black Culture,
The New York Public Library, New York.

Samuels Thoms, R.N. Mahoney was an inspiration to Franklin, Thoms, and the NACGN (*A Salute to Democracy*, 1951). These three women were early Black American leaders in nursing, and the cornerstones of the NACGN. They worked in support of each other toward the common goals of improving the status of the professional Black nurse.

Mary Mahoney was born during the pre–Civil War era and thus her early childhood years in racially shadowed Boston shaped her cause and concern for her race. In addition, the progressive feminist nondiscriminatory philosophy of her school of nursing (the New England Hospital for Women and Children) broadened her outlook and inspired her to believe that there was hope for her race in nursing. This hospital's philosophy, based on removing professional barriers due to sex and race, fostered Mahoney's initial interest in women's equality and suffrage. Mahoney also pursued these causes within her profession and is thus characterized as an architect for integration and equality.

Given a rare and unique opportunity to demonstrate that she could achieve and succeed, Mahoney channeled her professional goals into seeking equality for Black women in nursing through the NAGCN. Mahoney also sought equality for women and the right to vote; she was a firm believer in equal rights and inclusion versus exclusion.

Suffrage for the Black woman was desirable. However, as the women's national movement gained momentum, old notions about a woman's proper place, which really never ceased, resurfaced. Neverdon-Morton (1989) examined the two issues of relative importance of the vote for women: Black male suffrage and their own rights as Black women. According to Neverdon-Morton, such debates and choices were the subject of discussion but not continuous debate.

> At no time did feminist views largely articulated by white women become more important than racial issues. It was not a matter of choice for Black women; they understood clearly that advancement as women was meaningless if not accompanied by racial advancement. This was not to suggest that concerns unique to women were not important to them, but racial issues were of greater importance. More often than not, the women found time, energy and resources to respond to both gender and racial concerns (p. 177).

Religion and the church were central to Black family life and to women. Mahoney's personality, religion, and civic interest were revealed through her great-nephew's reflections. Mr. Fredrick Saunders speculated that if his great-aunt Mary were alive today, "she would be involved in feminist issues, civic issues concerning all races of people, and in particular the Black race" (Saunders 1987). Mahoney attended the People's Baptist Church, a historic Black church at 134 Camden Street in Roxbury, Massachusetts. She was a very religious woman and attended church regularly. Mahoney's family descendants today remain devoted to their religion.

Mahoney's family had very strong family ties and Saunders frequently visited his great-aunt, who lived about a half-block from his house. She often talked with her family, nieces, nephews, great-nieces and nephews, imparting her knowledge and wisdom. Mahoney typically dressed in long skirts, reflecting the style of her day. Mahoney loved to cook and she was a very good cook. She often cooked for her family and her patients. One of her favorite dishes was plum pudding. Mr. Saunders stated that his great-aunt Mary made "very good plum pudding and she often stored it in her basement" (Saunders 1987). Thus plum pudding was always on hand. Mahoney "never married, however; she had a personal life. She enjoyed being alone at times, valued her privacy, and enjoyed her own company." She knew many people, including those within her surrounding community. However, Mahoney was a business woman; "she was always about her business" (Saunders 1987).

Mary Eliza Mahoney was born in Dorchester, a part of Boston, Massachusetts, on May 7 (Certificate of Birth, 1845).[1] Her parents were Charles Mahoney and Mary Jane Steward Mahoney, and the family resided at 31 Westminster Street in Boston. Mary was the eldest of three, with a sister, Ellen, and a brother, Frank. Her parents migrated north to Boston from North Carolina soon after their marriage. This was a familiar migration pattern for many Black Americans hoping to escape the racially hard environment of the deep South. During Mahoney's early years, she attended the Phillips Street School in Boston.

It was the pre–Civil War era, slavery was predominantly flourishing in Southern states, and free Black Americans did not enjoy the rights and privileges afforded White Americans. Boston gained notoriety as one of the Northern states where free Blacks migrated and escaped slaves sought refuge. However, Boston was not free of racial problems that affected Black Americans. Boston's history of race relations is noteworthy. A closer scrutiny of Boston's environment provides insight beyond the notion of an escape haven for runaway slaves or migrating Southerners. The environmental history sheds light into the pre–Civil War atmosphere, setting the tone overtly and covertly for the post–Civil War era. This environment provides insight into Black family life in Boston—Mahoney's environment as a child, an adult, and a professional nurse.

Blacks in Boston were left behind in the crucial area of economic advancement. Dr. John S. Rock (1825–1866),[2] a prominent leader in the Boston Black community, concluded that Blacks were oppressed. This contrasts with the belief that oppression occurred only in the South. Black male Bostonians could vote, ride the bus, and after a legal battle in 1855, Blacks gained access to public schools. However, Dr. Rock, a sought-after public orator, advised that these were not reasons to conclude that there was less prejudice in Boston than further South. It was five times harder, he said, for a Black person to get a house in a good location in Boston and to acquire even menial employment. Black business in the capital was respected but not patronized. And it was not unusual for Black Bostonians to be openly assaulted by White persons without reason (Levesque 1994, p. 131).

In 1846, the Boston Black community was further described as a segregated population of degradation and dependency. "A prejudice existed in the community and still exists against them on account of their color, on account of their being the descendants of slaves. They cannot obtain employment on equal terms with Whites." Additional analysis of the Boston Black population revealed that "Even when all traces of the Negro is lost by intermixture—the knowledge of African ancestry is sufficient to place him in the proscribed list, to the difficult position sustained by the free colored people of the Northern States" (Levesque 1994, pp. 121–123).

In 1850, five years after Mahoney's birth, Boston's Black population totaled 1,999, by gender 919 males and 1,080 females. In comparison, the White population totaled 501,357, by gender 484,093 males and 501,357 females.

The fugitive slave law signed by President Millard Fillmore on September 18, 1850, provided that any federal marshall who did not arrest on demand an alleged runaway slave might be fined $1,000. Fugitive slave suspects could be arrested on request without a warrant and turned over to a claimant on nothing more than the claimant's sworn testimony of ownership. Officers who captured a fugitive slave were entitled to a fee, which caused unscrupulous officers to become kidnappers of even free Blacks, for it was easy to find dishonest claimants who would falsely swear to ownership and gladly pay a bribe for a new slave. Such was the celebrated case of Solomon Northrup, a free Black man captured, taken South, and enslaved for twelve years.

In two celebrated cases, the courts of Boston ruled in favor of sending the runaway slaves back South. The Boston court refused to accept payment for the slaves in order to prevent the slaves' return. Instead, the court ordered extra guards to the courthouse, held a trial and escorted the slaves to the boat docks where they were sent back South. These measures cost the City of Boston much more money than the monetary value of the slaves as they were designated. The Boston community had mixed reactions to these laws. Though some Bostonians agreed with the court's position, others made their objections known through nonviolent measures such as demonstrations outside the court and prayer vigils at the boat dock of departure until the slaves were out of sight at sea. The Black citizens of Boston compiled and published a Declaration of Sentiments, objecting to these "Negro snatchings" and held a meeting regarding the same at a local Boston church that was well attended. In addition, the Black community of Boston published a list of the state Congressmen who voted for the fugitive slave law, making their political misdeeds known to the public. Although these Congressmen were from the free states, their hearts obviously were with the Southern states. In actuality, any Congressman who voted for the fugitive slave law, was as bigoted as those who actually carried out the acts. To put it mildly, the Black population of Boston was frightened. They lived in fear and were warned not to talk to watchmen or policemen.

In 1851, the Vigilance Committee of Boston printed and posted signs of caution for the Black population. The Boston Vigilance Committee listed contributions to the underground railroad activities run by Harriet Tubman, which was a common avenue for escaped slaves. Many Bostonians were abolitionists, and others simply disagreed with the capture and return of runaway slaves and made their positions known by way of public postings.

In 1857, four of Boston's theaters relegated Blacks to segregated galleries, and two denied them admission. On January 22, 1857, when Mahoney was twelve years old, *The Liberator*, a Boston newspaper, surmised: "The manner and custom of hotels, churches, and theaters indicates accurately the degree to which caste prevails in Boston" (Levesque 1994, p. 129; *The Liberator* 1858).

On March 7, 1860, a feminist protest emerged in Boston. In the midst of a snowstorm, 800 White women who worked in the Lynn shoemaking industry went on strike. Their protest signs read: "American ladies will not be slaves. Give us fair compensation and we will labour cheerfully" (Sandroff 1977, p. 38).

Meanwhile, Black women in antebellum Boston and the North were relegated to labor that was deemed appropriate for their race and sex. Racism and sexism together forced them to work at menial jobs that paid little and conferred minimal status, power, or respect. Unskilled, and with few opportunities for advancement, domestic work was prevalent.

Antebellum nursing by Black women in Boston as reflected in probate records, indicated that home care was seen as employment. The clearest indications of a combined role (nursing and domestic) revealed five women—Elizabeth Riley, Chole Russel, Eunice Sexnex, Cathy Limes, and Ruby Lee— who rendered health care as untrained nurses and household services to the elderly and ill, converting their gender-designated role as nurturers into their livelihood. The dual role set a historic precedent that would later prove difficult to separate.

In 1863, enslaved Black Americans were emancipated. However, their desire and campaign for first-class citizenship was successfully undermined by status and social customs. During the 1870s, Blacks were ruthlessly disenfranchised, a practice designed to relegate them to a step above a slave and many steps below the U.S. White population.

The Civil War caused local conflict in the Boston community as in other New England states. The Boston Irish population blamed local Blacks for the Civil War and race riots ensued. In the Boston Draft Riot, Whites and Blacks clashed on the docks because the Irish felt it was not their war. The Civil War heightened racial antagonism between Blacks and immigrant Irish who demanded they be fired from jobs as porters and dock workers.

Post–Civil War, Black Bostonians charged discrimination at Brigham Restaurant and Globe Theater. In 1865, this led to the state legislature passing a law forbidding racial discrimination in licensed businesses and places of public accommodation. Thereafter, in 1885, multiple complaints of discrimination occurred at skating rinks.

In 1885, the New England Conservatory of Music tried to segregate Black students in its dormitories, and the nursing school of Massachusetts General Hospital denied the applications of Black women, which served to further broaden the bills implemented against discrimination. In 1893, Cambridge barbers refused to cut the hair of Black law students, which further expanded the laws and stiffened penalties in 1895.

No other Northern state passed as many civil rights laws or was as inclusive in its course of antidiscrimination acts as Massachusetts. However, discrimination lies in one's heart and mind. Post–Civil War Boston maintained its distinction of abolitionist Boston and the legal advance of Massachusetts Blacks. Therefore, when a Black Bostonian like Mahoney encountered someone, it either created obstacles or provided opportunities.

A critical analysis of the origins, history, and philosophy of the New England Hospital for Women and Children (NEHWC) provides insight in order to understand Mahoney's acceptance there.

In 1859, the New England Female Medical College invited Dr. Marie E. Zakrzewska to the Chair of Obstetrics (see Illustration 2–2). She was a German who had studied and worked in the hospital "Charite" of Berlin until she came to America to take advantage of the larger yet well-constrained opportunities for women. At her suggestion, the Trustees proposed to add a hospital or clinical department to the college, in which the students might receive practical

ILLUSTRATION 2–2.
Dr. Marie Zakrzewska
Physician, Nurse Educator
Courtesy of Sophia Smith Collection, Smith College.

instruction. Besides her duties as professor in the college, Zakrzewska took charge of the hospital department, with additional responsibilities as housekeeper and superintendent. At her request, eight ladies in the Boston community were elected to fill vacancies in the Board of Lady Managers who then took charge of the clinical department. After three years of service, Zakrzewska resigned her position at the New England Female Medical College and the clinical department was abandoned. However, the ladies connected with it, and some members of the community, had become so impressed with the value of the hospital both as a charity and as a means of furthering the medical education of women, that they were determined to establish a hospital on an independent basis. The friends of this enterprise organized a provisional committee that conducted the general affairs of the institution until its incorporation. The neighboring communities were buzzing with the potential and possibilities this new endeavor had for their community. The hospital work began July 1, 1862, in a small house on Pleasant Street. Four women of the committee assumed responsibility for the rent, and each of the ladies pledged to obtain and provide her proportion of the expenses from month to month.

The New England Hospital for Women and Children was incorporated by the Legislature of Massachusetts on March 18, 1862, with the following purposes:

- To provide for women, the medical aid of competent physicians of their own sex
- To assist in educating women in the practical study of medicine
- To train nurses for the care of the sick
- To prove to the world that a woman can be a good physician and skillful surgeon (*History and Description of the New England Hospital* 1876, p. 8)

Mahoney lived in the Boston community of Roxbury, and at the age of 18, when the NEHWC was incorporated, she began to show an interest in nursing as a career. In 1865, Mahoney began working as an untrained nurse. However, as a Black woman, her status in society was very low, and as a woman, domestic service was generally the primary means of making a living. Although she preferred nursing, she was also employed in the combined role of domestic worker to facilitate her income.

Zakrzewska stated that the most striking feature in the hospital's character was that it was designed to give educated women physicians an equal chance of proving their capacity as hospital attendants with their medical brethren, and to admit only female students to its wards, as all other hospitals closed their doors to women as medical students. This was clearly a feminist endeavor designed to provide equal access to the medical profession and counter the discrimination affecting women or medicine.

The NEHWC was the second of this kind in the United States, the New York Infirmary being its senior by several years. With small means, and with the help of a few friends and two liberal gentlemen physicians, there was a beginning; the hospital and dispensary were both under the direction of Zakrzewska, who had the assistance of two female students for more than a year. The hospital consisted of a dispensary, better understood today as an ambulatory out-patient clinic, and lying-in or hospitalized patients. The immediate care of the patients was in the hands of women, as all resident and attending physicians were women. However, the counsel and help of males was gladly welcomed, as attending in various specialties and as consulting physicians and surgeons (*Annual Report* 1865, p. 12).

According to Dr. Lucy Sewall, resident physician during 1867, a large proportion of the patient population suffered from "female diseases," in many cases for an extended period and with great suffering. When asked why they remained so long without treatment, many of their responses revealed the need for this institution, "Oh, I could not go to a man," stated in a tone so earnest that whether the feelings were wise or not, it was sincere (*Annual Report* 1867, p. 12).

It was questioned by some of the directors of the hospital whether it was not an inconsistency to have male physicians in attendance, as it has always been stated that the advantage of the hospital dispensary is that women can be attended by physicians of their own sex. Zakrzewska's response to this paradox was "patients have their choice of a woman physician" and are given prior notice of who is in attendance. A male physician was never in attendance without a female physician; thus, a woman could choose the female physician (*Annual Report* 1865, p. 18). Making certain the female patient had a choice, Zakrzewska would not promote exclusion.

The day-to-day, high-quality patient care for all established such an excellent reputation in Boston that the house on Pleasant Street was soon too small, and in 1864, the hospital moved to an estate on Warren Street. The benefits of the dispensary practice were fully appreciated by the poor, evidenced by the number of elderly patients who returned for care bringing with them friends who desired similar treatment. This was the only hospital in Boston that received the indigent woman. Zakrzewska, attending physician, stated that nobody who had charge of the poor and unfortunate could deny that this hospital was considered a necessity in a city like Boston.

Mahoney's entrance to this school of nursing was in contrast to American society during an era when Black women were not admitted to White nursing schools. Mahoney's graduation predates the existence of Black schools of nursing. From its small beginnings, this institution was progressive in its philosophy, as stated in its history, that "sect or party, color, or nationality have never been recognized as distinctions for admission to its benefits" (*History and Description* 1876, pp. 25–26).

Although this hospital was established for the care of women by female physicians who were not allowed to join the Massachusetts Medical Society, they welcomed the support of male physicians. They also welcomed all classes of patients, married and unmarried, during an era when an unmarried mother was held up to severe ridicule and scorn. Ednah Cheney, pre–Civil War abolitionist and the hospital's secretary during its early years (see Illustration 2–3), stated that, "Even error has not shut the poor suffering women out from maternity houses where during the solemn hours of her confinement her sister

ILLUSTRATION 2–3.
Ednah Cheney
Secretary, NEHWC
Courtesy of Sophia Smith Collection, Smith College.

women have stood by her." It has been interesting "to see how gently and kindly this class has been treated by the other patients in maternity houses" (NEHWC, History and Description 1876, p. 26).

The NEHWC had "visitors," a historic term very different from the current-day concept of someone visiting a patient in a hospital. These were women who were engaged for a short period of time without pay to talk and read to patients. The influence the visitors had on the patients was remarkable. However, it was difficult for the visiting women to give enough time to talking and reading with all of the patients; thus, a number of younger ladies were invited to join as assistant visitors. The visitors gave the patients that affectionate sympathy and moral encouragement that often tend to facilitate recovery. Their presence was appreciated, and the monthly visitor was always greeted with a warm welcome and praise from doctors, matrons, and nurses (*Annual Report* 1868, pp. 5–7; *Annual Report*, 1867, p. 5). This is the earliest documented description of what is today known as a hospital volunteer, and a clear indication that the hospital believed in the concept of holistic care of the mind and body.

An early annual report of 1865, thirteen years before Mahoney's entrance, revealed that this institution, unlike many other hospitals, embraced Black women and their infants. Their annual reports made special note of their exceptional pride in a racially mixed patient population. Black patients in American society were segregated in separate Black hospitals, separate wings of hospitals, or not admitted at all. Lady visitors commended the hospital's policy of equal access treatment and the racially mixed patient population. This philosophy was reflected in the hospital's annual reports. Table 2–1 presents various visitor views of the hospital.

Although the hospital was in a different location of Boston, the ladies of Roxbury where Mahoney lived were very involved and concerned with the well-being and success of the NEHWC. Who these individuals were was not recorded; however "lady" is a term historically applied to the middle-upper class White women involved in social and community affairs. According to the

TABLE 2–1.
Cultural Diversity: Excerpts from Annual Reports of the New England Hospital for Women and Children

Cultural Diversity and a Diverse Patient Population	**Excerpts from NEHWC Annual Reports**
Race and Race Relations Life Continuum New Life—Near Death	*NEHWC Annual Report 1865* "The hospital has represented striking contrasts the last month. In the lower ward, at either end of the little crib a tiny head protrudes. On closer view you find one of the little occupants is Black, the other White. No antagonism is manifested except in position. You pass from these little beings, just entering upon life, to the patient suffering longing for the last hour to come."
Upper Social Class and Illiterate	"Here is a woman delighting in the companionship of the Brownings; and nearby, another who has no such solace of her weary hours, being ignorant even of her alphabet."
Married, Home, and Children and Unmarried, Homeless	"One tells you of husband and children, longing to welcome her home, in improved health; and another you find looking out upon the world as a great wilderness, without home or friends for her. All agree, however, in testifying to the kindness and skill of [physicians and nurses] and expressing their gratitude that the doors of the hospital were opened to them."

TABLE 2–1. (CONTINUED)
Cultural Diversity: Excerpts from Annual Reports of the New England Hospital for Women and Children

Cultural Diversity and a Diverse Patient Population	Excerpts from NEHWC Annual Reports
Varying Social Class and Freed Slaves Celebrating Diversity	*NEHWC Annual Report 1867* "Our lying-in patients have been of various classes. We have had several colored patients, some of whom had known the bitterness of slavery, and rejoiced over the little ones born into freedom. It is very funny to see the little Black head and the fair White baby peeping out of their cribs side by side. One Indian patient was brought to us in labor by a policeman from the Providence Railroad Station—so that the three great races which divide the Continent were represented in our wards."
Educational Endeavors Open to Males	*NEHWC Annual Report 1874* "Nursing should be considered high and noble work, into which men or women fitted by nature and inclination may enter, without any loss of refinement or social position.

*Davis, A. T. (1996, Spring). Historical roots of cultural diversity in nursing. *Journal of Cultural Diversity*.

NEHWC Annual Report of 1865: "Again, and yet again, we have to thank the ladies of Roxbury for their generous efforts in our behalf. Their annual fair and entertainment gave great pleasure to numerous visitors and brought up the handsome sum of six hundred and eighty dollars" (*Annual Report* 1865, p. 9). This community involvement may have been influential in the hospital's eventually moving to Roxbury where Mahoney lived. Therefore, the Roxbury community was very much in touch with the services and educational endeavors rendered by this hospital from its inception.

Zakrzewska cherished the idea of training nurses, and by 1862, she had trained six. Zakrzewska's early methods of teaching were modeled after the nurses' training at the secular school of the Charity Hospital in Berlin where she had studied midwifery and medicine. These early attempts to train nurses had little or no distinct theory, and the major focus was practical experience. Zakrzewska was described as a strict disciplinarian with high standards for practical work; however, she was affectionately known as Dr. Zak. Her thorough methods produced experienced nurses who were described in the hospital's annual reports as excellent.

Prior to the Civil War, young women were averse to giving six months of work without pay in order to acquire practical knowledge. However, the experience of the Civil War convinced all classes of society that training nurses was as important as all other professions and a crucial factor in health care.

In 1867, the hospital annual report reflects a six-month nursing program with board and instruction that offered no diploma. By 1868, the hospital again considered the subject of educating nurses, offering the advantages of practice at the hospital with board and washing, and low wages after the first month of trial to those who wished to acquire skill in this important art (*Annual Report* 1868). At the time there were few applicants who were able to devote six months, and the hospital was not willing to accept responsibility for a nurse who had spent less than six months training. By 1870, the hospital's annual reports reflect that there was a great demand for competent nurses. The few who faithfully served this time found more than they could do and took rank at once as superior first-class nurses.

Cheney's thorough annual reports provided historical insight into this culturally diverse institution.

By 1872 Zakrzewska had trained thirty-two nurses, although these nurses did not receive a diploma. Some of these nurses were hired by the hospital as head nurses and assistant head nurses; others worked in homes.

On September 1, 1872, the hospital opened its school with a formal training program with a one-year curriculum. In order to fully carry out the purpose of preparing women thoroughly for the profession of nursing, the hospital made the following arrangements:

> Young women of suitable acquirements and character will be admitted to the school of nursing for one year. This year will be divided into four periods, three months will be given respectively to the practical study of nursing, in the medical, surgical, and maternity wards, and night nursing. Here the pupil will aid the Head Nurse in all the care and work of the wards under the direction of the attending resident physicians and medical students.
>
> Our plan is to train them thoroughly, theoretically, and practically. At the end of the year, if we are satisfied with their behavior and their knowledge, we shall give them certificates signed by the hospital doctors. In order to enable women entirely dependent upon their work for support to obtain a thorough training, the nurses will be paid for their work from one to four dollars per week after the first fortnight, according to the actual value of their services to the hospital (*Annual Report* 1872, pp. 7–8).

In September of 1872, the hospital moved to new buildings in Roxbury, the same community where Mahoney lived with her family. A bustling enthusiasm filled the Roxbury community on the hospital's moving day. Physicians, pupil nurses, and ambulatory patients all participated in moving everything that could be carried to this new location. This was the hospital's third and final location, consisting of a main building that would accommodate sixty patients, with a suite for the resident physician and rooms for interns and nurses. The servants lived in a small cottage near the main building.

Linda Richards, the first trained professional nurse in America, who had previously worked as an untrained nurse, entered the school of nursing on the first day it opened. Within 6 weeks, four more pupil nurses entered the school; thus, a class of five students entered the first formal program. These five students were a happy and united group. However, Richards reminisced that she received a cool reception from the previous graduates who did not receive diplomas (1915). Richards theorized that the prior graduates realized that the formalized program would produce better nurses.

The newly organized program included twelve lectures and supervised clinical practice. The physicians who taught Richards volunteered to teach the following classes:

1. Dr. M. E. Zakrzewska, on "Position and Manners of Nurses in Families"
2 & 3. Dr. Emily Pope, on "Physiological Subjects."
4 & 5. Dr. Augusta Pope, on "Physiological Subjects."
6. Dr. Sewall, on "Food for the Sick."
7 & 8. Dr. Dimock, on "Surgical Nursing."
9 & 10. Dr. Morton, on "Childbed Nursing."
11. Dr. Emma L. Call, on "The use of Disinfectants to prevent Contagion."
12. Dr. M. E. Zakrzewska, on "General Nursing." (Annual Report of the NEHWC, 1873, p. 8)

Richards summarized that the clinical instructions usually amounted to a consultation between the intern and the pupil regarding the best way to perform a procedure. The first group of pupil nurses had no entrance exams, textbooks, or final examination. They had no specific uniform; however, they were instructed to wear dresses that were washable. While this training appears to be primitive, it was an initial attempt to produce a formal training program. And, it was far better than what had previously existed, and surpassed any attempts by other American hospitals to train nurses. Upon completing the 1-year requirement, each of the first five pupil nurses were called one by one, and quietly given their diploma.

After the first formal class concluded in 1873, the hospital acclaimed having achieved great success in its new training methods and the 12 lectures. These lectures were required for pupil nurses and open to women in the community who desired this knowledge. These lectures were so well-attended by women in the community that tickets had to be issued for admission (Davis 1991, p. 159–160).

This institution, which pioneered the first formal nursing program, set the appropriate historic image and respect for nursing. The philosophy of this institution was that the education of nurses was as important as the education of their female physicians:

> Our second object is the training of nurses for their duties. This is hardly less important than the first; for the life of the patient often rests quite as much in the hands of the nurse as of the physician. A physician is nearly powerless if his orders are executed by unfaithful or unskilled hands.
>
> Nursing should be considered a high and noble work, into which men or women fitted by nature and inclination may enter, without any loss of refinement or social position, and in which they should receive ample compensation for superior and trained ability (*Annual Report 1874*, p. 6).

In 1875, the curriculum was extended to sixteen months, which was in effect when Mahoney entered this school of nursing. Annual reports revealed this extension was thought to be a step in the right direction. By this time, nursing at the NEHWC received high commendations and was being done almost entirely by pupil nurses, and graduates of the program found immediate employment.

Miss Hawley,[3] a family friend, stated, "Mary went to the hospital to work. She cooked, washed, and scrubbed, and—she got in. A woman doctor wanted her there and that was the only influence she had" (Chayer 1953, pp. 429–431). Mahoney worked at the hospital before becoming a pupil nurse and perhaps lived in the servants' quarters on the grounds of the hospital. When Mahoney became a pupil nurse, she was accepted on her own merits. The directors of this pioneer institution, which was founded by women in medicine, were sensitive to race discrimination in American society. These women physicians had also experienced prejudice (gender bias) in their efforts to practice their profession.

Mahoney was enrolled at the NEHWC on March 23, 1878. Pupil nurses were required to report two weeks earlier for a probationary period. By the time Mahoney entered the school, the women physicians had some fifteen years of experience in the preparation of nurses. Admission requirements were that the applicant must be well and strong, between the ages of twenty-one and thirty-one, and have a good reputation as to character and disposition. Mahoney was two years above the top age limit; however, personal interviews were employed with flexibility in the selection of applicants.

Applicants came from a high class of women with respect to character, intelligence, and kindness, of which all efforts were made to obtain only the best. New students were placed in a position of responsibility and observed to determine if they had the qualities of a nurse. The resident physician, Dr. Dimock (see Illustration 2–4), continued by stating that:

> A fair trial is given, and if they show themselves deficient, we consider that their place is not in this hospital. We are glad of the confidence and approbation which our trained nurses have earned in every direction, and while we feel that much is owing to our system of training, we know that more is due to the high characters and good hearts of the women who have entered our school (*Annual Report* 1874, p. 14).

No entrance fee was required. An allowance of $1 a week was given for the first six months, $2 for the second six months, and $3 for the last four months. This they thought would provide the requisite pupil nurse's uniform for hospital service, a simple calico dress and felt slippers. Twelve of the sixteen months of experience were to be spent in medical, surgical, and maternity wards. The student had 16-hour days and seven-day weeks, and night duty was required. The last four months were to be used to prove the students' competency in all these clinical areas by sending them into the homes of the community for private duty under the direction of the school. By 1877, the school was under the direction of Dr. Sarah M. Crawford; however, all bedside teaching was done by Zakrzewska.

ILLUSTRATION 2–4.
Dr. Susan Dimock
Physician, Nurse Educator
Courtesy of Sophia Smith Collection, Smith College.

Each nursing student was in charge of a ward of six patients, and was responsible for their complete care. There were twelve lectures on position and manners of nurses in families, physiological subjects, food for the sick, surgical nursing, child-bed nursing, disinfectants, and general nursing. In addition to the twelve hours of required lectures, women interns taught the pupil nurses to take vital signs, to bandage, and to perform various procedures. While most of the teaching done at the bedside appeared to be a free-flowing exchange between physicians and nurses, some information remained hidden to the nurses. Pupil nurses were not allowed to know the names of medications given to patients, and medication bottles were labeled with numbers.

Mahoney, like other students, spent twelve months in the hospital's medical, surgical, and maternity wards gaining experience and applying theory to clinical practice. Students made rounds with the doctors every morning and received orders for the patients' care. Physicians were precise, requiring good care for the comfort of their patients. In keeping with the hospital's philosophy, the life of the patient often rested quite as much in the hands of the nurse as the physician.

The head nurse's responsibility and list of duties, according to Helen Kimbal, a head nurse at the hospital during the time Mahoney was a student, was to assist in the education of nursing students. Head nurses at the NEHWC were always graduate nurses. The head nurse's role, in addition to the varied nursing clinical administrative responsibilities, was specifically to instruct and assist all students with their work (Chayer 1954, pp. 430–431) as outlined below.

1. To see that the nurses of the various departments are ready to enter upon their duties at six o'clock and that night nurses are relieved of all duties at the same hour
2. To see that each nurse is faithful in the discharge of her special duties until nine o'clock, when the night nurses are put upon duty, to have entire responsibility in every ward except where a special nurse is appointed
3. To visit wards and get records
4. To preserve or restore harmony
5. To receive new nurses
6. To instruct and assist all students with their work

Although the major responsibility for teaching the nursing program was with the physicians, the head nurse was involved in teaching and supervising the nursing students' clinical practice, providing a joint endeavor and collaborative approach. The value of this by current nursing standards is that the nursing student was provided with an appropriate role model for emulation.

The following account of the 1878–1879 nursing class of the NEHWC provides insight into attrition and the difficulties encountered in meeting the demands and requirements for graduation:

During the past year we have had forty-two applications from young women who were considering the matter of becoming nurses. Ten of these were from the Western and Southern States, and the remainder from residents of New England. Several of this number were, however, deterred from entering by the conditions. Others entered, and, after a month's trial, either were found in some way unequal to their duties, or were not sufficiently in earnest to promise well for their future career and were permitted to withdraw. Others, again, having enlisted in the cause, were called home by serious illness in their families, and in two instances, by failure of their own health. In view of these various contingencies it will seem less surprising that we can report only four nurses as having graduated with diplomas during the year, though several others have now nearly completed their course. These four graduates, Miss Edwards, Miss Mahoney, Miss Clough, and Miss Tarlton, it is believed, are fully entitled to confidence as efficient nurses, and will be sure not to disappoint those who may employ them (*18th Annual Report* 1879, p. 13; see Appendix A).

The requirements for admission appear simple, but the demands for performance were quite the contrary. Out of forty-two students who entered the school in 1878, three White students and one Black student, Mahoney, made the grade for graduation. Mahoney graduated on August 1, 1879, and she received a diploma with the full recommendation, confidence, and approval of the hospital. This must have been a day of acclamation for all four students, and a historic accomplishment in the life of Mahoney, her family, and subsequent Black nurses . . . her professional descendants.[4]

It should be noted that a 16-month course was no short course in comparison to 3-year diploma programs which subsequently evolved. Sixteen hours a day, 7 days a week, for 16 months add up to more than 5,760 hours in the historical 3-year nursing programs. Could Mahoney have known how much her enrollment in a school of nursing was to mean to the future Black nurse, and to nursing in general? Mahoney had a great deal of personal courage and perseverance. However, Chayer speculated that if Mahoney knew the groundwork and legacy she was creating, that knowledge might have helped her over the rough places she trod, eased her fatigue of the 16-hour day, the weariness of the 7-day week devoted to nursing theory and clinical practice.

Linda Richards, the first trained professional nurse in America, substantiated the quality of nursing taught to her at the NEHWC in her memoirs. She stated that she received the affectionate interest and cooperation of Dimock and other members of the NEHWC.[5] In addition, Richards conveyed her feelings about the long hours required while in training. Nursing students' rooms were between the wards and at first they were required to care for patients day and night. The hours of duty were from 5:30 A.M. to 9 P.M. with no particular appointed time off duty. Anna C. Maxwell, who was Assistant Matron at the NEHWC during the time when Mahoney was in training, thought so well of the nursing care given there that she enrolled for the three-month course in maternity nursing (Chayer 1954, p. 430; Richards 1915, pp. 174–176).

Historically, the New England Hospital for Women and Children has claimed three prestigious distinctions (Staupers 1961, p. 2):

- It was the first institution in America to conduct formal courses for nurses.
- America's first trained nurse, Linda Richards, graduated with a diploma from the NEHWC on September 1, 1873.
- America's first Black trained nurse, Mahoney, graduated with a diploma from the NEHWC on August 1, 1879. Mahoney's graduation predates the existence of schools of nursing for Black women.

In addition to these three achievements, a fourth distinction given little attention by scholars in the past is that the NEHWC is the historical root of cultural diversity in nursing. This institution demonstrated the first evidence of pride in a racially, culturally, and socially diverse patient population, and was the first to open its educational opportunities to a Black woman and encourage males to enter nursing.

That Mahoney was a credit to her school of nursing was substantiated by a number of people and events. Perhaps the most significant testimonial is that the New England Hospital School of Nursing continued to accept Black students. By 1899, the NEHWC had trained and graduated five additional Black nurses: Lavinia Holloway, Josephine Braxton, Kittie Toliver, Ann Dillit, and Roxie Dentz Smith (Staupers 1961, p. 2). In the listing of their names, no mention is made as to whether the student was White or Black. However, the early membership records of the NACGN reflected the Black graduates of the program. The school of nursing was organized by the same doctors that had organized the hospital. The hospital philosophy as stated in its history was that "Sect or Party, Color or Nationality have never been recognized as distinctions for admission to its benefits." One of its benefits was to prepare nurses; therefore, this philosophy flowed to the school of nursing.[6] Table 2–2 shows the variety of nationalities served by the hospital.

Although she graduated with the full recommendation of the hospital, discrimination was pervasive in Boston and in American society. It is plausible that Mahoney encountered discrimination with the refusal of hospitals to employ Black nurses. At a time when serious illness was often treated at home rather than in a hospital, Mahoney was almost entirely employed as a private duty nurse. Mahoney gave more than forty years of service to humanity and the nursing profession.

Private duty nurses were expected to work twenty-four hours a day for as long as their services were needed. The nurse was to walk softly, close doors quietly and oil noisy hinges, put things in their proper place, anticipate the patient's needs (without having to ask), and never contradict the patient even when delirious or disoriented. Literally moving into the household like family, the nurse was expected to be cheerful with a helping disposition at all times. How she answered when called was a major aspect of documented references regarding her disposition. The private duty nurse was responsible to the family and the physician.

TABLE 2–2.
Annual Report of the NEHWC
Reflecting the Varied Nationality of Patients Cared for by Pupil Nurses

	The Year Linda Richards Trained at the NEHWC 1872–1873			
Nationality of Patients	**In Hospital**	**At Home**	**In Dispensary**	**Total**
United States	136	208	1,193	1,537
Ireland	44	167	1,223	1,434
England	13	9	94	116
Germany	12	4	114	130
British Provinces	30	2	242	274
Scotland	2		15	17
Sweden	6	2	8	16
Wales	1			1
Bohemia		3	3	6
Russia			3	3
France			3	3
Poland			2	2
Italy			1	1
Switzerland			1	1
Denmark			1	1
Holland			1	1
Portugal			1	1
TOTAL	244	395	2,905	3,544

Private duty nursing facilitated independence and control of one's employment. After a prolonged case, nurses could take time off or temporarily remove their names from the registries to care for a sick relative or friend. Some private duty nurses exercised selectivity in various aspects to avoid unappealing situations, physicians they found troublesome, or cases they did not want. Doctors, nursing leaders, and registries complained bitterly about the practice of case picking. Surveys revealed that the majority of cases nurses refused were contagious, obstetrical, and mental. Other commonly rejected cases were night cases, twenty-four-hour cases, and male patients.

TABLE 2–2. (CONTINUED)
Annual Report of the NEHWC
Reflecting the Varied Nationality of Patients Cared for by Pupil Nurses

The Year Mary Mahoney Trained at the NEHWC
1878–1879

Nationality of Patients	In Hospital	In Dispensary	Total
United States	161	2,869	3,030
Ireland	38	959	997
England	23	134	157
British Provinces	25	259	284
Scotland	1	11	12
Germany	7	94	101
Sweden	6	9	15
Portugal		4	4
France	1	4	5
Poland		5	5
Holland		2	2
Italy		2	2
Fayal		2	2
Bohemia		2	2
Russia		2	2
Switzerland	1		1
Out patients, nationality not taken			354
TOTAL	263	4,358	5,475

*The culturally diverse training nurses received at the NEHWC prepared leaders for national and international contributions to the nursing profession. (A. T. Davis 1996, p. 18.)

Cases generally lasted three weeks or longer. Deprived of sleep, the nurse caring for a seriously ill patient remained awake at night (with two to six hours sleep during the day). During convalescence, the nurse slept on a couch near the patient and generally concluded a case exhausted. The nurse's time completely belonged to the patient and family. A daily walk for fresh air was granted at the patient's and family's discretion. Private duty nursing hours and the length of a case were unpredictable and therefore disrupted one's social life outside of work. "People are too busy to bother to keep up friendships with a person who is never able to say her time is her own" (Melosh 1984, p. 484).

A well-established nurse enjoyed a special status in her community. Her good reputation, excellent nursing skills, stamina, demeanor, and nature of her communication and responses preceded her and created talk within a community. Some nurses formed professional alliances with physicians, which facilitated the security of steady patient cases and congenial working relationships.

Some physicians would not take a case unless a private duty nurse was hired. On the other hand, some physicians complained that private duty nurses were paid too much money and were becoming exclusive. However, nurses took a firm stand on their salaries. This sparked the beginning of nurses taking the position that certain rights were exclusively within the domain of nursing, specifically their salaries.

When private duty nurses became ill, they were dependent on their own limited resources. Private duty nursing was isolating, insecure, and seasonal. Work was abundant in the winter months and less available in the healthier seasons of summer and fall.

Patients and families generally treated their nurses like domestic servants who should eat in the kitchen with other household servants. Asking them to mend, iron, cook, scrub, do laundry, and attend children in any free moment were tasks that made certain the private duty nurse was kept busy at all times.

Nursing manuals devoted to private duty nursing provided guidance on this difficult position. Nurses developed various clever ways to resist and circumvent household tasks, attempting to define and draw clear boundaries regarding their training and special nursing skills, which separated them from the domestic. However, private duty nurses had to tread carefully in defining their boundaries. Always present, the untrained nurse would happily replace them, compounded by old-fashioned physicians who would agree with their patient that household work was par for the course, to be expected and a part of the nurse's duties.

Some advice given to private duty nurses by colleagues was that in order to succeed, one must provide some satisfaction to the patient and family, even when the requests were inappropriate. Therefore, the private duty nurse had to be skilled at negotiating compromising situations with inner professional conflict.[7]

Upon graduating, Mahoney registered with the directory for nurses at the Boston Medical Library (Countway Medical Library, pp. 114–115). Thereafter, she may have also registered with other directories to provide a steady source of income. The Massachusetts Medical Society organized a library of old and new medical books so that doctors would have a place to study and meet. In November 1879, Drs. F. C. Shattuck and C. P. Putnam of the library committee organized and maintained a directory for nurses. This directory was the first of its kind in the United States and it was later emulated by many libraries. The purpose of the directory was to register nurses who were competent and

ILLUSTRATION 2–5.
No. 19 Boylston Place, circa 1890.
Courtesy of the Francis A. Countway Library of Medicine, Boston,
Massachusetts.

could be recommended through an organized headquarters to those who
wished to hire a nurse. Thus, the directory would furnish the nurse's name, references, address, and stated fees. When Mahoney registered with this directory,
she was living at 39 North Russell Street, Boston, Massachusetts.

Nurses paid the directory an annual fee for their registration. Records were
maintained on which nurses kept their fees up to date. The family also paid a fee
for the recommendation the directory provided. These fees were used to maintain the directory and any excess money was used to maintain the medical
library. When the nurses' directory was organized in 1879, it relieved the
library's financial condition. The directory was located at 19 Boylston Place in
Boston, Massachusetts (see Illustration 2–5).

One month before the nurses' directory came to fruition, the library had no
telephone. The telephone was first beginning to take hold upon American society
as the major instrument for communication. Embarking upon this new endeavor,

the library installed a telephone and received an early Boston phone number exchange 113. This telephone was crucial for the success of the directory, allowing it to function as a headquarters for registration, referrals, and a repository for written references. The records show such references for Mahoney as having a "good temper, discretion, and loyalty which were well-tested in the case of a weak, nervous self-indulgent invalid." Further commendations stated "high recommendation," "no faults noticed," "excellent nurse," and "would employ again."

Looking toward Boylston Street, the Medical Library, which organized the first nurses' directory, was located at 19 Boylston Place, the third bay window from the right. With many doctors' offices nearby, Boylston Place was an important thoroughfare, and many patients and family members passed the library daily.

Established on a busy street lined with doctors' offices, the directory was successful from the start. The library committee was assisted by three public-spirited and experienced ladies: Miss M. A. Wales, Miss A. P. Dixwell, and Mrs. M. R. Towne. Their untiring self-sacrifice contributed a great deal toward the success of the directory. By 1881, 412 nurses were registered with the directory, which had high standards and was well managed. Between January and November 1881, seventy-four nurses were referred and hired per month.[8]

The graduates of the NEHWC usually registered at the bureau, so the hospital had the opportunity to follow their subsequent careers, which in most cases, according to the 1883 annual hospital report, was again satisfactory. Whether this was the same directory referred to as a bureau or another one that was organized was not specified.

Mahoney was the only "colored" nurse listed with the directory and her references specified that she was colored. When Mahoney began working for the directory, she charged $1.50 per day and $8 per week (see Illustration 2–6). Some nurses with the directory specified that they charged more for male patients, and they would not accept infectious cases, commonly referred to as communicable diseases. Reflecting her school of nursing's philosophy, Mahoney charged the same fee for male and female patients and she accepted all cases. In 1892, Mahoney increased her wages to $2.50 per day and $15 per week, which was in line with her colleagues.

Families who had employed Mahoney were eager to have her again and employed her frequently. Her well-known calm, quiet efficiency instilled confidence and trust, which in some instances overcame the barrier of color. The Arms family for whom she worked many times gave testimony to her skill as an excellent nurse. A lifelong friendship was established between Mahoney and the Arms family and they were like her family. Mr. Arms said, "I owe my life to that dear soul." Sarah Beatty of the NEHWC staff wrote, "I used to hear her praises sung everywhere around Boston and its suburbs" (Chayer 1954, p. 431). There was a legendary aura to Mahoney's nursing practice. As a private duty nurse, she was very successful in Boston and nearby towns where she was usually employed by the best families (Thoms 1929, p. 9). She gained a notable reputation for quality nursing; she was called to New Jersey by a patient who had been one of her "babies." Whether she delivered this baby at birth and/or cared for the baby as a baby nurse, or both, is unknown. She would have been exceptionally skilled in nursing care of the mother and newborn being a graduate of the New England Hospital for Women and Children, since most of the patients were maternity and newborn. Mahoney was called once to Washington by a friend whose husband, an Army surgeon, had become ill with tuberculosis. She accompanied him to North Carolina when his prognosis indicated that he would not recover.

Although varied health care concepts were couched in different terms historically, Mahoney had progressive ideas about nursing and health care. Applying present-day concepts to Mahoney's nursing care, she believed in and practiced holistic health care, the philosophy embodied in death and dying, and concepts reflected in the philosophy of Hospice. Her sister Ellen Mahoney Foster had similar beliefs. Saunders stated that his great-aunt Mary's motto was service for humanity, which was clearly manifested in her nursing care

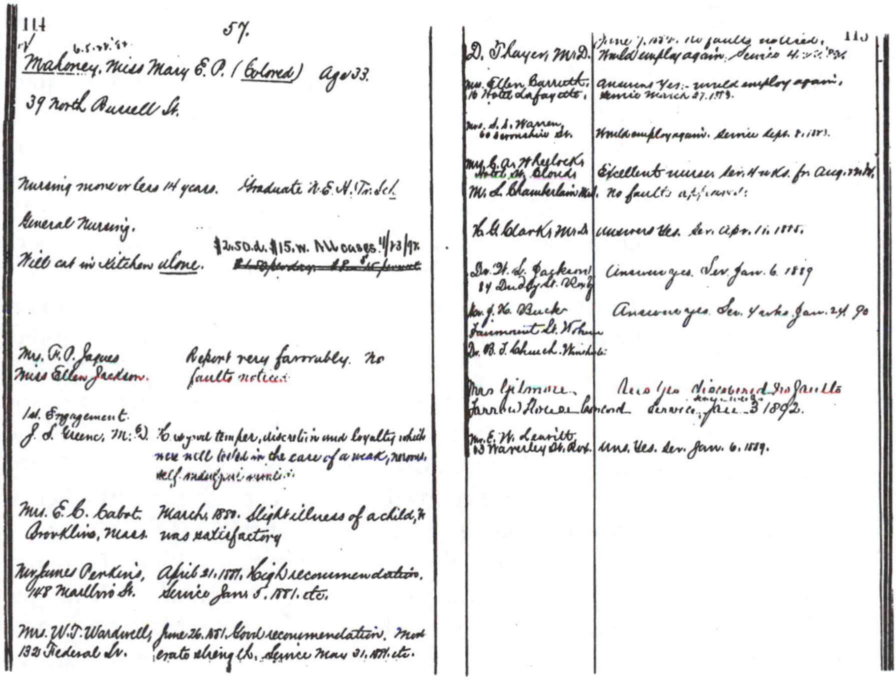

ILLUSTRATION 2–6.
References, Mary Eliza Mahoney.
The directory organized a book entitled **The Directory,** *which contained the names and references of the nurses registered with the directory. Mary Mahoney was the 57th nurse to register with the directory.*
Courtesy of the Francis A. Countway Library of Medicine, Boston, Massachusetts.

(Saunders, Personal Interview 1987). Mr. Fredrick Saunders stated that his grandmother, Ellen Mahoney Foster, also practiced nursing. Ellen Mahoney married, becoming Mrs. Ellen Mahoney Foster. She bore five children, one of whom is the mother of Mr. Fredrick C. Saunders (Saunders, Personal Interview 1987). Ellen Foster lived to be 91 years old.

Mahoney was an avid believer in the role of the professional nurse. She believed that nursing was not a domestic job and, in fact, the historic domestic aspect of the nurse's role should be eradicated or diminished. Mahoney protested the prevalence of domestic responsibilities in the nurse's role. Mahoney, a very calm woman, did not believe in making much of a fuss. She once cautioned Thoms to be calm, stating, "You won't get any place by fussing." Mahoney would and did make her point when she chose to. As a trained nurse, her protest took an interesting form. Although Mahoney performed required domestic responsibilities in addition to direct patient care, she performed them with dignity. One way of distinguishing herself in protest was by refusing to eat in the kitchen with the household help, separating herself and choosing to eat alone[9] (Friends, Relatives Pay Tribute 1973, pp. 9, 14; Saunders, Personal Interview 1987). Mahoney also indicated on her reference that she would eat in the kitchen *alone*. Distinguishing herself from household servants, in quiet protest, Mahoney would eat alone. And, she answered "yes" when called.

Mahoney had ties with Boston's Black medical circle through her good friends Dr. John B. Hall and his wife. Hall was a prominent Roxbury physician and leader in the National Medical Association. He was also a noted scholar and publisher. He wrote articles about tuberculosis as Boston's major health problem among the Black population. No doubt Mahoney was abreast of current health problems through nursing meetings which, in addition to business, encompassed health care problems and visits to hospitals and patients' homes (Staupers 1961, pp. 19, 206). In addition, this friendly alliance would have afforded her the medical view on current health care matters; therefore, she was more than likely prepared to care for patients with tuberculosis. Hall and his wife lived approximately a half-block from Mahoney.

Mahoney's graduation in 1879 occurred sixteen years after the Emancipation Proclamation. It is noted in history textbooks that this was the beginning of a pathway for Black women to obtain a career in nursing. Linda Richards, America's first professional nurse, and Mary Mahoney graduated from the same school of nursing only six years apart. However, it took Mahoney's professional descendants seventy-two years to achieve membership in the American Nurses Association (ANA), and in some Southern states, longer. It was the post–Civil War era; segregation and discrimination were prevalent in American society, and like other aspects of society, nursing was affected.

It is apparent that Mahoney loved nursing sick people; however, she also had other concerns. She recognized the need for nurses to organize and work together, and that a mechanism was needed to improve the status of Black nurses in professional life. One of the problems that always distressed her was that when Black women applied for admission to schools of nursing, they usually were not accepted. This was a major concern for Mahoney; even though her school was not prejudiced, she knew other schools of nursing were and rejected Black applicants. In addition, many Black women experienced rejection from White nursing students regarding their acceptance (see Appendix B).

New schools of nursing were established in other localities but their student bodies were, with few exceptions, entirely White. It was soon apparent that for Black students to obtain a nursing education, separate Black schools would need to be established. Goodnow reported that it had never been the custom in America to take colored females, even those with a small amount of Negro blood, though no objection was made to females of other dark-skinned races. The belief was that Black individuals were intellectually inferior to White individuals (Kalisch 1978, p. 559; Myrdal 1944, pp. 137–153). This discriminatory attitude forced most Black women to train at all-Black hospitals. However, like most but not all nursing schools of the late nineteenth century and early twentieth centuries, the nursing school focused on the need for patient care at the expense of the education for Black nursing students.

Mahoney was able to become a member of the Nurses Associated Alumnae of the United States and Canada organized in 1896 (which became the ANA in 1911) through her alumnae association. She was one of the few early Black members of the ANA. However, because of her own personal experiences and in communication with her colleagues, she was convinced that if Black nurses in every section of the nation were to have the privilege of ANA membership and the other professional expectations that White nurses were granted, Black nurses would have to organize.

Mahoney enthusiastically welcomed and supported the organization of the NACGN founded by Martha Franklin, R.N., in 1908, to collectively improve the status of the Black nurse. The first meeting of the NACGN was held in New York City in 1908. Mahoney's good friend, Dr. John B. Hall of Boston, was in town for the National Medical Association Convention, a Black physicians' organization. He invited the group to hold its next annual meeting in Boston in 1909.

In 1911, Mahoney's compassionate interest in women and children emerged in a different form. Although she is best known for her many years of private duty nursing in homes in which she was loved by the babies and families she nursed, she was also employed in other areas. Mahoney was in charge of the Howard Orphan Asylum in King's Park, Long Island, New York, in 1911. At the Annual NACGN Convention in 1911, Mahoney's honored presence was acknowledged: "We have the first colored graduate in America" (*Minutes of the NACGN* 1911, pp. 37, 40). At this convention, Mahoney reported on the work being done at the Howard Orphan Asylum (Of Interest to Nurses 1911, p. 400).

Newly emancipated Black women who were destitute came North to establish homes for their children. Unable to place them in the colored New York Asylum run by White administrators, twenty children were taken into a home owned by Mrs. S. Tillman, a philanthropist, who lived at 104 East 13th Street in New York City. Tillman cared for these homeless children for six months. This home converted to an orphanage was later moved to Brooklyn, New York, with Tillman as its first director.

The orphanage was located on Dean Street and Troy Avenue, in an area now known as Crown Heights.[10] Subsequently, it was organized into an association that lasted until it was incorporated by a general act of the legislature, under the name and title of the "Brooklyn Howard Colored Orphan Asylum of Brooklyn, New York, September 7th, 1868." Their major philosophy and goals were as follows:

- shelter, protect and educate the destitute orphan children of colored parentage
- to instruct said children in useful trades and occupations, and
- to receive, take charge of and disburse any property or funds which at any time and from time to time, may be entrusted to such society for the purpose aforesaid. (*17th Annual Report* of the Howard Colored Orphan Asylum, 1885, p. 21)[11]

The Brooklyn Howard Colored Orphan Asylum, though it always had some private financial support, for many years had all or nearly all Blacks on its board and primarily all Blacks on its staff. In contrast to the New York Colored Asylum, which employed mostly White staff, the Brooklyn Asylum had closer ties to the Black community and was distinctly poor in comparison to the New York Asylum. In 1906, the orphanage moved to St. James, Long Island, as a farm school with aspirations for being a great industrial school for Black youths in the North.

This orphanage, born out of a humane interest for Black women and children in need, had a mission and a cause, which Mahoney was a part of as the head of this orphanage. Mahoney was in this position for one and a half years and retired in 1912 (Walton 1929, p. 10).

Mahoney rarely missed a national nursing meeting. Her local and national involvement was extensive. Mahoney represented the NACGN at the Conference of Health Officers in Boston, Massachusetts, June 3–5, 1921 (Nurses Section: Nurses Notes 1921, p. 218). Her presence was always especially noted and held in high esteem. She was a great force in getting other nurses to join the NACGN, and she presented a challenge and an inspiration to its members.

Mahoney was a pioneer for civil rights in nursing and she worked diligently for the acceptance of Blacks in the nursing profession and for the improvement of the status of the professional Black nurse. The last national meeting Mahoney attended was in August 1921 in Washington, D.C., when the association was a guest of the Freedman's Hospital Alumnae Association. At this convention, the nurses of the NACGN had a meeting at the White House with President and Mrs. Warren G. Harding.

During the early years of the NACGN and within society in general, Mahoney was concerned about the progress of women as citizens, and worked diligently for their equality. She was a strong supporter of the women's suffrage movement. The 19th Amendment giving women the voting franchise was ratified in 1920. In 1921 at the age of seventy-six, Mahoney was among the first women in her city to register to cast her vote for the first time. On this historic occasion, she was accompanied by her good friends who lived nearby, Dr. and Mrs. John B. Hall.

After the death of her parents, Mahoney leased a small apartment at 48 Warwick Street in Roxbury where she lived until her death. She became ill in 1923, suffering with metastatic cancer of the breast for three years. After many years of remarkable service, her life was near its end. A close family, Saunders continued to visit his aunt when she became ill. On December 7, 1925, Mahoney entered the NEHWC, where her career had begun. She was brought to the hospital by a social worker, delirious and so ill that she was taken to her room on a stretcher and immediately placed on the critical list. During the admission process, she gave the names of her sister Ellen Mahoney and Mr. Arms, a family she had nursed that was like a family to her, as the next of kin. She was given the most expert medical and nursing care; however, she was beyond help. Mahoney died at the New England Hospital 25 days after her admission, on January 4, 1926, at the age of 81 (Death Certificate #E001828 1926, p. 12).

Mahoney was an architect and a pioneer in nursing; her graduation, and almost forty years of nursing thereafter inspired many Black women to pursue successful careers in nursing. The NACGN established an award in Mahoney's name in 1936, in recognition of her example to nurses of all races (see Appendix C). The award was established to honor her active participation in nursing organizations and her efforts to raise the status of Black nurses in the nursing profession. The Mary Mahoney Award recognizes significant contributions by an individual nurse or a group of nurses to integrate within the profession. Adah Belle Samuels Thoms was the first nurse given the award. Thoms described Mary Mahoney as her friend with an unusual personality and a great deal of personal charm. When the NACGN dissolved in 1951, the award was continued by the ANA. It is presented biennially. The committee for the Mary Mahoney Award reviews all nominations for the award and selects a nominee for endorsement by the ANA board of directors. The criteria for the award reflect Mahoney's professional endeavors:

1. The nurse nominee or nominees must have made a significant contribution to opening and advancing opportunities in nursing to members of minority groups.
2. The nurse nominee or nominees must also have made a significant contribution to nursing.
3. The contributions or the impact of the contribution of the nurse nominee or nominees toward integration, retention, and advancement of minorities in nursing and nursing in general must be current and demonstrated.
4. The contribution of the nurse nominee or nominees must reflect that the outcomes had an influence on nursing and on the advancement of intergroup relations. (ANA, National Awards Pamphlet 1983–1984)

Further recognition of Mahoney include the naming of several local affiliates of the NACGN in her honor. The Mary Mahoney Club of Omaha, Nebraska, was organized in 1937. Since the organization was formed, it has been concerned with general community welfare. Among its many community projects are the following:

- Annually sponsoring a boy in day camp
- Making layettes for the Visiting Nurses Association
- Awarding a $100 scholarship to assist a student entering a school of nursing
- Sponsoring visits by each of the National Executive Secretaries, resulting in improved relationships between the nurses and hospitals in Omaha

This local club in Nebraska is indeed an honor to Mahoney, who had a special love for babies and children. Thus, sponsorship of a boy in day camp and making layettes for the Visiting Nurses Association are a reflection of her major interest in nursing. Mahoney was also concerned about the education of Black nurses and their status thereafter. She would have enthusiastically supported a scholarship fund as well as any endeavor to improve working relationships.

The Mary Mahoney Nurses Local of the NACGN in Boston was reorganized in 1944 with the following objectives:

- To function fully in the recruitment of prospective student nurses
- To move towards 100 percent participation in local, state, and national organizations
- To provide information concerning educational and employment opportunities
- To stimulate professional development
- To further intergroup relationships that the nurse may become a vital part of the community whole

The group presented its first conference on Saturday, June 10, 1944. The program pamphlet was indeed an honor to Mahoney and complimented the characterization of an architect. The program head in bold typeset print stated:

<u>Building Today for Tomorrow's World</u>
The Mary Mahoney Nurses Local of the NACGN presents a Conference on Nursing Problems Today and Tomorrow

Mabel Staupers, then executive secretary and later president of the NACGN, knew Mahoney very well, and honored her by sharing her experience in a lecture entitled "Ten Years with the NACGN." The cost of attending the program was fifty cents, and for nursing and high school students, there was no charge, providing access to most interested nurses. The goals of this conference were indeed a reflection of Mahoney's goals as the first Black professional nurse with an interest to pave the way for future Black nurses.

She was also honored in 1954 by the ANA on the 75th anniversary of her graduation. Among many other honors, the Community Health, Education, and Welfare Department established a center in her memory located in Oklahoma. This center provides health care services to isolated communities.

An additional honor is the Mary Mahoney Life/Health Care Center located on the same vast historic grounds of the NEHWC. In 1969, the in-house patient services of the NEHWC closed. The center was reestablished as an out-patient facility and renamed the Dimock Community Health Center. This facility is a comprehensive family center, a major regional center for alcoholism, a regional health vocational training center, and a comprehensive day-care and child development center with a senior citizens' office. This facility directs and operates its own programs, and serves as a site for low-cost space to thirteen other independently operated community health programs. Thus, the Dimock Community Health Center is the modern incarnation of the NEHWC, old in tradition yet young in enthusiasm. In addition, it offers health care services on a continuum throughout the developmental life cycle.

> What began more than 100 years ago as a reaction to discrimination against women continues today, in part, as a reaction to discrimination against middle and low income populations who do not receive adequate health care. What once was a training center for nurses is today a center for training manpower in several health fields (*Annual Report* 1984–1985, p. 33; *The Dimock Story* 1985, p. 33).

The main administrative building of this historic complex is the life center, named in shared honor, The Mary Mahoney Health Center and Clinics, which is housed in the Linda Richards building. Richards was a pioneer in mental health nursing and education in the United States and in Japan. Richards and Mahoney both rose to national prominence through their professional involvement in nursing organizations.

Mahoney is buried in Sable Path, Woodlawn Cemetery, Everett, Massachusetts. Mahoney's family members also purchased burial plots near her resting place. In August 1973, the ANA and Chi Eta Phi, a Black nursing sorority affiliated with the National Council of Negro Women, Inc., restored Mahoney's gravesite. Mahoney's family assisted in locating the grave that was made into a shrine, with a private unveiling ceremony held on August 15, 1973. The gravestone is a gray granite, four-foot, sculpted monument that features a hand-carved bust of Mahoney with the legend, "The First Professional Negro Nurse in the U.S.A." On the reverse side of the monument is an image of the Mary Mahoney Award (see Illustrations 2–7 and 2–8).

In 1976, Mahoney was posthumously admitted to nursing's prestigious Hall of Fame along with Martha Franklin and Adah Belle Samuels Thoms. In 1979, honorary membership was posthumously bestowed on Mahoney by Chi Eta Phi, Alpha Chapter, Washington, D.C.

Mahoney's honors have never ceased.[12] On September 1, 1984, the ANA and Chi Eta Phi held a national rededication ceremony in honor of the high ideals for which Mahoney stood and for the professional foundation Black nurses inherited. The theme of the ceremony was *From Whence We Came*. Mahoney earned the title Architect of Integration and Equality. Nurses from all over the United States traveled to Boston, over the 1984 Labor Day weekend to join in the first national pilgrimage to Mahoney's gravesite. Many Black professional nursing descendants, nurses of all races, and Mahoney's family descendants were present. In addition to many speakers from Chi Eta Phi and the ANA, Mabel Staupers, who knew all three architects, addressed the gathering in Mahoney's honor. Mr. Fredrick C. Saunders, Mahoney's great-nephew, also addressed the gathering; this was one of the weekend's highlights as he shared with the group his personal familial knowledge of his aunt. A well-planned tribute in prayer, ceremony, and song reflecting Mahoney's courage and perseverance was held at her gravesite, including this excerpt (also see Illustration 2–9):

> LEADER: In the grand order of the universe, our Lord God wisely has chosen women and men to serve him in each era. Such a servant of our Lord God was Mary Eliza Mahoney.
>
> AUDIENCE: In the life of Mary Mahoney, let freedom ring.

ILLUSTRATION 2–7.
Mary Eliza Mahoney Grave Site, Front View.
Courtesy of the American Nurses Association, Washington, DC.

ILLUSTRATION 2–8.
Mary Eliza Mahoney Grave Site, Rear View.
Courtesy of the American Nurses Association, Washington, DC.

LEADER: Mary set on a journey. A journey as a role model that was destined to have an impact on the future of nursing and the Black nurse. Her calm efficiency instilled confidence and trust, which overcame the barrier of color. It was a journey that carried her from Boston to Brooklyn to Washington, portraying the attributes of an expert practitioner, an exemplary citizen, an untiring worker in both local and national professional organizations.

AUDIENCE: In the name of Perseverance, let freedom ring.

LEADER: And now we come to the one hundred fifth anniversary of Mary Mahoney's graduation from the New England Hospital for Women and Children. We are thankful for a woman of Mary Mahoney's stature, a sound builder for the future, a builder of foundations on which others to follow could safely depend.

AUDIENCE: In the name of Personal Courage and Perseverance, let freedom ring.

LEADER: We are thankful for Ms. Mahoney's contributions to nursing, to the cause of freedom, and to the history of Blacks in professional nursing. We are thankful for her noble legacy to continue the journey of full participation in nursing for all nurses.

ILLUSTRATION 2–9.
Paying Tribute at Mary Eliza Mahoney Gravesite.
Courtesy of the American Nurses Association, Washington, DC.

ALL: We are grateful for the exemplary and distinguished
life of Mary Eliza Mahoney!
IN THE NAME OF PERSONAL COURAGE AND PERSEVER-
ANCE, LET FREEDOM RING! (ANA and Chi Eta Phi, Program of
the National Pilgrimage, 1984)

Notes

1. Research by the author at the Boston State Archives revealed an Eliza
   Mahoney born October 1846, in Springfield, Massachusetts, mother's
   name Ellen and father's name Dennis (Vol. 16, No. 38, p. 219). Mahoney's
   middle name was Eliza; thus this document was considered. Also listed is
   another Mary Anne Mahony (note last name does not contain an *e* and is
   thus spelled differently), both September 28, 1847, in Roxbury, Massachusetts. Mother's name is also Mary, father's name is John (Vol. 23, No. 22,
   p. 133). Mary Ellen Chayer, Professor Emeritus, Teachers College, Columbia University, cited that an unverified report gave Mary Mahoney's birth
   date as April 16, 1845, in Roxbury. Dorchester is near Roxbury in Boston,
   and the close proximity of dates lends credibility to the date cited above in
   Dorchester since the April 16 date is unverified. The mother's name on the
   Dorchester birth certificate is Mary, providing additional correlation.
2. Dr. John Swett Rock, a celebrated Black Brahmin, was a practicing dentist, physician, lawyer and one of the most sought after lecturers. He was
   the first Black lawyer allowed to argue cases before the U. S. Supreme
   Court. (Grain and Pub 1994, p. 113)
3. Mahoney's brother Frank married and relocated to Portland, Maine, in a
   two-family house with the Hawley family. A lifetime friendship was
   established between Mahoney and the Hawley family. Through this
   friendship, we are indebted for some intimate details of Mahoney's struggles for an existence in the field of nursing. Miss Hawley relocated with
   her family to Brooklyn, New York, and became a schoolteacher.
4. Retracing Mary Mahoney's footsteps on the grounds of the New England
   Hospital for Women and Children, now known as the Dimock Health Center, Boston, Massachusetts, located on the same grounds, was a fascinating
   experience. A visit to this historic hospital (by the author on January 16,
   1987, accompanied by Mary Mahoney's great-nephew, Mr. Frederick C.
   Saunders) provided a sense of knowing Mary Mahoney and, in addition,
   insight into the setting where Mahoney's nursing training took place. The
   same buildings that were built in the 1800s are still standing, clearly reflecting
   nineteenth-century architecture and the connecting ground-level tunnel-like
   pathways. The main administrative building, the Dimock Building, is named
   in honor of Linda Richards, who was the first trained nurse in America. This
   building houses the Mary Mahoney Clinics and Health Care Center.
5. This support was counterbalanced by the sullen disapproval of the older
   type of (nondiploma) nurses whom Linda Richards was to supersede, and

the stubborn resistance to change of the more conservative doctors. Thus, her fond memories also included challenges.

6. There was, however, a quota system of accepting two Black nursing students per year, later altered to one Black student and one Jewish student.
7. Mahoney enjoyed cooking and cooked for her family and patients.
8. After being in existence for thirty-five years, the profits from the directory began to decrease. This was due to increasing competition from the large number of nurses' directories or registries that sprang up in Boston. On December 31, 1914, the directory closed its door after a long honorable career. Dr. C. P. Putnam remained the director of the directory during its entire existence.
9. Harriet Brent, pre–Civil War nurse, experienced being told to eat in the kitchen with the servants; thus, this household servant designation persisted as well as the dual connotation for Black women.
10. This community area is noted historically because it includes the first settlement area where Blacks who migrated North after the Civil War in Brooklyn resided. It was named Weeksville.
11. In early 1917, Blacks pouring into Northern cities looking for war work brought many more Black children who needed shelters. The Brooklyn Howard Colored Orphan Asylum had severe financial problems. As an asylum it eventually closed during World War I under tragic circumstances in which lack of money and wartime shortages led to permanent injury to children. However, Howard exists today in the form of Howard Memorial Fund and its primary function is scholarship aid to needy children.
12. In March of 1985, the ANA sought a commemorative postage stamp in honor of Mary Mahoney. The request was denied by the U.S. Postal Service.

Chapter 3

Martha Minerva Franklin, 1870–1968

> What has counted for women historically is to organize,
> organize, and then organize some more.
>
> *Laura Liswood*

Martha Franklin was one of the first nurses to campaign actively and nationally for racial equality for Black nurses (see Illustration 3–1). She was the architect for collective action by Black nurses in the early twentieth century. Through her pioneering interest to improve the status of the Black nurse, she was the founder and organizer of the National Association of Colored Graduate Nurses (NACGN). Through this organization, a unified movement of Black nurses sought the needed respect, dignity, and equality within the profession and in American society. "Martha Franklin, whose light and life enriched the nursing tradition, was the Bernadette who envisioned and founded this remarkable unit" (A Salute to Democracy at Mid-Century 1951).

Through Martha Franklin's roles as founder and organizer of the NACGN, she came to know Adah Belle Samuels Thoms, R.N., author of *Pathfinders*, and Mary Eliza Mahoney, the first Black professional nurse in America.

ILLUSTRATION 3–1
Martha Minerva Franklin, 1870–1968
Previously from the collection of the Connecticut Afro-American Society,
New Haven, Connecticut. Courtesy of Dixwell Community House, New
Haven, Connecticut.

These three nursing pioneers had a special friendship and alliance of support and respect for each other with common goals that would improve the status of the Black nurse in American society. They were all posthumously admitted to the Nursing Hall of Fame in 1976.

Franklin was born on October 29, 1870, in New Milford, Connecticut. Her parents were Henry J. Franklin and Mary E. Gauson Franklin. Mr. and Mrs. Franklin both lived in New Milford and were married there on November 7, 1866. To the Franklins, three children were born. The eldest was Florence, born July 24, 1868,[1] Martha was the middle child, and the youngest was William, born July 4, 1873 (see Illustration 3–2). Martha Franklin's father was a laborer. During the Civil War, he served as a private of Company K, 29th Connecticut Volunteer Division.

History texts have given but fleeting attention to Martha Franklin, but lent mass confusion as to her race. Franklin was light in complexion and mistakenly characterized as White (Stewart & Austin 1963, p. 211). Specific family documents, however, provide family history, primary data, and evidence that immediately substantiate her race as Black. Martha Franklin's maternal grandparents and mother were designated as colored on the certificate of birth of Martha's mother. Henry Franklin (Martha's father) was designated as colored on the certificate of marriage for Martha's parents; thus, his parents would have been designated as colored (see Illustrations 3–3 through 3–5).

Franklin's light complexion was the result of fair-skinned Blacks marrying fair-skinned Blacks. This pre– and post–Civil War historic phenomenon was analyzed by William Gatewood (1996) through the prism of a Southern community:

> Although the White ancestry of mixed slaves was of varied social origins, well-to-do white fathers of fair-complexioned mulatto children sometimes granted them freedom and provided them with education, property, and opportunities unavailable to other Blacks. There came into existence throughout the South free mulatto families who tended to marry other light-skinned individuals. Viewed with favor and leniency by the white establishment, they intricately related to one another by blood and marriage and were sometimes so fair in complexion that it was impossible to discern any African ancestry (p. 2,445).

When abolitionist crusades moved through the South and the opposition to miscegenation heightened, sizable numbers of light-skinned Blacks migrated out of the South. Mulatto and light-skinned Blacks were believed to have a higher level of intelligence than darker-skinned Black and were favored in employment.

Light-skinned Black individuals coped with perceptions of marginality in various ways, from embracing Black identity and assuming leadership roles in movements combating anti-Black discrimination to disappearing from the Black world and assuming White identity. It is evident from Franklin's family

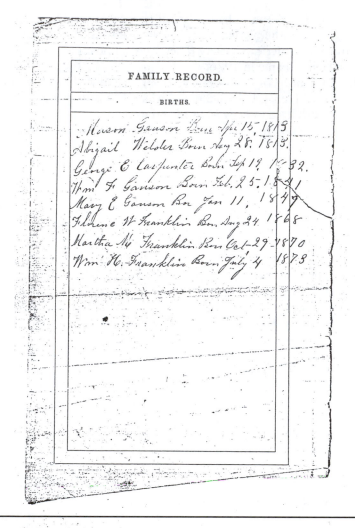

ILLUSTRATION 3–2.
The Franklin Family Tree
Mason Gauson and Abigail Welder (who married Mason Gauson) were Franklin's maternal grandparents. It is unknown to the author who George C. Carpenter was in the family; however, the surname Carpenter appears again in Martha Franklin's family Bible under marriages. William F. Gauson was Franklin's maternal uncle, and Mary E. Gauson was Martha Franklin's mother. Franklin's name then appears in her family Bible, along with her siblings, her older sister Florence Franklin, and her younger brother William Franklin.
Previously from the collection of the Connecticut Afro-American Society, New Haven, Connecticut. Courtesy of Dixwell Community House, New Haven, Connecticut.

State of Connecticut, } ss. Town of New Milford.
County of Litchfield,

I, JOHN S. ADDIS, Town Clerk of said Town, and *ex-officio*, Registrar of Births, Marriages and Deaths, and Custodian of the Records thereof,

Do Hereby Certify, That it appears from the records of⎽⎽⎽⎽⎽**BIRTHS**⎽⎽⎽⎽⎽for said town that Mary Gauson was born January 11th, 1848

FATHER: name, Mason, Gauson; age, 36; color, Colored; occupation, days workman; residence, In the District

MOTHER: name, Abigail, Gauson; age, 34; color, Colored. Residence in the District

IN TESTIMONY WHEREOF, I have hereunto set my hand, and affixed my official seal, this⎽⎽⎽6th⎽⎽⎽ day of ⎽⎽⎽⎽June, 1927⎽⎽⎽⎽

Attest,

⎽⎽⎽⎽⎽⎽⎽⎽⎽⎽⎽⎽⎽⎽⎽⎽⎽⎽⎽⎽⎽⎽⎽⎽
Registrar of Births, Marriages and Deaths.

ILLUSTRATION 3–3.
Certificate of Birth of Mary E. Gauson.
Previously from the collection of the Connecticut Afro-American Society, New Haven, Connecticut. Courtesy of Dixwell Community House, New Haven, Connecticut.

State of Connecticut, } ss. Town of New Milford.
County of Litchfield,

I, JOHN S. ADDIS, Town Clerk of said Town, and *ex-officio*, Registrar of Births, Marriages and Deaths, and Custodian of the Records thereof,

Do Hereby Certify. That it appears from the records of ....**MARRIAGES**........ for said town that Henry J. Franklin and Mary E. Gauson were married November 7, 1866.

GROOM: name, Henry J. Franklin; age, 21; color, colored; birthplace, New Milford, Conn; Residence, New Milford, Conn;

BRIDE: name, Mary E. Gauson; age, 19; color, colored; birthplace, New Milford, Conn; residence, New Milford, Conn;

Minister or Magisteate, Rev. D. Murdoch; licensed and recorded by C. C. Noble, Regrs.

IN TESTIMONY WHEREOF, I have hereunto set my hand, and affixed my official seal, this............ 6th ....day of............ June, 1927 ....

Attest,

John S. Addis.
............Registrar of Births, Marriages and Deaths.

ILLUSTRATION 3–4.
Certificate of Marriage, Mary Gauson to Henry Franklin, Martha Franklin's Parents.
Previously from the collection of the Connecticut Afro-American Society, New Haven, Connecticut. Courtesy of Dixwell Community House, New Haven, Connecticut.

State of Connecticut,

County of Litchfield, } ss. Town of New Milford.

I, JOHN S. ADDIS, Town Clerk of said Town, and *ex-officio*, Registrar of Births, Marriages and Deaths, and Custodian of the Records thereof,

Do Hereby Certify. That it appears from the records of_____BIRTHS_____for said town that   a female child was born October 29, 1870.

FATHER,   name, Henry J. Franklin;   birthplace, New Milford, Conn; age, 25;   color, colored;   residence, New Milford, Conn;   occupation, laborer.

MOTHER: maiden name, Mary E. Gauson;   birthplace, New Milford, Conn; age, 22;   color, colored;   residence, New Milford, Conn;

Physician certifying, James Hine, M. D.

IN TESTIMONY WHEREOF, I have hereunto set my hand, and affixed my official seal, this_____6th_____day of_____June, 1927_____

Attest,

John S. Addis.

Registrar of Births, Marriages and Deaths.

ILLUSTRATION 3–5.
Martha Franklin, Certificate of Birth. (See Illustration 3–2.)
Previously from the collection of the Connecticut Afro-American Society,
New Haven, Connecticut. Courtesy of Dixwell Community House, New
Haven, Connecticut.

documents that she was Black, and it was quite clear from her endeavors that Franklin had a firm Black identity.

The Franklin family resided at 63 Cherry Street in Meriden, Connecticut. Martha Franklin attended Meriden Public High School and graduated on April 9, 1890, with a diploma "as most honorable testimonial of her scholarship and character" (see Illustration 3–6). Franklin's father died in 1892 and Mrs. Franklin encountered grave difficulty in collecting her husband's Civil War pension. Franklin was very helpful to her mother in this endeavor and aided her in writing numerous letters to the government to collect her husband's pension, and additional letters to acquire the correct amount. On February 18, 1893, Mrs. Mary Franklin was granted a pension of $8 a month. In 1917, this pension was increased to $25 per month. However, Mrs. Franklin never received the increase and by 1925 many letters had been written and she sought a pension attorney to handle the matter. In 1928, after a long battle of wits and writing, her pension was finally increased to $40 a month.

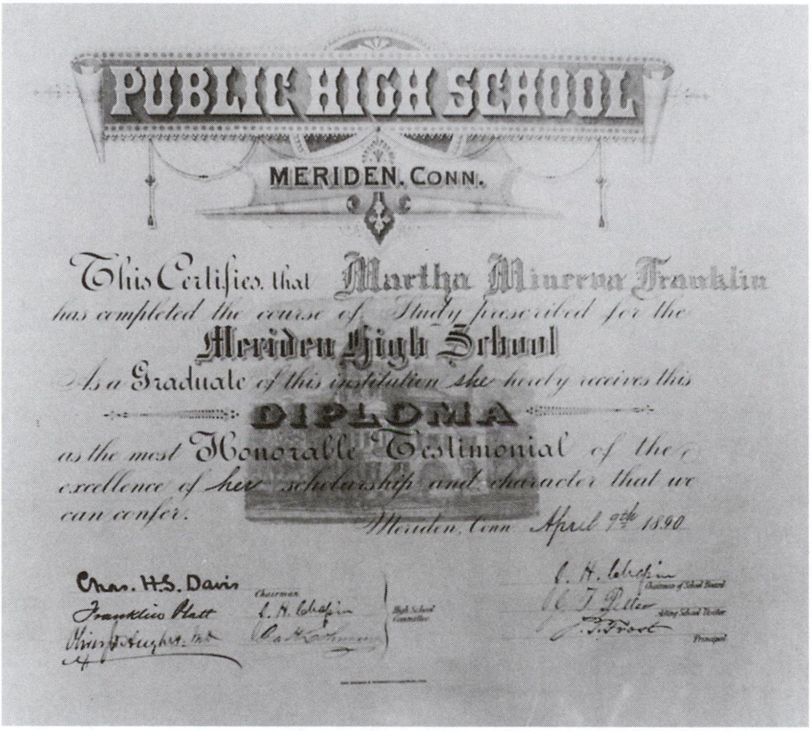
PUBLIC HIGH SCHOOL

MERIDEN, CONN.

This Certifies, that Martha Minerva Franklin
has completed the course of Study prescribed for the
Meriden High School
As a Graduate of this institution she hereby receives this

DIPLOMA

as the most Honorable Testimonial of the
excellence of her scholarship and character that we
can confer.

Meriden, Conn April 9th 1890

Chas. H. S. Davis
Franklin Platt

ILLUSTRATION 3–6.
Martha Franklin, High School Diploma.
Previously from the collection of the Connecticut Afro-American Society, New Haven, Connecticut. Courtesy of Dixwell Community House, New Haven, Connecticut.

Connecticut's history in general of race relations is noteworthy, particularly in Meriden where Franklin grew up as a child and in New Haven where she later relocated. Martha Franklin was born in 1870, the post–Civil War era. The history here could possibly shed light on the pre–Civil War era, which inevitably set the tone overtly and covertly for the post–Civil War era. This environment provides insight into Black family life in Connecticut—Franklin's environment as a child, an adult, and as a professional nurse.

Connecticut was one of the first colonies to pass a law against the slave trade in 1769. In 1784, the legislature of Connecticut passed an act declaring that all persons born of slaves after the 1st of March in that year should be free at the age of twenty-five. This act was amended in 1797 to the age of twenty-one, at which time gradual emancipation was legalized in Connecticut.

While these early anti-slavery laws are impressive, Connecticut restricted the importation of slaves primarily because it inhibited the flow of Whites to the colonies, and simultaneously made it difficult for the poor White population already there to find jobs. Thus, its primary motives were economic and political.

As a whole, Blacks were not welcome in the North. Throughout the pre–Civil War era, there was increasing competition between free Blacks (like the Franklin family) and foreign immigrants for manual labor work. Racial prejudice became more common as Irish and German immigrants feared that former slaves would come north in great numbers and take their jobs. And three states—Connecticut, New Jersey, and Pennsylvania—which once allowed Blacks to vote, amended their constitutions restricting suffrage to White males only. Barred from regular elections the Black population developed mock imitations of the election proceedings; the winners were accorded unofficial power within the Black community.

Travel for a Black person, enslaved or free, was precarious and dangerous. In 1774, Connecticut enacted statutes that specified any Negro, Indian, or mulatto servant found off his master's property without a written pass could be returned by anyone to his owner who was then compelled to pay a fine. These statutes also included "free Negros" stopped without a pass who would be fined themselves. This, of course, requires analysis. Clearly the "free Negro" was not truly free and required written passes to move about town or risk the threat of being taken into slavery or being fined.

> Any negro, Indian or mulatto servant found wandering out of the town or place to which he belonged, without a written pass was liable to be seized by anyone, taken to authorities and delivered to his master. The master must then pay an accrued charge, in other words, a fine. [. . .] Any free negro traveling without a pass shall be stopped or taken up. He shall pay all charges rising thereby.

This law was in full effect when the U.S. Constitution was adopted and was not rescinded until 1797. Therefore, up until that time, free Blacks and mulattos were associated with servants and slavery by the police and established Connecticut laws.

By the late eighteenth century, Connecticut's Black population had reached a definitive status in which they were characterized as free people of color. The Black population lived a life totally separate from the rest of the community in that they were more or less forced to develop their own social and political customs.

In 1819, there was intense anti-slavery agitation in many parts of Connecticut. New Haven recorded resolutions that declared slavery an evil of great magnitude, and that it was the solemn duty of the government to prevent its existence by all constitutional means.

During the early to mid-nineteenth century, Connecticut maintained separate educational facilities for the White and Black populations. The struggle in Connecticut to secure equal educational opportunities for the Black population preceded the national emancipation of slaves. About 1830, the subject was broached of a founding college in New Haven for the education of Black people. Bitter opposition, racial prejudice, and discrimination were so high that in 1833, the legislature of Connecticut passed an act that made it illegal to establish schools in the commonwealth for the education of Blacks from other states. The passage of this law was celebrated in Canterbury by the ringing of the church bells and the firing of cannons. This law was specifically aimed at Prudence Crandall.

Connecticut is well known for two celebrated legal cases that received significant attention and made history. Prudence Crandall, a schoolteacher in 1831, admitted a Black student to her school in Canterbury, Connecticut. White parents removed their children. Crandall then proposed a school for Black children. Although these events happened before the 1833 Connecticut bill making the same illegal, Crandall was condemned by her peers and fellow residents, intimidated, harassed, and finally jailed. Thereafter, an angry mob burned down Crandall's school. Perhaps fearing for her safety, Crandall left Connecticut.

New Haven also made history when it tested the international laws of slavery. An unprecedented trial took place in the New Haven federal court—the Amistad, which Steven Spielberg recreated as a multimillion dollar movie production. In 1839, Cinque, a captured slave, led a successful mutiny on board the ship *Amistad,* killing the captain and the cook. Tricked by the remaining crew, the Africans were steered to Long Island, New York, rather than toward their homeland. The slaves were captured, jailed in Connecticut, and tried for mutiny and murder. Court proceedings lasted all winter and generated so much interest and excitement that law students at Yale University were excused from classes to attend the trial. Abolitionists came to their defense, and an Amistad Committee was formed that contributed legal defense funds. A dream team of brilliant lawyers was responsible for the Africans' defense. Cinque and other slaves were acquitted; however, countersuits and appeals followed. The case was ultimately argued before the U.S. Supreme Court. Moved by the plight of the captives, John Quincy Adams, then seventy-three, and a

Congressman from Massachusetts and nearly blind, argued the case before the U.S. Supreme Court. On March 9, 1841, after an eight-and-a-half-hour eloquent argument by Adams, the Supreme Court ordered Cinque and his fellow Africans freed. They returned to Sierra Leone in 1842.

Temple Street Church in New Haven was one of the foremost stopping-off points for fugitive slaves en route to Canada. It was founded by two underground railroad agents, Reverend Simeon S. Jocelyn and Amos G. Bemen, the latter of whom was the church's first Black pastor. New Haven certainly was not without racial bias and prejudice. However, it is said that the town of New Haven lived up to its name both prior to and during the Civil War, providing shelter to many slaves bound for freedom. Many New Haven citizens were involved in this work.

In 1850, New Haven had 989 free Black Americans. Of these, 360 attended school and 167 were considered illiterate (Wesley 1908, p. 173). In 1865, five years prior to Franklin's birth, Connecticut by popular vote denied Black residents the right to vote. In New Haven, Black residents petitioned for the end of discrimination and segregation in public schools and on July 7, 1869, the Board of Education moved to incorporate the colored children into the regular school system. However, throughout the the 1880s the school laws of Connecticut made no distinction as to race and color and continued to establish separate schools.

Meriden, Connecticut, where Franklin lived during her early years, was a stopover point for the underground railroad. At this time, the Black population of Meriden was strikingly the minority. In 1810, the general population had 1,249 residents. By 1870, the year Franklin was born, there were only 77 Black residents. In 1880, the general population of Meriden had 18,000 residents and of those 18,000, there were 162 Blacks. In 1890, the year Franklin graduated from Meriden Public High School, there were 227 Black residents in Meriden. By 1900, the general population totaled 28,000, of which only 207 residents were Black. (U.S. Census Records of Meriden, Connecticut).

The Women's Hospital of Philadelphia was incorporated on March 22, 1861, by a group of twenty-four women, a feminist movement designed to counter the discrimination affecting women in medicine. It was stipulated that the chief resident had to be a woman. The unique purposes for which the hospital was established were as follows:

- The treatment of women's and children's diseases by women physicians
- To furnish facilities for clinical instruction to women engaged in the study of medicine
- The practical training of nurses (History of the Nurses Training School, p. 7)

Informal efforts to train nurses began as early as 1863; however, it was 1872 before a formal curriculum was developed with a systematic course of lectures given by resident physicians. In 1877, the program was extended from one to two years, the latter being in effect when Franklin entered the program.

In 1895, when she was twenty-five years of age, Franklin entered the Women's Hospital Training School for Nurses of Philadelphia. The school of nursing was under the direction of Dr. Anna M. Fullerton, as chief resident physician and superintendent of nurses. Application for admission to the school was made to the chief resident physician. The hospital records noted with much satisfaction that applications came from young ladies whose intelligence and education qualified them to be teachers, but who turned from that over-crowded profession into this new vocation where the demand far exceeded the supply and where there was ample opportunity for intelligence and refinement to give distinction (*Annual Report* 1877, p. 8). Applicants had to be between twenty-one and forty-five years of age and have good character and habits, for which references were required. Applicants were cautioned that something more than health and strength were required as qualifications for a pupil nurse. "The nurse must love her profession. If she adopts it merely as a means of live-lihood, her interest may soon lose itself in the peculiar test of her temper and courage of her patience and her fidelity" (pp. 7–8). There were thirty strict rules and regulations that governed the pupil nursing from entry to gradua-tion. Pupil nurses had to sign a written agreement to remain under instruction for one year, and to give one additional year in the service of the school. After the initial first month of probation and five months of instruction, a small com-pensation was considered a fair equivalent for their services. During the last six months of training, students received an increase in pay and an additional increase during the following year of service.

The curriculum included twenty-two lectures:

1. Application of bandages
2. Making a patient's bed and changing linen without disturbing the patient
3. Preventing and dressing bed sores and arranging positions
4. Frictions—their manner of application, duration, and repetition
5. Application of cups and leeches
6. Fomentations, poultices, blisters, etc.
7. Dressing of bruises, sores, and wounds
8. Administration of enemata
9. Use of a catheter
10. Method of giving baths, partial and general; their temperature and dura-tion, including moist-air, dry-air, and medicated baths
11. Attention before, during, and after parturition
12. Care of newborn infants
13. Method of ascertaining and noting pulse, temperature, and respiration
14. Ventilation
15. Disinfectants; their preparation and use
16. Method of stopping hemorrhages
17. What to do in emergencies and accidents
18. Observations on the general condition of patient with regard to appetite, skin, secretions, appearance of eruptions, chill and fever, effect of medi-cine, and diet
19. Fever nursing

20. Surgical nursing
21. Preparation of food
22. Massage

Pupil nurses were required to be present at all nursing lectures unless detailed for special duty at the time. Students were required to serve the prescribed length of time in the diet kitchen, where they were to prepare all gruels, beef teas, egg nogs, etc. Each student was required to be present at the morning visit in her assigned ward. During the evening visit, the student nurse was required to accompany the physician through all the wards and receive bedside instruction at the resident physician's direction, and the wards were to be kept perfectly quiet between 8 P.M. and 5 A.M. If assigned night duty, the day was entirely at the students' disposal for rest and recreation.

A strict watch of each patient and her every symptom was to be kept and reported to the resident physician. Gentleness and kindness to all patients were strictly enforced upon the student; no personal remarks of criticism, expressions of foreboding, nor comparisons with other cases were allowed. In addition to the structured nursing curriculum, the head nurse was responsible for training and supervising pupil nurses. The head nurse during the time Franklin was a student was Miss A. I. Fetting.

Students were allowed one afternoon in each week and part of alternate Sundays for their own disposal unless an emergency required their services. Upon the approval of the Examining Board of Physicians and Managers, a diploma with the seal of the hospital, signed by the resident physician and Examining Board, was granted to each graduate.

From its early beginnings, Women's Hospital Training School of Philadelphia Graduate Nurses established a reputation for earnestness and efficiency. The hospital's annual report of 1877 substantiated that the school of nursing held its graduate nurses accountable for the quality of nursing care they delivered. The training school asked that all who employed its nurses return an exact statement of their conduct in the paper sent for that purpose. The school's position was that it was in the highest interest of the school and of the nurse herself that entire frankness on the part of the employer be observed. In addition, the school requested that "all persons who employ nurses claiming to have graduated from this school require to see their diploma." The school's interest to protect the public from fraudulent representation and services was remarkable for its time, in comparison to the rare yet continuous exposure of fraudulent representation in the health profession that we see today.

Franklin graduated with the full recommendation of the hospital and a diploma dated December 15, 1897, stating: "Miss Martha Franklin has served for two years as Nurse Pupil on duty in the wards of the Women's Hospital and she has passed a satisfactory examination before the medical examiners." She was the only Black graduate of her class (see Illustration 3–7). After graduation, Franklin returned to her home in Meriden. Franklin, like Mahoney, did private duty nursing in the patient's home. Therefore, both women shared common

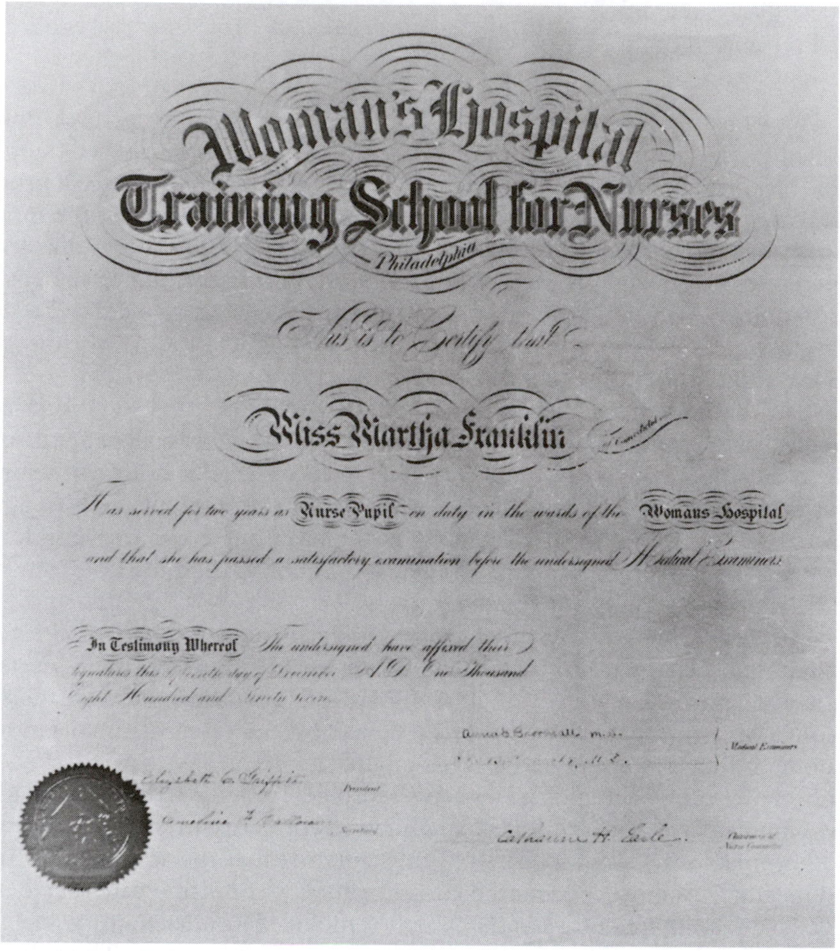

ILLUSTRATION 3–7.
Martha Franklin, Diploma.
Women's and Children's Hospital of Philadelphia.
Previously from the collection of the Connecticut Afro-American Society,
New Haven, Connecticut. Courtesy of Dixwell Community House, New
Haven, Connecticut.

experiences that a Black nurse may have been subjected to as a private duty nurse. She later pursued the same type of work in New Haven (Thoms 1929, pp. 143–144), where she relocated, residing at 61 Drexel Avenue.

At the turn of the century, there were several Black social groups that formed in New Haven in response to racial and social needs. The Tents and the Household of Ruth were two groups of all Black women with similar goals. Dues were collected, and funds allocated to members when one became sick.

These groups also undertook to bring Black women to Connecticut from the South. The Women's Twentieth Century Club, organized in 1901, was one of the most active clubs in the Black community. The group founded the Hannah Gray Home for Aged Black Women because Black women could not get into White nursing homes. This group maintained the home for over seventy years, and it is still in existence today. The Reading Circle was a group of educated Black women who met to review the latest books. The Eastern Stars and the Pocahontas Temple, formed in the early 1900s, were the female counterparts to the Masons and the Elks formed in the 1800s (Interview with Mrs. Edna Carnegie, 1986). Although it is not known how many of these social groups Franklin belonged to, it appears from early group pictures that she was a member of the New Haven Twentieth Century Club. This endeavor, concerned with the care of the aged Black woman, was closely aligned with her profession as a nurse.

Franklin was a religious woman and a member of the Dixwell Avenue Congregational United Church of Christ, located at 217 Dixwell Avenue, New Haven. In addition to being a woman of the church, "Martha was a very refined woman who had class. She was polite, very sophisticated, and in sum, she was a dignified black woman" (Interview with Reverend Edwin R. Edmonds, June 13, 1986).

Franklin had many friends in Connecticut; in particular was Dr. Ernest Saunders and his wife Georgie Saunders. Franklin did not marry; however, Dr. Saunders was like a grandson to Franklin, and she was like a grandmother to him. Dr. Saunders was one of the founders of the Connecticut Afro-American Historical Society in New Haven (Interview with Georgie Saunders, October 14, 1985; Interview with Mr. and Mrs. Williams, October 13–14, 1985).

What specific experiences Franklin had as a Black nurse that prompted her to become a pioneer for civil rights, as the organizer of the NACGN, have not been recorded. However, during the era between 1879 when Mary Mahoney graduated as the first Black professional nurse and 1908 when the NACGN was organized by Franklin, America developed rigid patterns of racial discrimination and segregation. This was a deterrent to Black Americans, precluding them from participating as totally free citizens. Every facet of society was affected, and nursing was no exception. Black codes were instituted as the law in the South, and practiced as a custom in the North. Mabel Staupers clearly summarized the problem by stating that hospitals and nursing schools followed this pattern both in admission of Black students and in the care of Black patients. This exclusion inevitably forced the establishment of hospitals and nursing schools for Black patients and student nurses.

In addition, in many Southern states, Black nurses were prohibited from membership in the State Nurses Association because of their race. Since this was the only avenue to membership in the American Nurses Association (ANA), they were therefore precluded from joining that prestigious group, although they qualified for membership in every other aspect. This discrimination in part urged Franklin to begin her quest for a movement to organize the NACGN.

It was in the fall of 1906 that Franklin began to study the actual status of the Black graduate nurse of America. Her interests were to unite on a national level. She sent more than 500 letters[2] to graduate nurses, superintendents of training schools, and many nursing organizations. Through this process, she wanted to make a general survey of the field. Although the study was limited, it was done with the expenditure of a great deal of Franklin's time and energy. Nurses were very slow in replying to her letters and many did not reply at all.

Being a woman with insight, initiative, and an unusual amount of executive ability and determination, Franklin continued to seek the information that she wanted to acquire. Although education offered more opportunities for White women historically, Franklin knew that facts would be needed to convince others that nursing education and subsequent employment were serious problems for Black women.

By 1907, as a result of her two-year survey, Franklin recognized that her group of Black nurses were concerned as she was and needed help. Moreover, she realized that if this help were to materialize and be effective, it must be initiated by Black nurses themselves. She believed that only through collective action could their problems be identified, analyzed, and thus eliminated. She further believed that the organization of a National Association of Negro Nurses would gain recognition for them, and would in time make it possible for them to serve the American public without racial bias. Franklin felt that, since segregation and discrimination were impeding them from this goal, something would have to be done immediately. She took the initiative and became the motivating force in the development of the NACGN. She sent out 1,500 letters, asking nurses to consider the possibility of a meeting in the near future.

Adah Belle Samuels Thoms, R.N., president of Lincoln Hospital School of Nursing Alumnae Association, responded, cordially inviting Franklin and interested nurses to meet in New York City as its guest. With the sponsorship of this alumnae group and Lincoln Hospital, a meeting was called to order at 10:30 A.M. on Tuesday, August 25, 1908, at St. Mark's Methodist Episcopal Church on West 53rd Street, where Thoms was a member. Fifty-two nurses were present, and their meeting began with a prayer, led by the pastor, Dr. William H. Brooks of New York City (Franklin, *Minutes of the NACGN*, 1908, p. 10).

The purpose of the NACGN meetings was etched in each nurse's conscience, through life and professional nursing experiences that brought them together in unison. The details of the meeting minutes provide insight into Franklin as a leader and an organizer. In addition, the details give further insight into this organization in its infancy, including its goals and purpose, Franklin's influence, and Thoms and Mahoney as significant participants in this major professional endeavor.

Franklin presided as with all other sessions that followed. As one reads the minutes, there is clearly a perception of reverence and respect for Franklin present. In addition, there was obvious cohesion between Franklin and Thoms. Thoms gave the welcoming address and Franklin responded to Thoms's address.

Immediately thereafter, temporary officers were appointed. Franklin was appointed temporary president and Ms. Effie B. Watkins temporary secretary. This was followed by registration of the nurses who were present—the charter members.

The first session of six of the three-day convention was bustling with excitement. In her modest way, she made a presentation, setting forth the purpose of the meeting. She suggested that a permanent national organization of colored graduate registered nurses should be formed, and that forming a national organization was the only way to bring the nurses together to share and understand their problems. Her interest was to develop leadership among them, and promote higher standards along administrative and educational lines. In addition, she thought collective action would secure cooperation, and more professional contact with nursing leaders of the world. Franklin convinced the group that this was the only way to stimulate nurses toward a higher standard of nursing, and to raise the requirements for admission to schools of nursing. The nurses were very interested, and many lengthy discussions followed. This national endeavor was welcomed; nurses in a few local communities believed in this concept and had already begun to organize. The Norfolk local began in 1901, and in New York, Chicago, and Washington, graduates of established Black schools had all organized alumnae associations by 1908.

A few nurses from the less qualified schools were concerned that they would be excluded from joining. Franklin and many others realized that these nurses were victims of the very discrimination they were rallying to organize against. Since Black women in general were not accepted to White schools of nursing, these less qualified schools were the result of discrimination and separate learning facilities established for Black nurses and were not equal in quality to White schools of nursing. These schools did not meet the qualifications for state registration and thus were inferior. The group decided a concerted effort would be made to improve these inadequate schools, with the hope that if these efforts were not successful, a way might be found to encourage their closing. The group decided to accept these nurses; however, in the future, others who might desire to join the NACGN must meet the prevailing standards for all nurses. The group decided that in the future, state registration should be a qualification for membership.

The convention process was democratic, using what appears to be synonymous with Robert's Rules of Order. It was motioned and decided that a committee of five, later increased to nine, be appointed by the chair (Martha Franklin) "to frame the object of the Convention" (*Minutes of the NACGN* 1908, p. 10). Franklin appointed a committee and designated Thoms as the chairperson, a sure indication of trust. A paper was then presented on "The Colored Visiting Nurses of Philadelphia," followed by many questions, answers, and discussion.

Dr. John B. Hall of Boston, a noted physician and lifetime friend of Mahoney's, addressed the NACGN and extended greetings from the National Medical Association (NMA). Black doctors also experienced discrimination in practicing their profession and had organized the NMA. Black physicians wrote in their journal that the door of the American Medical Association (AMA) was closed to most of them because membership was contingent upon membership in a constituent medical society. They were not admitted to many societies in the North and to none in the South. In 1908, the annual NMA meeting was held in New York City at the same time the nurses were having their meeting. Dr. Hall invited the nurses to have their annual meeting in Boston the next year in 1909, at the same time and place as the NMA. Many Black doctors from the NMA came to the nurses meeting to give encouragement and pledge their support for this new endeavor.

The NMA developed a very serious interest in the NACGN and invited the NACGN to have their national conventions at the same time and place as the annual NMA Convention. The NMA sent representatives to the NACGN meetings and the NACGN sent representatives to the NMA convention meetings. Representatives generally addressed the group and reported the particulars of the meeting back to their respective organizations. The NMA invited the NACGN to contribute articles to their publication, the *Journal of the National Medical Association*. During the early years through the 1920s, the *JNMA* contained full sections on the NACGN and nursing entitled "Of Interest to Nurses" or "Nurses Section." Many members of the NACGN subscribed to the journal. At a later date, the NACGN developed its own journal. The NMA's interest and good wishes were well taken and appreciated; however, their interest included a long-term goal to merge the two organizations that was ultimately rejected by the NACGN. The NMA's interest was in later years contained in the NACGN's best interest to retain the organization's identity as a group of nurses.

Black doctors accompanying Dr. Hall with greetings, well wishes, and support for this new organization included Dr. Daniel Hale Williams, a noted surgeon from Chicago who performed the first heart surgery. Also, Dr. E. P. Roberts of New York came and spoke about the new employment opportunities developing for nurses in the New York City Health Department, in which he had been recently appointed as the first Black physician in the clinics. Also bearing well wishes were Drs. Mar of Washington, D.C., and Boyd of Nashville, Tennessee, chairman of the National Medical Association.

At this time, the high number of deaths from tuberculosis among the Black population in cities of the North and the South, and the high infant mortality rate were the subjects of a great deal of discussion. These nurses knew from first-hand experience that the health problems of the Black population were aggravated by inadequate housing, lack of proper health facilities, and inability to find employment. In many sections of the country, Blacks were living under conditions little better than they had been subjected to during slavery. Many Black families had migrated from the South to large Northern cities. In addition to other problems, they battled prejudice from other immigrants, who, like themselves, were seeking a better way of life. The NACGN, from that first meeting until its dissolution, dedicated itself to improving the health care of the Black population (Staupers 1961, p. 19). The members realized that if the health of Americans were to be improved, every segment of the population must be given equal opportunity to receive adequate health care.

During the three-day convention in 1908, this new founding group discussed their goals, objectives, a constitution, and membership eligibility. However, the meeting was also about continued learning, sharing, exchanging ideas, experiences, and professional attributes. There were a number of interesting papers presented, including "Community Nursing on St. Helena Island," "Settlement Work in New York City (New York West Side Settlement)," "Advancement of the Profession of Scientific Nursing," "Professional Etiquette," "Massage," "Obstetrical Nursing," and "Training Schools for Nursing." Thoms presented a paper entitled "Is Trained Nursing a Necessity?" Thoms addressed the nurses at the Wednesday afternoon session. Franklin then, on behalf of the Visiting Nurses, thanked the Lincoln Alumnae Association for their hospitality.

The intellectual exchange following the presentations was so stimulating that by Thursday morning, August 27, a motion was put forth that discussion of papers be limited to two minutes to a speaker. Time was of the essence, important business was still at hand, and the motion was carried. It was now the third day of the convention and the morning session which began with a prayer at 10:30 A.M., was in progress with Franklin presiding. An important motion was put before the body: "On motion by Mrs. Mary Tucker, R.N. of Philadelphia, The Association elected Miss Martha Franklin of New Haven, Connecticut, President of the Association by acclamation" (*Minutes of the NACGN* 1908, p. 13). This must have been quite an honor for Franklin who was now thirty-seven years old and had practiced nursing for eleven years. It is clear from the minutes that support, admiration, and respect for Franklin was so high that no actual election by ballot was required or desired, and she was put into office by acclamation.

There were well wishes and greetings received from many, including the Nurses' Aid Association of Charleston, South Carolina. Perhaps these were women who aspired to be nurses. Another friend at that first meeting was Mr. Fred R. Moore, editor and publisher of a magazine, *The Colored American*, which carried the first story of the founding of the NACGN. Mr. Moore continued his interest in nursing and health care programs. As editor and publisher of the *New York Age*, he worked for better health conditions for Blacks in New York City.

The Thursday afternoon session was called to order at 2:15 P.M. The minutes of the morning session were read and adopted. On motion it was decided to go into the election of officers by ballot. The minutes note that:

> Miss Franklin having been elected, the following officers were elected by ballot.
> 1st Vice President—Miss Vida V. Symore, Ohio
> 2nd Vice President—Miss Edith M. Carter, New York
> Recording Secretary—Miss Mary F. Clarke, Virginia
> Corresponding Secretary—Miss L. Viola Ford, South Carolina
> Treasurer—Miss Adah Belle Samuels Thoms, New York

In addition to these, an executive committee, a membership committee, and an auditing and finance committee were elected.

It was determined which nurses were eligible for membership, the financial role was called, and dues were collected from the membership list. From its small and humble beginnings a total of $57 was collected in dues from which the cost of the convention was applied as follows in disbursements:

Church Rental	$10.00
Programs	3.00
Advertisements	4.00
Hangers	5.50
Stationery	13.50
Janitor	1.50
Announcements	2.00

After three days of stimulating discussion, the NACGN became a reality with twenty-six charter members. Many of these charter members had also been members of the Nurses' Associated Alumnae of the United States and Canada, which later became the American Nurses Association. It was thought that these women could provide this new organization with leadership by interpreting the current trends in nursing and developing professional standards within the NACGN. They believed that in time these standards would overcome the barriers of inadequate educational facilities that were impeding their progress.

The group agreed that the goals of the NACGN would be as follows:

1. Advance the standards and best interests of trained nurses
2. Break down discrimination in the nursing profession
3. Develop leadership within the ranks of negro nurses (Staupers 1961, p. 17).

At the close of the convention, the group decided to have its first Annual National Meeting in Boston in 1909. A very pleasant and interesting social program closed the convention. The nurses were given a luncheon by Lillian Wald and the Henry Street nurses at 265 Henry Street. The luncheon was an experience that would always be remembered. They were also given a clinical demonstration and a tea at Lincoln Hospital, which was a delightful learning experience. The convention culminated in a sightseeing trip to Coney Island and a reception for the nurses that rewarded them for their long, tiresome trips to New York City and prepared them for their return trips home.

Between the August 1908 meeting and the August 1909 First Annual Convention, there were two documented executive board meetings. The executive board of associations or organizations is generally a very influential and powerful deciding body. Franklin and members of the NACGN believed that the executive board could determine and advise on the proper development of the Association. On April 28, 1909, Franklin called the first executive board meeting to order. The meeting took place in New York City with four members present, and Franklin presiding. Present for the roll was: Miss M. M. Franklin,

CONSTITUTION OF THE NATIONAL ASSOCIATION OF COLORED GRADUATE NURSES

ARTICLE I.

Name

We, the graduate nurses of the various training schools for nurses throughout the country, do pledge our support by personal efforts to our organization to be known as The National Association of Colored Graduate Nurses.

ARTICLE II.

Object

The object of the Association shall be: To advance the standing and best interests of trained nurses, and to place the profession of nursing on the highest plane attainable.

ARTICLE III.

The officers of the Association shall consist of a President, First Vice-President, Second Vice-President, Recording Secretary, Treasurer, and Executive Board.

CODE OF ETHICS

SECTION 1. There is no profession open to women, from the members of which greater purity of character and a higher standard of moral excellence are required than that of nursing, and everyone who has entered the profession has incurred an obligation to maintain its dignity and honor.

SECTION 2. A nurse can best do honor to her Association by her personal conduct and by the high character of her professional work. When a nurse becomes a member of the Association she tacitly admits that she owes to it her allegiance.

SECTION 3. Every member of the Association should feel it her duty to further its interests, not only by attendance at the meetings and payment of dues, but also by giving her hearty support to all work for the elevation and advancement of the Association, and by interesting the public in such work in all legitimate ways.

SECTION 4. A nurse as a good citizen should do all in her power to improve the moral and hygienic conditions of the community in which she resides.

EXHIBIT 3–1.

Miss A. B. Samuels, Miss A. Marrin and Mrs. M. B. Edwards (*Minutes of the NACGN*, p. 17). The group made plans for the First Annual Convention. They discussed sending out notices for the annual convention to superintendents of all training schools and graduate nurses of those schools. Their interest was to increase support and participation. As in the case with any new organization, money was a problem. There were members who were delinquent with their dues. They were notified of their delinquency and of the upcoming meeting in Boston. The meeting lasted until 11 P.M. This late hour for business surely suggests dedication to a cause and a movement. The executive board met again on August 22, 1909, at the Lincoln Hospital Nursing Home at 61 West 134th Street in New York City. This meeting was in preparation for the First Annual National Convention two days later in Boston, where Franklin and Thoms would encounter Mary Eliza Mahoney for the first time.

The First Annual National Meeting of the NACGN was held in from Tuesday, August 24, through Thursday, August 26, at the Twelfth Baptist Church of Boston. The meeting was called to order at 10 A.M. by Franklin, who was presiding. This national meeting also began with a prayer by Dr. Neil Shaw of the Twelfth Baptist Church. There were twenty-six charter members present including Thoms, who had supported Franklin from the outset of this endeavor, and Mahoney, a new and inspirational ally (see Illustration 3–8). There were twenty-five new members added to the membership list and ten states were represented. In those ten states, a great deal of enthusiasm had developed over the past year. As the convention proceeded, Franklin capitalized on the opportunity to encourage this enthusiasm at the state level. This provided grassroots involvement as well as local and national communication.

Mahoney was introduced as the first Black professional nurse, and the oldest practicing nurse in Boston. She delivered the welcoming address, stating:

> . . . one of the problems which had always distressed her was the condition in the early days of her training, when colored girls who applied for admission to good schools usually found the doors closed against them, though she said my school was not so selfish, she knew other schools of nursing were (Thoms 1929, p. 9).

At sixty-four, Mary Mahoney was pleased to know that the nursing profession was progressing. However, an analysis comparing her training experience and era to that of 1909 revealed that she thought the current day training lacked the quality of her own nursing program thirty years prior. Thoms, recorded her first impressions in *Pathfinders*, stating: "Miss Mahoney was small of stature, about five feet in height and weighed less than one hundred pounds. She was most interesting and possessed an unusual personality and a great deal of charm."

Mahoney's interest in and support of this new organization's endeavors were immediate. She joined in concert with Franklin and Thoms, forming an

ILLUSTRATION 3–8.
Members of the NACGN, 1909 Convention Meeting in Boston,
Massachusetts. Franklin and Thoms are seated in the first row, fourth and
fifth from the right, and Mahoney is directly behind and in between
Franklin and Thoms.
Courtesy of Schomburg Center for Research in Black Culture, The New
York Public Library, New York.

alliance in support of their common goals to improve the status of the Black nurse. Their work together spanned many years through the service of this organization. Franklin was inspired by Mahoney, as was Thoms. In fact, Mahoney was one of Franklin's and the organization's continuing inspirations (A Salute to Democracy at Mid-Century 1951). The three architects who were the cornerstones of the NACGN were now together, and the prism through which they are conceptualized and visualized began to take shape.

Many speeches, presentations, and committee and officer reports followed, including the treasurer's report by Thoms, which showed the financial status of the Association was improving. Perhaps members who were delinquent sent in their dues when reminded subsequent to the executive board meeting. This was followed by a report and address by Franklin that was very interesting and well received. Dr. John B. Hall presented an inspiring paper entitled, "Mutual Cooperation Between Nurses and Physicians." All three architects were center-stage as Franklin presided over the First Annual Convention; Mahoney and

Thoms jointly responded to Dr. Hall's presentation. This was very much like conferences of today in which a response is planned to an oral presentation. How much preplanning went into their response has not been recorded; however, along with two other nurses, a vibrant and full discussion ensued. Mutual cooperation between nurses and physicians is a topic that continues to be alive today in the health profession.

As the convention progressed, there were other interesting presentations: "Nursing Conditions in the West Indies," "The Origins of Trained Nursing by Colored Women in Chicago," coupled with words of encouragement and interest in the association that were greatly appreciated. In addition, excellent papers were presented on "The Importance of Cooperation in the Work of the Visiting House and Children's Diseases." Thoms gave a presentation entitled "The Education of the Probationer" at the Wednesday afternoon session, followed by questions, answers, and a great deal of discussion. The educational process for nurses today in the academic setting was clearly one of the organization's main concerns as well as nursing practice subsequent to nursing education.

The NMA was developing a strong interest in the NACGN. Again the NMA, as in the 1908 convention, attended sessions of the NACGN. Dr. McGuire of Boston gave an address that was considered charming, and congratulated the NACGN on the efforts it was putting forth to bring the benefits of their profession to the public. Dr. McIurdy of Boston was then introduced and extended a very cordial invitation to the nurses to the planned entertainment for the local medical association. In return, the NACGN sent the NMA greetings by three appointed delegates.

At this convention, chairmen from each state were appointed by Franklin to make an investigation and report on tuberculosis work and clinics being conducted in their own states. This was a follow-through from major concerns voiced and discussed at the 1908 NACGN convention in New York regarding the high mortality among the Black population from tuberculosis. In light of the health care the Black population was often denied, Black nurses had reason to be concerned. In 1904, when the National Tuberculosis Association was organized, there were 111 hospitals, sanitariums, and day camps for the care and treatment of patients suffering from tuberculosis in the United States. By 1919 there were 600 such institutions. Despite the increase, for Black patients these institutions were inadequate because only a few of them admitted Black patients. By 1921, Metropolitan Insurance Co. reported that tuberculosis claimed two-and-one-fourth times as many victims among Black policyholders as among White policyholders (van de Vrede 1921, pp. 55–57).

Franklin began to increase the effectiveness of her organization by intricate networking. Franklin suggested that the chairpersons of all special and standing committees be members of the executive board, and that such chairpersons be appointed by the chair (Franklin). This was posed in the form of a motion and carried. Franklin would obviously appoint chairpersons on committees whom she trusted and in whom she had confidence. Thus, the executive board would be a major support system for Franklin.

On Franklin's suggestion, a motion was made and carried to appoint a local chairperson from each state to organize local branches of the NACGN among the graduate nurses. A roundtable discussion was held on forming local clubs for graduate nurses in cities where groups made up of all graduate nurses from accredited schools might be brought together for closer affiliation and a better understanding between them. It was also decided to get in touch with superintendents of all schools with a request that the graduates of each school should organize an alumnae association.

To encourage state level enthusiasm, it was decided that local organizations whose purposes were the same as the national organization, would be permitted to send one voting delegate to national meetings. In this manner, the national program would be strengthened and in turn the national organization would give its full cooperation to local problems. The members also believed that on the local level, citizens together with nurses could work for the improvement of existing nursing schools and for better community facilities. It was believed that segregation and discrimination, like most national problems, could only be eliminated if there were close cooperation between the local and the national organizations. From this point on, local NACGN organizations contributed toward the national budget of the NACGN. A nurse could join the national organization as an individual member, but endorsement by her local organization was required.

To further shape the direction and goals of this new organization in its second year, Franklin appointed three nurses to review the constitution in detail, one of whom was Thoms, her trusted friend and confidant. Changes were made in specific use of terminology, thus refining its purpose and lending precision to the constitution of the NACGN.

An excerpt from the minutes of the 1909 national convention provides insight into the well-planned program as well as the trips that provided learning and social networking. Mahoney planned a tea for the NACGN at her alma mater. The Wednesday afternoon session was in progress (Franklin 1909, p. 21):

On Constitution Committee Miss Samuels [Thoms] of New York, Miss Davis of Norfolk and Miss Strickland of New Jersey were appointed by the Chair. After much discussion the meeting adjourned to take a trip to the New England Hospital for Women and Children, where a beautiful tea was served on the lawn after a tour of the hospital. Short talks were made by Miss Eliza Gardenia, the Superintendent of the hospital, Mary Mahoney and Martha Franklin. The Superintendent of the hospital and her corps of nurses were tendered a standing vote of thanks for their kind hospitality by the entire body of nurses. On motion it was decided to meet Thursday Morning at 10 A.M., August 26th, 1909.

Miss M. M. Franklin, President
Miss M. F. Clarke, Sec.

The nurses visited the wards and dispensaries, acquiring valuable information to take back to their own schools or hospitals. Many of the group were either head nurses or superintendents of small hospitals in the South and gained knowledge from the advanced methods that they observed.

This must have been an exciting, inspirational visit. This hospital was an important part of American nursing history. It was Mahoney's alma mater and the group had the honor of a tour of the very hospital school of nursing that trained the first Black professional nurse in America, that developed the first training program for nurses in the United States, and that was also the alma mater of Linda Richards, the first graduate professional nurse in America.

Mahoney was awarded life membership in the NACGN, was exempted from dues, and was unanimously elected the national chaplain. As chaplain, Mahoney often opened the meetings with a prayer. She was responsible for the induction of new officers, instructing them in their newly elected duties and responsibilities to be carried out faithfully, which she would emphasize. In addition, Mahoney had a major interest in increasing the membership of the NACGN.

The Thursday morning session began and was called to order by Martha Franklin, president (*Minutes of the NACGN* 1909, p. 23).

> The body was temporarily dismissed to take a trip down Long Island Sound to the Boston Leity Hospital. The morning session was continued on board the government launch. Business continued with Committee Chair reports. At this juncture we arrived at the State Hospital. The visit of the NACGN to the state hospital on Long Island Sound was never to be forgotten. The nurses received a most hearty welcome. A reception was tendered to the nurses at the Nurses Home overlooking the Sound. During the intermission a tour of inspection was made of the beautiful home followed by a delicious dinner. Speeches were made by Mrs. Jones, Mrs. Allan, and Miss Franklin. After dinner the Association was conducted through every department of the hospital, then entertained by the band who gave a concert on the campus overlooking Long Island Sound. Upon the arrival of one of the monitors the entire body was accompanied by Miss Chilsom and her assistant who watched everyone safely aboard. It was with reluctance that the scene of the day's pleasure faded from sight, after many a pleasant goodbye. Once more aboard the boat, business resumed. The first business was a suggestion by Martha Franklin. A motion was made and carried to appoint local chairmen from each vicinity represented at the NACGN to organize local branches among the graduate nurses. Nurses were appointed by Martha Franklin (Chair) from each state represented . . . Upon arriving in Boston, business was temporarily suspended until they reached the church: there Martha Franklin appointed numerous committee chairpersons for Printing, Program, Membership, Banking and Auditing. This was followed by elections . . .

Franklin was again unanimously elected president, unopposed. She thus served the first two years of this organization as its president. Franklin, who was

Black, was very light in complexion and slender. As the NACGN gained national recognition, Franklin was mistakenly characterized as a "white nurse friend of colored nurses" by nursing leaders (Stewart & Austin 1962, p. 211).

After elections, it was decided that the NACGN have an emblem to be worn as a pin (see Illustration 3–9). As a group of professional nurses and women who had experienced racial discrimination and segregation, they sought as an organization visual identity of a movement and their unity. Franklin assigned three members to this task, one of whom was Thoms, as a committee to purchase pins. On this note, the organization adjourned to meet in Philadelphia in August 1910.

When the 1909 meeting adjourned, the members had decided to work actively for state registration laws, since these were the developing standards of practice for nursing. The NACGN's plan was to insist that there be no double standard of practice based on race. Therefore, the group determined and set another goal that Black nurses must meet the required standards for all nurses. A plan was developed in Boston whereby Black nurses would be encouraged to recognize the value of state registration. Information would be disseminated

"NOT FOR OURSELVES, BUT FOR HUMANITY"

ILLUSTRATION 3–9.
The Emblem and Motto of the NACGN
Courtesy of Schomburg Center for Research in Black Culture, The New
York Public Library, New York.

through the Black press about state board examinations in local areas. Also, coaching classes would be organized to help nurses prepare for these examinations (Staupers 1961, p. 20).

In a few Southern states where state registration was established, Black nurses were either barred from taking the examination because of their race and color or were given a special examination. This form of discrimination was recognized by the NACGN as a deterrent to the future progress of the Black nurse. In addition, the NACGN's position was that the entire profession of nursing could not progress as long as any one group of nurses was required to face a double standard. There were many White nurses in these states who believed this practice was wrong. It was through their cooperation that the Black nurses were able to counter the problems and work toward their elimination. Black nurses desired no special privileges or waivers and made their position known to the members of the various state boards of nurse examiners through the NACGN. They also served notice that, if necessary, they would fight for the privilege of taking the same examinations given to all other nurses within these states.

In Georgia, a courageous Black nurse, Mrs. Ludie Andrew of Atlanta, a NACGN member who was in charge of the Colored Division of Grady Hospital, instituted legal proceedings against the Georgia State Board of Nurse Examiners. After legal proceedings that cost $200, she was successful in getting registration for the nurses of Georgia, which brought this discriminatory practice in that state to an end. After a ten-year legal battle, her victory was a victory for all Black nurses in Georgia and any state who practiced this segregation, Black nurses in Georgia would now be allowed to take the state licensing exam and register. Efforts in other states, although not as dramatic, nevertheless were successful. It was through the persistence of the Black nurses of the NACGN that throughout the United States, all nurses who graduated from accredited nursing programs, regardless of race, qualify for the practice of nursing in the same manner. Dr. Clark Hine (1989) analyzed Andrew's ten-year plight: "Andrew's career illustrated that Black nurses had to fight for every bit of recognition and fair treatment they received throughout the period 1900–1950, professionalization for them was synonymous with struggles" (p. xxi). That struggle, in different forms, continues today.

The NACGN met in Philadelphia, Pennsylvania, August 16–18, 1910, as a guest of the Mercy Hospital and Douglass Hospital nurses. Under Franklin's guidance, the association began to take further shape and form (Thoms 1929, pp. 206–207). Franklin presided during the entire convention, and nurses came from every section of the country. Many good presentations were given and freely discussed, including reports on care of patients with tuberculosis in different locales. This was a follow-through from the previous annual convention in which Franklin had appointed chairpersons to research and investigate the work being done with the tuberculosis population in their respective states.

There were interesting discussions of concern regarding protecting graduates from imposters, a problem that still exists today, and establishing a nurses' directory. The NACGN discussed an invitation received from Lavinia Dock, secretary of the International Council of Nurses (ICN), to send a delegate to the ICN in Cologne, Germany, in 1912. Franklin appointed a memorial committee to draft resolutions on the death of Florence Nightingale who died in her sleep on August 13, 1910, and Edith Elliot of Boston, an NACGN member.

A clinical and demonstrations were held at Douglass Hospital to update and facilitate their clinical practice. These were very helpful to the group. Much like today's ANA conventions, attractive booths were arranged by the ways and means committee. Dolls dressed in the uniform representing each school for Black nurses were made for sale, and other articles were contributed by several firms. Although hampered by prejudice, Black nurses were very proud of their school uniforms and caps. With the funds acquired through these sales, the NACGN opened a bank account.

A trip to Atlantic City closed a very successful and harmonious convention. Franklin had given the association a great deal of her personal time, energy, and organizational and administrative knowledge. Franklin had also formed two invaluable alliances with Thoms and Mahoney. In unison, these architects of integration and equality influenced, shaped, molded, and built the NACGN from its infancy and for many years to come (see Illustration 3–10). Mary Tucker, R.N., of Pennsylvania was elected president at the close of the 1910 convention. In 1911, the NACGN met in Washington, D.C., as a

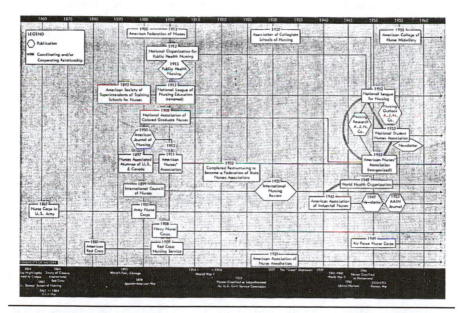

ILLUSTRATION 3–10.
The Growth and Development of Nursing Organizations in the United States.
Courtesy of Nursing Outlook.

guest of Freedman's Hospital. This convention was full of interest with organizational and professional concerns. In addition, Congress was in session at the time and the nurses had the added pleasure of seeing the chief executive conduct this session. The membership of the NACGN had increased from 51 to 125. Franklin's leadership skills were superior and apparently were quite missed during her first year away from the presidency. She was nominated and urged to serve a third term as president. There appears to have been a persistent and continuous request for Franklin to reassume the presidency; however, she refused. Absent any explanation, one can assume that Franklin believed that someone else should take over this tremendous task. The NACGN minutes of 1911 state, "It is to be noted that Miss Martha Franklin positively refused all nominations." Franklin remained very involved in the organization; she was named honorary president for life, and was later designated the organization's historian.

One of the first nursing leaders to recognize the NACGN was Lillian D. Wald of the Henry Street Settlement. Another leader and early friend was Lavinia Dock, who gave the officers of the NACGN advice on organization. The recognition by these two outstanding leaders was a valuable asset to the NACGN. Dock as secretary of the ICN invited the NACGN to send a representative to the 1912 ICN meeting in Cologne, Germany. The NACGN sent one representative, Rosa L. Williams, and Lincoln Nurses Alumnae Association sent two representatives, Adah Belle Samuels Thoms and Ada Senhouse. Two of these three nurses were early supporters of Franklin and charter members of the NACGN. This was the first opportunity Black nurses had to meet other nurses at an international meeting. A valuable contact with nurses in other lands was made with the Black nurses in America. They were well received and their presence was celebrated. The NACGN was now internationally recognized and this was the beginning for Black nurses universally to join and participate in the ICN (Staupers 1961, pp. 20–21).

Several national organizations emerged from 1861 to 1920 that shaped and organized the nursing profession. Organizations that had early interaction with the NACGN in support of its goals were the ICN, the Henry Street Nurses Settlement, and the NMA.

The International Council of Nurses (ICN). The idea for the ICN arose at the Columbia Expedition held in Chicago in 1893. After the success of the International Council of Women in 1899, the council appointed a provisional committee to work out a plan for an organization. This committee invited nurse representatives from nine countries. The professional committee convened in London, and in 1900 the constitution was adopted. The purpose of the ICN was to band together, advanced by greater unity of thought, sympathy, and interest of the nursing profession. Members of the NACGN attended the ICN. One of the first to attend was Adah Belle Samuels Thoms.

The Henry Street Nurses Settlement was founded in 1895 by Lillian D. Wald. Wald and a friend, Mary Brewster, opened Henry Street Settlement House on New York City's Lower East Side in September 1895. This successful historic endeavor was financed by Mrs. Solomon Loeb and her son-in-law, Jacob H. Schiff, a banker and philanthropist. By 1913, the Henry Street Settlement Visiting Nurses Association had ninety-two nurses, with branches in upper Manhattan and the Bronx. Lillian Wald also supported and facilitated the NACGN, which was reflected in the minutes of the NACGN Annual Conventions.

The Nurse Corps in the U.S. Army, founded in 1861, became the Army Nurse Corps in 1901, now the oldest of the federal corps. It excluded Black nurses from service until 1918. Entrance to the service could only be acquired through enrollment in the American Red Cross Service, which also excluded Black nurses. The Reserve Nurses were established by President Taft in 1911.

Navy Nurse Corps. On May 13, 1908, President Theodore Roosevelt signed the Naval Appropriations Bill that established the Navy Nurse Corps. As in the Army Nurse Corps, Black nurses were excluded from the Navy Nurse Corps and denied access until 1945.

National League for Nursing (NLN). On June 13, 1893, twenty superintendents met at St. Luke's Hospital in New York at the invitation of Katherine Lett, then director of nurses. At this meeting, a temporary organization was formed with Anna L. Austin as Chairperson. In 1912, the name was changed to the National League of Nursing Education, and in 1952, to the National League for Nursing.

American Nurses Association (ANA). Seven members of the Society of Nurses, Superintendents, and Alumnae delegates laid the plans for a National Association of Graduate Nurses. The delegates met in New York in September of 1896 and organized the Nurses Associated Alumnae of the United States and Canada. Isabel Hampton Robb served as first president of this organization. Its purposes were to foster high standards of nursing practice and promote the welfare of nurses so that all people would have better nursing care. The name of the organization was changed in 1911 to the American Nurses Association.

American Red Cross. In May of 1881, Clara Barton, a Civil War nurse, and several of her associates organized the American Association of the Red Cross. The purpose of this organization was to respond to natural and unnatural disasters. Barton's idea emerged after traveling to Europe and observing the International Red Cross, established by Henry Donant. The American Red Cross was established by an act of Congress in 1900.

The Red Cross Nursing Service is a branch of the American Red Cross. In 1905, a need was identified for a reserve body of nurses trained, prepared, and ready for service in the event of a war. The Red Cross asked the ANA to collaborate in developing a uniform basis for nursing service. The collaborative efforts organized the Red Cross Nursing Service with registered nurses, officers, and a national committee. Jane Delano was the first chairperson of this branch of the Red Cross, a position she held until her death in 1919. Thoms and Jane Delano were in continuous communication during World War I regarding the initial and prolonged rejection of Black nurses for service.

National Organization for Public Health Nursing (NOPHN). Early in 1912, a group of public health nurses advised the NLN and the ANA of their interest for a national public health organization. Membership would include public health nurses and board members. In 1912, the National Organization for Public Health Nursing came to fruition.

The NACGN had a valid, yet monumental task to improve the status of the Black nurse. From its small beginnings, the association grew to a membership of 2,000 during World War I and over 12,000 nurses by 1940, representing virtually every state in the union. The NACGN was able to counter some of the problems adversely affecting the Black nurses. As the NACGN progressed and its membership increased, the national registry was set up to aid the Black nurse in securing positions. The NACGN developed local community and national support systems by establishing a local citizens committee in New York state and an advisory council on a national level.

By 1928, Franklin herself relocated to New York and resided at the YMCA at 175 West 135th Street, New York City. She enrolled in a six-month postgraduate course at Lincoln Hospital, became an R.N. in New York State, and was employed as a school nurse in the public school system in New York (Thoms 1929, p.144). At the age of fifty-eight, still interested in continuing her education, Franklin applied and was accepted as a student at Teachers College, Columbia University. She was enrolled in the Department of Practical Arts, today known as the Department of Nursing Education, from 1928 to 1930 (Interview with Dr. Roland Rinsland 1985; Student Directory 1930).

Thoms, one of the architects and Franklin's good friend and confidant, as president of the NACGN encouraged nurses to educate themselves for the specialties in nursing, one of which was the school nurse. In addition, Thoms highly recommended Teachers College, Columbia University for this specialized preparation. What influence Thoms had on Franklin's decision to enter Teachers College is unknown; however, it is clear that Thoms thought the school nurse invaluable and higher education at Teachers College a quality decision of decision. Thoms stated:

> I know of no greater contribution to offer society than the school nurse. She is a most important factor in our health program. She is in a large measure responsible for the moral, mental, and physical growth of our boys and girls. With her clear conception and cooperation with the physician, much can be done to guard against all diseases due directly to school life.
>
> There are 15 colleges throughout the country offering special training to nurses who wish to engage in special work. Columbia College is the first of its kind and it is most liberal in its views. It offers an equal opportunity to all who can meet the requirement . . . (President's Address, Adah Belle Samuels Thoms 1920, p. 74).

In 1925, Adelaide Nutting, head of the department of nursing at Teachers College, retired after eighteen years of pioneering service as a professor of nursing. By this time, under Nutting's direction, the department of nursing at Teachers College had grown from the smallest division in the college to its largest single unit. The curriculum had thirty-five nursing courses offering a wide range of subjects from the university departments and seven distinct majors representing fifteen to twenty vocational fields. During Nutting's years of service, admission standards steadily rose, and the certificate student had by and large become the degree student.

Teachers College graduates were making their greatest contributions in establishing new university centers of nursing education, improving standards of teaching in both hospitals and homes, and in extending the public health idea to all phases of nursing. Professor Nutting trained Isabel M. Stewart, her assistant who succeeded her in 1925 as head of the department in nursing education. Among others on the Teachers College nursing faculty, Nutting also trained Lillian A. Hudson, whose special field became Public Health Nursing (Cremin, Shannon, & Townsend 1954, pp. 54–56). When Franklin entered Teachers College in 1928, Isabel Stewart was the department head and Professor Hudson, Franklin's advisor, was in charge of all public health nursing courses. The Public Health Nursing program of study was open only to qualified nurses. It was designed to offer fundamental work required in preparation for public health nursing in its general and special forms such as child welfare, school, rural, industrial and visiting nurse.

Franklin was a candidate for a Bachelor of Science degree majoring in Public Health Nursing (see Illustration 3–11). Franklin worked as a school nurse while she attended Teachers College. All nursing students were required to take a two-credit nursing history course, a requirement that should be nationally reinstituted today. Tuition at Teachers College was then $10 a credit with a college fee of $80 per semester.

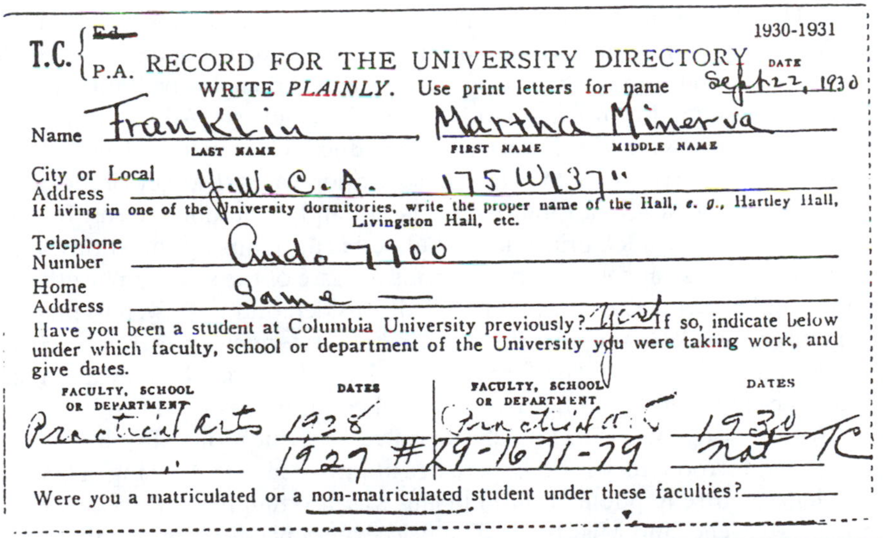

T.C. { ~~Ed.~~ P.A. RECORD FOR THE UNIVERSITY DIRECTORY — 1930-1931

WRITE PLAINLY. Use print letters for name — DATE Sept 22, 1930

Name Franklin (LAST NAME), Martha (FIRST NAME) Minerva (MIDDLE NAME)

City or Local Address Y.W.C.A. 175 W137th

If living in one of the University dormitories, write the proper name of the Hall, e. g., Hartley Hall, Livingston Hall, etc.

Telephone Number Audo 7900

Home Address Same

Have you been a student at Columbia University previously? Yes If so, indicate below under which faculty, school or department of the University you were taking work, and give dates.

FACULTY, SCHOOL OR DEPARTMENT	DATES	FACULTY, SCHOOL OR DEPARTMENT	DATES
Practical Arts	1928	Practical Arts	1930
	1927	#29-1671-79	not TC

Were you a matriculated or a non-matriculated student under these faculties?

ILLUSTRATION 3–11.
Martha Franklin, Student (University) Directory.
Courtesy of the Registrar, Teachers College, Columbia University, New York.

The Public Health Nursing major at Teachers College had various components, offering a diploma as a public health nurse, a supervisor of school nursing, a teacher of home nursing and child care, and supervision and organization in public health nursing. The public health nurse degree program had specific requirements. At least one month's experience in an approved field was advised before entering the college. The public health nurse track coursework required the following: Principles of Public Health Nursing, Special Fields in Public Health Nursing, Field Work in Public Health Nursing, Preventable Diseases and Public Health Administration, Child Hygiene School Nursing, Field Work in School Nursing, Food Economies, Family Social Work, Practice in Family Social Work, Mental Hygiene, and recommended electives.

In the fall of 1928, Franklin enrolled for three courses, Principles of Family Care Work, in the social science department, English Literature, and Psychology, totaling eight credits. Principles of Family Care Work was a two-credit course taught by Mrs. Grove. The course provided a general survey of social disabilities, outlining the effects on family, the individual, general principles and methods of intermediary social service and individual adjustment. The course encompassed case methods/studies with typical problems of social disability, standards of living in relation to relief, and promoting helpful human relations by various types of social agencies. In the spring of 1929, Franklin enrolled in two courses, Survey of English Literature and Psychology of Mental Hygiene, for six credits. No doubt this first year's coursework enriched Franklin's background and performance as a public school nurse and broadened her general knowledge as a professional.

In the fall of 1929, Franklin enrolled in two more courses, Principal of Public Health Nursing No. 141 and Philosophy of Education, for six more credits. She was now fifty-nine years old and she continued working as a public school nurse while studying at Teachers College. Principles of Public Health Nursing was taught by Professor Hudson, Franklin's advisor. Additional instructors in the course were Miss Favelle and Mrs. Buell. Class met on Tuesdays and Thursdays from 3:10 to 5 P.M. The course included a brief survey of the development of public health nursing to meet family and community needs. In addition, the course included principles of Public Health Nursing, functions of the public health nurse in community programs for care of the sick, and health promotion and prevention of disease. Detailed consideration was given to practical programs of work as they developed in maternity, infant, preschool, school, industrial health services. The formulation of a well-rounded family and community health service in both urban and rural communities was included.

In the spring of 1930, Franklin enrolled in Educational Psychology for Nurses and Introductory Field Experience in Public Health Nursing. This field experience course in public health nursing was also taught by Professor Hudson, Miss Favelle, and Miss Buell. The field experience was arranged in cooperation with the Visiting Nurse Service at the Henry Street Settlement, which was under the direction of Lillian Wald. Edith Maude Carter[3] was supportive of Franklin in public health nursing and a good friend who lived in New York.

Carter was one of the first three Black nurses appointed to the Henry Street Settlement in 1906 by Lillian Wald. In later years, when Franklin trained at Henry Street, Carter was a senior nurse at the Henry Street Visiting Nurses Service of New York.

The course included demonstrations, individual and group conferences, and supervised field work during a 41-hour period weekly for two months or twenty-eight hours weekly for three months. The 1929–1930 academic year in which she studied with Professor Hudson, a protégée of Adelaide Nutting, no doubt was a fruitful year that further enriched Franklin as a public school nurse. The details of how Franklin worked and managed these extensive hours is unknown and remarkable; although she did not complete the Bachelor's degree at Teachers College, she successfully completed all courses taken, and can be viewed as having continued her education, updating her knowledge and skills.

After living and working in New York for many years, Franklin returned to New Haven, perhaps to retire. She resided with her sister Florence Franklin, who was a poet and also never married (Interview with Leroy Pierce, 1986). They resided at Heritage Home, a convalescent home at 1354 Chapel Street.

At ninety years of age, Martha Franklin withdrew to her home and was unable to attend church regularly on Sundays. Reverend Edwin Edmonds,

ILLUSTRATION 3–12.
Dr. (Reverend) Edwin R. Edmonds, a prominent Black clergyman in New Haven, Connecticut. An inspirational, caring leader, loved by his congregation and in the community, Dr. Edmonds visited Franklin each week for eight years before her death. Dr. Edmonds stated, "Martha Franklin was a proud woman; as an aged woman, Franklin retained her dignity and polished mannerism." Courtesy of Edwin R. Edmonds.

pastor of the Dixwell Congregational Church of Christ where Franklin was a member, knew her very well (see Illustration 3–12). Dr. Edmonds visited Franklin at her home regularly for eight years prior to her death. "Martha was a proud woman," and as an aged woman, Franklin retained her dignity and polished mannerisms. "At times Martha reminisced about the Depression, a difficult time in which she maintained her dignity and refused to be made into a field hand" (Interview with Dr. Reverend Edwin R. Edmonds 1986). This interview revealed that Franklin was a very determined woman.

Franklin lived to the ripe age of ninety-eight, and she died on September 26, 1968. The cause of death is listed as senility, and the major contributing factors were the physiological aging process and anorexia. Her private attending physician was Dr. William J. Massie, M.D., for the nine months prior to her death (Interview with Dr. William J. Massie 1985; Death Certificate #18466). Franklin outlived her family and siblings. Franklin is buried in the family plot along with her brother William who died in 1905 and her mother who died in 1934 (see Illustration 3–13). The names of Franklin's mother and brother are inscribed on the gravestone. There appears to have been no surviving relatives and, to date, this great nursing leader's name has not been added to the family gravestone. Her gravesite is at Walnut Grove Cemetery in Meriden, Connecticut.

ILLUSTRATION 3–13.
Gravesite of Martha Minerva Franklin
Walnut Grove Cemetery, Old Colonial Road, Meriden, Connecticut,
Section C West, Lot 298.
Picture taken by author.

Notes

1. The County Registrar recorded Florence Franklin's birth date as July 24, 1868, while Franklin's Bible recorded it as August 24, 1868.
2. This correspondence and the subsequent 1,500 communications were handwritten.
3. Carter was a charter member of the NACGN, elected second vice president in 1908 when the organization began.

Chapter 4

Adah Belle Samuels Thoms,
Circa 1870–1943

Women are the architects of society.

Harriet Beecher Stowe

Adah Belle Samuels Thoms was a crusader for equal opportunity for Black women in nursing, and she felt a deep sense of responsibility to improve relationships among all races (see Illustration 4–1). As president of the National Association of Colored Graduate Nurses (NACGN), she campaigned for the acceptance of Black nurses to become members of the American Red Cross and the United States Army Nurse Corps during World War I. She authored *Pathfinders*, the first book ever to record the Black nurses' experience. Like an architect, she created the groundwork that facilitated membership into the American Nurses Association (ANA) and the National Organization for Public Health Nursing.

Through Thoms's pioneering interest to improve the status and acceptance of the Black professional nurse, she came to know and work with Martha Franklin, R.N., and Mary Eliza Mahoney, R.N. Thoms had a great deal of admiration and respect for Franklin whom she considered a friend. Thoms praised

ILLUSTRATION 4–1.
Adah Belle Samuels Thoms (circa 1870–1943)
Courtesy of Schomburg Center for Research in Black Culture, the New York Public Library, New York.

Franklin, giving her full credit for the NACGN, stating, "The Association [NACGN] is the result of the efforts and ideas of Miss Martha M. Franklin." Thoms considered Mahoney a role model and her "dear and trusted friend." An eloquent public speaker, Thoms's love for nursing, her personality, leadership, stamina, and concern for her race, were revealed through her thoughts, words, and deeds. In addition, Thoms, one of the strongest presidents of the NACGN, was highly respected by nursing leaders, and is one of the best-known Black nurses in America (*A History in the Making* 1929, p. 560; Thoms 1920, p. 53; 1929, p. 11).

Thoms was born on January 12, circa 1870, in Richmond, Virginia. Her parents were Harry and Melvina Samuels. Although little is recorded about her early years, it is known that Thoms had at least one sibling.[1] Her early education was in the elementary public and normal school of Richmond, Virginia. She had aspirations of becoming a teacher. Richmond Normal was the only Black school for preparing teachers in a two-year program, and it was then comparable to a two-year technical college. "Richmond Normal was established in 1865 to serve the colored children of that generation and to educate the children of the new generation. The Richmond Normal is now known as Armstrong Public High School and is located on the same site" (Charles, Interview 1985). After completion, Thoms taught school in Richmond before choosing nursing as a career. She was briefly married to a physician, Dr. Thoms, and carried the surname Thoms throughout her nursing career.

Thoms's career as a pioneer for civil rights in nursing evolved through varied life, educational, and professional nursing experiences. "Immediately after graduation from the Lincoln Hospital and Home, Thoms began a life of pioneering for civil rights in nursing" (Staupers 1961, p. 10). Although little is recorded about her parents and family life, her early childhood-adult environment was spent in post–Civil War Richmond. This environment helped shape her character, her support of civil rights, and her concern for her race. In addition, both the normal school and the health care facility with a school of nursing she attended had the philosophy of and emphasis on improving the status of Blacks in society through education and health care. Although Thoms experienced double standards during her nursing career, she continuously sought education as a way to self-improvement and success. She was an energetic woman, capable of wearing many hats at one time. Thoms was a pathfinder, a leader, and an architect of integration and equality.

In post–Civil War time, Richmond's advantages in life were largely enjoyed by the upper-class White male. As a result, able-bodied Blacks left Richmond, going North to seek better economic opportunities far sooner than any other Southern state. William Sanders, an Englishman visiting Richmond, stated:

> Impossible barriers existed, and segregation was the rule of city life with no social intercourse between the two races.
> "I never saw white and colored men in friendly conversation [. . .]

So great the separation that,
    "Not in a single instance did I find white and colored children
playing together."

Obviously children were taught segregation at an early age in Richmond.
The education system and churches were also segregated except for a few
White ministers who led Black congregations.

Richmond's history of race relations is indeed noteworthy. As in the case of
Mahoney and Franklin, the environmental history sheds light on the pre–Civil
War era that inevitably set the tone for the post–Civil War era. This environ-
ment thus provides insight into Black family life in Richmond, Virginia,
Thoms' environment as a child and as a young adult.

In 1860, ten years prior to Thoms's birth, there were 14,275 Black residents of Richmond of whom 11,699 were slaves and 2,576 free. There were
23,635 White residents in Richmond, the entire population totaling 37,910. In
1870, the year Thoms was born, Virginia was readmitted to the Union, and
there were 23,110 Black residents and 27,928 White residents, totaling 51,038.

Thoms was born in 1870 during the post–Civil War period, an era well
depicted by Michael Chesson in *Richmond after the Civil War, 1865–1890*
(1981). According to Chesson:

Before the war, slavery in heavily industrialized Richmond, where
nearly 20% of the black residents were free, differed from the peculiar
institution on southern plantations and farms. The immediate changes
wrought by emancipation were not as evident in Richmond as in rural
areas of the deep south.

The first rule of post-war southern whites was to keep the region a
white man's country, and the principal goal of most white Richmonders was
to keep the capital of Virginia a white ruled city (Preface, Chesson 1981).

Segregation in Richmond extended to public accommodations. Blacks
were not welcome in Richmond's better establishments. When the New Richmond Theater and the Monumental Hotel opened in 1865, antebellum rules
were put in effect. In 1867 and 1869, to counter discrimination, Black business
in Richmond built two hotels.

According to Chesson, public transportation caused the most trouble in
Richmond. Blacks were not allowed to ride inside the carriage of horse-drawn
cars, but could ride outside. This rule did not apply to "Black mammies attending White children"—their passport to civility.

These segregated policies led to minor conflicts in 1866 and two riots in
1867. During the riots, it was noted that while Blacks fought with police, White
civilians could walk undisturbed through their midst. Richmond's Civil Rights
Act stated: "Two [railroad] cars were to be reserved for White ladies, children,
and Black nurses, anyone could ride in the other cars." This, however, was largely
ignored and White men rode in the ladies' car and Black men were excluded.

The quality of life for Blacks in Richmond was degrading. During the 1870s, the Black population experienced widespread arrest, police brutality, and theft of their money taken in the process. Fear was utilized to subordinate the Black population cloaked in civil police duty. Richmond had little regard for its Black population in life and no respect in death. Since people were buried in segregated burial grounds, grave robbers employed by medical schools stole Black corpses. This became the subject of bitter editorials in the *Virginia Star*, a Black newspaper published in Richmond during the 1870s. In 1880, housing developments that tore up historic Black cemeteries were built without regard for the Black population, nor was information provided regarding if and/or where they were reinterred.

Race relations worsened during the 1880s. Blacks were laid off and disqualified from city jobs and employment in city hall because of their race and political affiliations. Discrimination compromised their political involvement and interest. Thus, Black Richmonders focused on surviving, making a living, raising their families, and educating their children rather than on politics.

Black life in antebellum Richmond revolved around the church, and fraternal and benevolent groups. Post–Civil War, these organizations continued and operated openly. Education for Blacks was the only one of the Freedman's Bureau programs that survived Reconstruction, as part of the city school system. However, the hostility of White Richmonders was an obstacle to the Freedman's Bureau Schools. The White population of Richmond did not like Northerners teaching the Black population and the city's gentlemen (who were not gentlemen) assaulted male teachers who taught in these schools. Boys jeered women instructors in the streets and pelted them with rocks.

In the Southern post-bellum period, there was a unified movement for universal education for ex-slaves. Their aspirations that had been constrained by 400 years of enslavement could be achieved. Southern popular demand for free schooling in the late 1880–1890 era was indebted to the ex-slaves' educational movement of the 1860s–1870s. This movement shaped the early education Thoms would obtain in Richmond and inspired her toward lifelong learning.

In 1877, Thomas Muldrop Logan, a former Confederate general and then an industrialist in Richmond stated: "Wherever public schools have been established, the industrial class has become more intelligent and have proved more skillful and efficient."

Southern ex-slave communities stressed leadership training as they pursued their educational objectives. They believed the masses could not achieve political and economic independence or self-determination without first becoming organized, and organization was impossible without well-trained intellectuals—teachers, ministers, politicians, managers, administrators, and businessmen.

To achieve their goals, Black leaders and educators adopted the New England classical curriculum taught in Northern White schools for the elementary Southern public schools. American missionary associations concentrated their efforts and financial aid on normal and higher education, which offered a traditional classical liberal curriculum and prepared educators. The normal school curriculum included the standard English component with additional courses as well as the practice of teaching, Thoms' initial career choice.

The short-term goals of Black education were to provide the masses of ex-slaves with basic literary skills and expectations of citizenship in a democratic society. The long-term goals were intellectual and moral development for responsible leadership that would organize the masses and lead them to freedom and equality. Unfortunately, the democratic society for which they were preparing to be members did not plan to provide them with access to full participation.

Being educated and literate had an important cultural significance to Black Americans and they pursued these goals in opposition to the economic interest of the plantation-dominated South. This drive and quest for education has continued through to the present.

In summary, when slavery ended, Jim Crow began in Richmond and separate but equal was, of course, not equal. All aspects of Richmond were segregated and health care for the Black population was severely deficient or inaccessible, resulting in a high rate of infant and adult mortality. This was explained and rationalized by the Richmond White community as a natural weakness of the Black race and that they were better cared for when they were property, as slaves.

The Black population trend of Richmond reflected a need to leave for better opportunities and was in contrast to other Southern populations. In 1870, Richmond was 45 percent Black, in 1880 it was 44 percent Black; in 1890 it was 40 percent Black, and in 1900 it was 38 percent Black. According to Richmond's Sheriff John Wright during the 1890s: "Best Negroes gone North . . . best keep going."

Thoms came to New York City in 1893 and was fascinated with the city, specifically Harlem, residing at 317 West 138th Street. "She came to New York during the gay 90s but much of the gaiety was not seen by Thoms, who was a most serious minded young woman" (Hernandez 1930, p. 5). During the 1890s, Thoms studied elocution and public speaking at the Cooper Union in New York City. Why Thoms chose to leave teaching and enter nursing has not been recorded. However, during the late nineteenth and early twentieth centuries, many women made career changes from teaching, which was an overcrowded profession, to nursing where the demand far exceeded the supply. Thoms entered the Woman's Infirmary and School of Therapeutic Massage in New York for a course in nursing and she was the only Black student in a class of thirty (Thoms 1929, p. vii). She graduated in 1900, and thereafter spent three years in varied work as a nurse in New York City and in North Carolina. Thoms worked at St. Agnes Hospital in Raleigh, North Carolina, for one year as a head nurse. St. Agnes was organized in 1895, a small fifty-bed Black hospital that later expanded to seventy-five beds.

After three years of employment, Thoms was not satisfied with her informal nursing course, and she decided to seek further training. The exact nature and length of her nursing course at the Woman's Infirmary and School of Therapeutic

Massage has not been recorded. However, the course offered was more than likely a course in the literal sense, and not a full two- or three-year R.N. program.[2] According to Marian Hernandez, R.N., "it was interesting to hear Adah tell that practically all the nursing consisted of was a few simple treatments and keeping the patients happy. The students had few very sick patients, for in those days people did not go to hospitals as they do now" (Hernandez 1930, p. 5).

Historically, the ANA and the American Hospital Association recommended short courses of training in nursing to women who were not qualified by varied criteria for the full course, or who chose not to take the full course. These courses included cooking, household care, diet therapy, basic science classes, and clinical experience in simple nursing procedures (Dolan 1958, p. 328). In addition, some schools of nursing offered a short nursing course, separate from their full R.N. program, for women who wanted some nursing skills for the care of their family.

When Thoms determined that nursing was her chosen career for life, she realized that her course of nursing at the Woman's Infirmary was inadequate preparation. Thoms's evolving experience at this point could be comparable to the mid-twentieth century and present-day experience of women who enter practical nursing programs. They soon find their knowledge, skills, and/or scope of practice limited, relevant to their aspirations in nursing, and decide to continue their education.

In 1903, Thoms entered the newly organized school of nursing at Lincoln Hospital and Home in New York City. This hospital was originally founded in 1839 by a group of White women who met in New York City to consider the destitute condition of the local Black population, and to plan a relief program. Subsequently, an organization was formed, consisting of nine women known as the Society for the Relief of Worthy Aged and Indigent Colored Persons. The goal of the society was to raise money to organize a relief program. One of the organizers, Mrs. Jay, donated the initial large sum of $1,000. However, the society's initial resources were so small that the first year's endeavors were visiting cellar and garret homes of twenty-five pensioners. The help offered in actuality was more like friendly interest and encouragement than tangible aid.

In 1840, during the society's second year, it received a gift of $2,000 that was used to form the first building fund. At this time, the list of infirm visited increased to sixty-three, and the Alms House allocated two rooms for the care of Black patients. During the succeeding years, the society continuously grew and change followed change in corporate name, location, and size of the successive homes. However, the original philosophy was maintained without change—to care for the sick and infirm among the Black people of New York, and to develop among them simple practical methods of self-help and aid for each other.

In 1841, the society rented a house on 51st Street near the Hudson (North) River (known today as 51st Street and the F.D.R. [Franklin Delano Roosevelt] Drive). This facility was used for two years and aged Black men and women were encouraged to come. Those who were sick and in need of medical attention were sent to Bellevue Hospital because the house could not accommodate them. In 1843, a two-story frame building located on 40th Street and Fourth Avenue was purchased for $5,620. Shortly afterward, a third floor was added. It contained two rooms that were used as an infirmary. They were now able to care for a well or sick Black patient population. However, five years later in 1848, the society purchased a new location for $13,000 at 64th and 65th Streets between First Avenue and Avenue A to alleviate overcrowded conditions. The patient population was booming, and in 1858, the society added a three-story wing to the main building. The hospital remained on this site for forty-nine years.

The cost of hospitalization differed at times. Unlike today, for a period of time, patients were admitted with a permit from the Alms House Department, or if their board were paid by friends. By 1846, an agreement was made with the Alms House to accept the city's indigent Black and hospital dependents. Support for this endeavor also came from donations, subscriptions, and bequests. Hospital cases were taxed from $1.05 up to approximately $1.85 per month each, until 1866. All other costs ranged from 50 to 80 cents per day plus a small fee for board.

By 1898, the institution was caring for 200 patients and, at that time, the fourth and final move to its present location at Southern Boulevard and 141st Street took place. Also at this time, a school in the nursing arts for Black women was added. In 1902, the then Colored Home and Hospital was reincorporated as Lincoln Hospital and Home, named after Abraham Lincoln.

The stated purpose of the hospital was to:

■ Provide for the support and comfort of aged or infirm and destitute colored persons of both sexes.
■ Maintain a hospital infirmary and dispensary for the relief of sick or disabled persons without distinction as to race, creed, or color.
■ Maintain a training school and home for nurses.
■ Aid in maintaining a social service department (Lincoln's School for Nurses on the Occasion of Its 100th Anniversary 1939, Folder 1132).

Lincoln School for Nurses has a long, proud, and interesting history. This nursing school was one of approximately ten Black schools of nursing formed during the 1890s in response to nationwide patterns of racial discrimination and segregation. Lincoln quickly became known as a leader, and it was the only Black school of nursing in New York during that era. Lincoln School of Nursing was nationally known, praised, and highly acclaimed for its graduates' quality and performance, and Lincoln received accolades from such noted nursing leaders as Isabel M. Stewart, in a 1939 address at Lincoln's 100th[3] Anniversary, who stated:

There is ample evidence in the history of this school that the Board Members and faculty are sincerely interested in their students, that they have made an effort to study their needs as individuals and as prospective professional nurses, and that they have been ambitious to make this school not only a leader in the education of colored nurses but one of the leading schools of nursing in the country; and much has been accomplished in the forty-one years of the school's existence. The school has won the respect of the community and has proven that its graduates can hold their own as nurses with the graduates (Stewart 1939, MC1237).

In May 1898, the first young woman arrived to start nurse's training. Shortly afterward, she was joined by five other student nurses, constituting the first class of nurses. Two years later, this first class of six nurses graduated. The first student nurses received a great deal of help and encouragement from Mrs. Margaret Rogers, one of the early supervisors, Dr. John A. Hartwell, and Dr. Louis Bishop. The nurses received very little compensation and indeed survived circumstances that did not enhance the learning process. There were no classrooms for student nurses, so they were given classes on the ward at night. Their pleasures, quite controlled, were reading fine books, attending the museum, seeing good plays, and attending religious services. About once or twice a month, they met to discuss the books. In addition to nursing, Lincoln sought to refine them as women.

Their living conditions were meager and rather overcrowded; student nurses lived across from the hospital on Concord Avenue. At a later date, they occupied part of the third floor of the new hospital, which later became male and female medical wards. The student nurses all lived together in a dormitory that consisted of thirty beds. The bathroom had three bowls, two bathtubs, and two toilets. In order to study, the students made a makeshift desk. This was perhaps their first lesson on improvising—an art required in nursing.

The training school continued to develop under various superintendents of nurses. The requirements set down for admission as of 1901 were as follows:

- The term was two years and two months.[4]
- The age limit was from twenty-one to thirty-five years of age.
- Candidates had to bring letters from their minister, dentist, and doctor.
- A personal interview was required when possible.
- Students were told to bring washable dresses for ward work.
- An entrance examination in English, writing, and oral reading was given.

The preliminary course was six months, after which the superintendent of nurses decided whether the student should be retained. If the student were accepted, she had to sign an agreement promising to stay for the remaining two years. The allowance for the first year was $6 and for the second year $7 a month. Each student was given two weeks of vacation a year. Learning continued to be at the bedside and examinations were held frequently. Graduation for each student was contingent upon passing the final examination with a grade of 75 percent or above.

Lincoln graduate nurses organized their Alumnae Association on December 1, 1903, and by 1905 its membership included more than fifty nurses. The Lincoln Alumnae were accepted for membership in the New York State Nurses Association, and thus the graduates were eligible for membership in the ANA.

In 1905, the training school was registered by the Board of Regents and students then had to be accepted by the New York State Board of Education.

During Thoms's two years of training from 1903 to 1905, she was said to have exhibited superior quality and was a dedicated nursing student (Staupers 1971, pp. 455–57). In her second year of training, she was appointed head nurse on a surgical ward. Historically, in the early years of training schools, the second year nursing student was often given the task of being a head nurse. However, identified leadership skills obviously played a role in which students were chosen for this role.

Thoms graduated from Lincoln School of Nursing in 1905 and was employed at the hospital as its operating room nurse and supervisor of the surgical division. She was the first appointed operating room nurse and she received a salary of $25 per month. In this position, she was responsible for the entire surgical division twenty-four hours a day. This twenty-four-hour responsibility is equivalent to the present-day concept of the on-call system. In 1906 Thoms was given added responsibility and appointed the assistant superintendent of nurses. During World War I, Thoms was superintendent of nurses until a new superintendent was chosen (Walton 1929, p. 10). Thoms held the position of assistant superintendent of nurses for eighteen years until her retirement.

During these eighteen years and until a director was selected, Thoms served as the acting director of the nursing school from 1906 through 1923. Despite her longevity in the role and her obvious competence, it was not the custom then to promote a Black woman to a major administrative position.

This acting position was later analyzed by Mabel Staupers, executive secretary and president of the NACGN, who personally knew Thoms:

> Segregation and discrimination worked against negroes in another way also. Since the larger schools of nursing were either controlled chiefly by white boards of directors or by white public officials, seldom was a qualified negro nurse appointed to a high level position. Mrs. Thoms's experience was an example of this type of discrimination. Even though the School of Nursing at Lincoln Hospital was set up as an institution for negro students, although qualified, Adah Thoms was never appointed as a director. She served in the capacity as director, but was given the title of acting director (Staupers 1961, p. 22).

In addition to practicing double standards relevant to Thoms and other Black nurses, Lincoln Hospital and Home refused to hire Black doctors for internships. The Lincoln Hospital and Home was admonished in an article entitled "Why No Interns," that appeared in the 1910 *Journal of the National Medical Association*:

> Today no negro doctor is permitted to be an intern at the institution. This is a fact. It is a painful and palpable violation of the principles of Lincoln's founders and we want to know why. It cannot be said that

there are not competent negro doctors or that they have not applied for admission. Such have applied and the evasion they have received has been a practical expulsion. There is neither right nor reason to this injustice to young negro doctors who deserve and are entitled to the practice which the institution affords. Lincoln Hospital cannot longer afford to continue this discrimination (Why No Interns 1910, p. 152).

Thus Black nurses observed moments of shame, denying equal rights for internship to Black physicians, while paternalistically educating Black female nurses (Sloan 1977, p. 82).

Although Thoms was only given the title of acting director of the nursing school, she took the initiative, evaluated and reorganized the curriculum, and instituted a graduate nurse program to meet the needs of society, health care, and new trends in nursing education. Within this role Thoms was able to utilize her previous career as an educator and a teacher, combining it with nursing education.

In 1913, Thoms started a six-month post-graduate course for registered nurses. Thoms announced her new program at the NACGN convention stating, "Opportunities for post-graduate work which heretofore have been denied colored nurses in most hospitals, are now presenting themselves, and Lincoln is offering its advantages" (Of Interest to Nurses 1913, p. 271). Thoms gave the program high visibility by advertising the program frequently in journals to attract applicants. The graduate program was frequently advertised in the *Journal of the National Medical Association (JNMA)*, which had a large graduate nurse subscription. This gave the program nationwide visibility in attracting graduate nurses.

In addition, one of Thoms's major contributions was her early recognition of the importance of public health nursing as a new and growing field in nursing. In 1917, just five years after the establishment of the NOPHN, Thoms added a course in this new field to the school's basic nursing curriculum, which by this time had increased to three years. Thoms and Lillian Wald of the Henry Street Settlement, which provided public health visiting nurse services, had a long-term relationship of professional respect for one another. Upon Thoms's request, Wald provided an instructor, Jane Hitchcock of the Henry Street Settlement, who taught the course on public health nursing. Thoms in her constant quest for new knowledge took the first course along with her pupils. Thereafter, Thoms took various post-graduate courses in public health.

Much debate today is still generated by the issue of mandatory continuing education for professional nurses. Though one cannot speculate which position Thoms would have taken on mandatory continuing education, it is clear that she needed no mandate to continue her own. Thoms took special continuing education courses at Hunter College and what is now known as the New School for Social Research in New York (*A History in the Making* 1929, p. 560; Thoms 1929, p. ix).

Thoms began working for equal opportunity for Blacks in nursing almost immediately after her graduation from Lincoln Hospital. "She inspired many young nurses to continue their education and to get more and better preparation. A perfectionist, she believed that in nursing there was a great future for young black women" (Staupers 1969, p. 10). Thoms predicted that the future Black nurse would make a real contribution to racial progress through teaching and by her personal example.

In 1908, Thoms played a key part in the organization of the NACGN. Thoms responded to a two-year survey by Martha Franklin of New Haven, Connecticut, regarding the status and employment of Black nurses, and her interest in starting a colored nurses association.

As president of the Lincoln Nurses Alumnae, a position she held for ten years, Thoms invited Franklin and interested nurses to have the first meeting of the NACGN in New York under the sponsorship of Lincoln Hospital Alumnae Association. Although Thoms was an early member of the ANA, she had major concerns about the status of Black nurses who were less fortunate. Specifically, the Black nurses' professional progress was impeded by the racial attitudes that permeated American life.

Thoms was a woman with deep religious conviction. Thus the first meeting took place on August 25, 1908, at St. Mark's Methodist Episcopal Church on West 53rd Street in New York City, where Thoms was a member. Thoms, a charter member of this new organization, was elected its first treasurer, a position of trust. Thoms then organized the New York Local of the NACGN, and the national body met on an annual basis. Thoms worked closely in concert with and in support of Franklin who was the founder, organizer, and first president of the NACGN.

Thoms was a pioneer in the participation of Black women in international organizations. In 1912, the International Council of Nurses (ICN) met in Cologne, Germany, and she was one of the first three Black delegates to attend. Thoms was sent by the board of managers to represent the Lincoln Hospital and Home and to describe its field of service and teaching. Lincoln Hospital also sent another Black delegate who traveled with Thoms, Ada Senhouse, also a Lincoln graduate. Lavinia L. Dock, first secretary of the ICN and a political activist, asked the NACGN to send a delegate representative to the ICN. The NACGN elected Rosa Williams Brown and sent her as their first delegate. She was also a graduate nurse of Lincoln Hospital and Home, and like Thoms, a charter member of the NACGN.

These Black delegates received spontaneous admiration and were held in high esteem by the European nurses and physicians. In a stately pageant representing the historic evolution of nursing, these Black delegates were placed in the center of a modern group as being the newest racial group on an international organizational level to enter nursing.

Always seeking new knowledge, Thoms was able to travel widely in Europe on this trip. She broadened her knowledge of nursing and hospital administration by visiting prominent hospitals in Europe—gathering valuable material for her work. Their attendance at the 1912 ICN meeting is said to have subsequently led Black nurses from Africa, South America, and the Caribbean to become members of the ICN and to attend subsequent ICN meetings. In addition, a valuable contact with nurses in other lands was made with the Black nurses in America (Staupers 1969, p. 20).

Thoms, a charter member of the NACGN and its first treasurer, was elected president of the NACGN at the Eighth National Convention held from August 17 to August 19, 1915. That year's convention was sponsored by St. Agnes Hospital in Raleigh, North Carolina, where Thoms had once been a head nurse. This must have been a triumphant return to old familiar places but with new and exciting beginnings. The convention meeting took place in the Chapel of Shaw University in Raleigh. The newly elected officers were installed by the Reverend Dr. Whitehead of Raleigh. It was now Thursday afternoon and Thoms, the newly elected president, took the gavel and in a few choice remarks accepted the presidency, then proceeded with the final business of the association. After what was said to be a most harmonious and profitable meeting, the NACGN adjourned to meet in New York City in 1916. The invitation to meet in New York City was extended by the New York State Local Colored Graduate Nurses Association which Thoms organized, and the Lincoln Alumnae Association, of which Thoms was president (Of Interest to Nurses 1915, pp. 326–27).

Thoms's presidency made history. She served as president of the NACGN for seven years, from 1916–1923. During her presidency, Thoms set forth many new ideas and established many new policies that in later years became the foundation for advances in education, employment, and community alliances made by its members for Black nurses. Like an architect, Thoms seemed to have a blueprint with specific goals. Some of her efforts were realized during her presidency, some after her presidency, and others after her death. The idea that a national advisory council be organized as a means of developing greater interest in and support for programs of the NACGN was first proposed by Thoms during the early years of her presidency. Thoms was obviously politically astute with this interest to get the community involved in the NACGN. This council later materialized in 1939.

Thoms was a leader in improving conditions within segregated health delivery systems and in combating segregation. In 1916, at the beginning of her first presidency, Thoms began working with the National Urban League and the National Association for the Advancement of Colored People (NAACP) in an effort to change the conditions of Black hospitals and training schools for Black nurses. Surveys of Black hospitals revealed deplorable, inadequate conditions. Black patients and students were subjected to these facilities. Black patients were predominantly hospitalized in all Black hospitals, or in Black wings of established hospitals. An obvious alternative to these disgraceful conditions was integration with institutions already functioning as health care facilities. The NACGN position was that sickness was a personal problem affecting the human race, not a racial problem afflicting one individual race.

Pain, healing, and convalescence are human experiences whether the patient is Black or White. However, nursing administrators had an inveterate image of the Black nurse. They thought that Black nursing students could only adequately care for Black patients, and that they were in fact happier and/or more comfortable in Black schools of nursing. This notion was indeed self-serving and designed to preserve segregation and the status quo.

Thoms was concerned with increasing the NACGN's membership and organizing local and state associations of colored nurses associations. As president, Thoms traveled extensively and addressed state and local nurses' associations. In January 1916, shortly after being elected president, Thoms traveled to Norfolk, Virginia, and met with the Norfolk Nurses Association. In April of that year, the Norfolk Nurses Association planned and organized an active state colored graduate nurses association. The NACGN interest was to increase its membership in unity and organization.

In 1909, at the second NACGN meeting that had been held in Boston, Franklin, then president, had begun the process of building the organization. Franklin had appointed chairpersons of ten different states to organize state level associations of colored graduate nurses, with their purpose being the same as the national body. Like Franklin, Thoms's interest was to increase its membership and organize. And like Franklin, Thoms believed that building the organization was important for its success. Grassroots involvement was key to organizational success and there was much work to be done in order to organize all the states.

At the Ninth Annual Convention of the NACGN held in New York City from August 15 to August 17, 1916, Thoms, having completed her first year as president, dedicated a song that she composed to the NACGN. It became the association's national hymn:

Dedicated to the
National Association of Colored Graduate Nurses
(Tune of Cairnbrook)

Words by ADAH B. THOMS

In this warfare we have listed
Sisters, one and all;
Let us always be united,
Waiting for the call.
Ever seeking to relieve thee,
Onward thus we go;
By His aid we will restore thee,
Trusting ever more.
Never doubting never fearing,
Ours the onward march;
Ask His guidance, always trusting
Jesus, all in all.

> We with gentle hands care thee
> Happy to be near thee,
> Never doubting, always trusting,
> Trusting God, our all.

It was proudly recorded that on the Tuesday afternoon of the convention "The body then arose and sang our national hymn which was composed and dedicated to the NACGN by our honored president, Mrs. A. B. Thoms" (Of Interest to Nurses 1916, pp. 203–207).

Thoms's first speech to the national body provides much insight into her as a person, her broad knowledge and concerns in nursing, her beliefs about nursing as a career for women, and the ideals of womanhood. It was the Wednesday afternoon of August 16, 1916, when:

> . . . promptly at two o'clock the vice president Miss York of Washington, D.C. called the afternoon session of the Association to order, "after which our honored president, Mrs. Adah B. Thoms delivered in her charming, dignified way her annual address which was filled with good things and gave us much food for thought" (*JNMA* 1916, pp. 206–207).

PRESIDENT'S ANNUAL ADDRESS

by Adah B. Thoms

Sister Nurses, Ladies and Gentlemen: It is my pleasure to greet you at this, our Ninth Annual Convention, to present to you some of our problems of the past year, which has indeed been one of great moment, and very eventful to the nursing world at large.

We have faced difficulties of various kinds, those that have confronted us most gravely, being State Registration and Post-Graduate Work in some of the larger training schools, the latter being so necessary to those of us that have graduated from small schools. While they have offered the best at hand, our nurses feel that in order to meet the present day demands and keep abreast of the times, they must seek admittance to some of the larger schools offering a Post-Graduate Course, or if there be no such course offered, make appeals to the governing board asking that such a course be established in these respective schools.

Now that training schools are being conducted in a manner that calls for the most favorable references and the highest standards of efficiency for the pupil, the States, likewise, demanding registration of its graduates; I fail to see why there should be any question about any qualified nurse sitting in examination with her more fortunate sisters, just as her physicians and surgeons.

Is it not a fact that the two professions go hand in hand? It is not a small thing to be admitted into the homes of rich and poor alike, to be left in charge by day and by night with some loved one of that home, with an occasional visit from the family physician who depends entirely upon the watchfulness of the nurse, and accuracy of her reports for the safe restoration to health of that dear one, and yet feel that there is a law, or an examining board in any State, controlled perhaps partly by the same physician who knows the value of that nurse if no other. Must we feel that he would sit idly by and permit that board, without raising a dissenting voice, to abrogate so valuable an assistant?

I feel that the time has come when we as graduate nurses of Standardized Training Schools should take up this matter very seriously and seek an interview with the Board of Nurse Examiners in every State in the Union where registration is required, for it is my unbiased conviction that nursing is the broadest professional field open to women today. Therefore I urge you to prepare yourselves to meet the present day needs and future demands.

While we have faced these problems, they have been equally balanced with brighter outlooks for our future. We may congratulate ourselves upon the work that we are doing along special lines, yet I do not feel that we should be satisfied until we have placed our National Association on a much stronger basis and raised its tower so high that it will stand out like a beacon light.

The field for nurses today is very wide; it is no longer confined to the sickroom. It covers the nurseries, the milk stations, the schools, the playgrounds, factories, stores, the districts, the courts; social service and various avenues now open to the graduate nurse. And by united effort of the members of this association, more of us shall engage in these activities.

We as nurses should stand very close together, closer than any other women in public life; we should have deeper sympathies, more interests in common. For no other women pass through the same discouraging period of loneliness and criticism of uphill struggles and ingratitude as the nurses; not only through her training, but in after life.

It has been my pleasure during the past year to search for those that were apparently lost from our ranks. Of the 742 letters sent out by your presiding officer, 512 replies have been received from my co-workers, each one expressing her faith and loyalty and pledging her support towards standardizing the profession of nursing along social, moral, economic and Christian lines.

I also visited many of the homes of our members; wherever I went the welcome was most cordial, each one seemed interested and doing a splendid work, not only happy to be one of us but eager too, that others should be. Each time I returned home stimulated and encouraged, feeling that my efforts were not in vain.

This spirit of co-operation was further verified a few weeks ago, when we seemed on the verge of a dreadful calamity, and indeed to us it was, when six of our "Gallant Tenth" spilled their life's blood on Mexican soil in defense of their country.

On June 29th the managers of Lincoln Hospital offered to equip a "Base Hospital Unit" and give colored registered nurses an opportunity to become members of the Red Cross Corps. This offer was accepted at Washington at a cost of $25,000,000 with an enrollment of 65 nurses. I am pleased to inform you that within 28 hours 31 of this number had offered their names in answer to the appeal and at the present time there are 87 of these noble women ready to enroll for duty at the front if called.

This proves loyalty, in loyalty there is unity, in unity there must be strength.

It may also interest you to know, that of the 100,000 nurses of which this country is proud today; that we number about 920.

I further welcome this opportunity to express my sincere thanks to the officers and members of this Association for their loyal support during the year, and deeply appreciate the honor bestowed upon me at our last meeting to serve you in this capacity. If in the slightest degree I have met your approval, permit me to say, it is due entirely to your excellent and hearty co-operation, for which I offer my heart-felt thanks. And this thought I leave with you: If we wish to succeed in this great work that we have undertaken, we must be earnest, we must be courageous, we must be imbued with absolute determination.

Remember that every door of opportunity is open to women, and the professional nurse may find therein a place for herself.

Let unity and service be our watchword, and may this Association always stand for the highest standard of nursing, and for the purest ideals of true womanhood.

Thoms, a charismatic leader, used the feminist concept of sisterhood as a unifying motivator for the NACGN. She began her national speeches addressing the assembled group as sisters. As defined in *A Glossary of Feminist Theory*, the term sisterhood was powerful in mobilizing women and encouraging solidarity where it was extremely difficult in the face of widespread cultural disparagement of women. Above all, sisterhood pointed toward political projects of alliances that might be forged (Sonya 1977, p. 278).

Thoms ended her 1916 national speech using the feminist concept of unity and womanhood. Like sisterhood, the concept of womanhood was a powerful motivating term.

The NACGN convention meetings during Thoms's presidency were dynamic, exciting full schedules. In addition to conducting the business of the organization at hand and hearing presentations of various committee reports, nurses presented papers and clinical demonstrations and the group made trips to hospitals to update their clinical knowledge. Doctors and civic guests also made presentations of interest to nurses professionally, theoretically, and socially. In addition, the NACGN sent letters and telegrams of protest or concern about professional and civic issues to appropriate elected officials, individuals, and organizations. This collective political action and unified voice made their presence known.

At the 1916 convention, during Thoms's first year as president, there were various standing committees and committee reports. Thoms expressed that she had received loyal support from officers and members of the association. There was an executive committee called to order by Thoms one-and-a-half hours before the national body convened at 9 A.M. on Tuesday, August 15, 1916. This committee dealt with a number of propositions brought before the committee. Their actions were reported to the national body as the convention began. This committee not only met before the national body was called to order, but they also met during the year, at times and places convened by the president. At the beginning of the convention, Thoms appointed an ad hoc committee for the entire three days (Tuesday–Thursday) of the convention to facilitate the smooth progress of all matters. The report of the national organizer, Eva P. Lewis of Virginia, stated that there were several organizations of colored graduate nurses, both state and city, in good and flourishing condition. What was developing here analytically was comparable to the ANA, New York Nurses Association, and a district nursing association. The presidents of several local organizations gave encouraging reports about their Associations. The membership committee read their minutes in a report to the national body, keeping them abreast of their growing numbers of support and interest in their united cause. The Commission on State Registration and Post-Graduate Work committee had encouraging results. The national organization was pleased to learn that a great many Black nurses were able to register in states where it was thought they could not, especially in the South. State registration and acceptance into post-graduate nursing courses was a major concern for Black nurses because of discrimination in the state registration practices and admission to not only generic nursing programs but post-graduate nursing courses as well. The secretaries of all other various committees presented their reports, including the treasurer's report, to the national body. The association acknowledged that too much credit cannot be given to these officers who were handling the business end of the association. In addition, there was a nominating committee that handled the election procedures of the organization and new officers were elected and installed each year.

Some of the papers presented by nurses were "Public Health Nursing and Sanitation in the South," "The District Nurse as an Educator," "The Nurse in Social Service," "Nursing Tuberculosis in the South," "Pioneering Community Work," and "Post-Graduate Work: Its Present Importance and Future Demands." Nurses who were out of training school for a number of years were urged to return for post-graduate work to prepare themselves to provide better service. Papers were also presented on "The Call of the Profession," "How We May Raise the Standards of Nursing, Discipline," "Social Disease Among Children," "Care of the Convalescent," and health care issues related to women.

Thoms had high ideals regarding womanhood and during her presidency. The NACGN fostered decision-making and choices for women by organizing family planning clinic demonstrations. These demonstrations were often incorporated into the programs of their annual convention. Thus, not only did these Black nurses meet for a convention, but they simultaneously reached out to women in the community for health care guidance and education. Local and state NACGN organizations also followed this pattern of community outreach to women.

At this time, the United States was embroiled in the birth control controversy. In October 1916, Margaret Sanger and her sister Ethel Byme opened a birth control clinic in Brownsville (Brooklyn), New York. Sanger and her sister were arrested for violating the Comstock Law by opening a clinic and teaching birth control. Evolving names for Sanger's efforts were family planning and planned parenthood. During Thoms's residency, the NACGN continuously provided community education on family planning.

During Thoms's years as president, some notable Black doctors addressed the NACGN.[5] At the 1916 convention, there were presentations of papers by doctors of both races, some of which were "Child Hygiene," "Poliomyelitis," "Proper Care of the Feet," "Care of the Eyes," "Care of the Teeth," "Relationship of the Nurse with the Physician," and "Unity in the Relationship Between the Nurse and Physician." The relationship between the nurse and the physician was evident in each convention during Thoms's presidency and it was presented each year either by a nurse or a doctor. Thoms had a strong interest in collaborating with civic groups. Eugene Kinkler, executive secretary of the National League on Urban Conditions Among Negroes, addressed the national body and discussed the phases of work his league was in. He pointed out the many ways in which the social workers and visiting nurses could affiliate with his organization.

The organization also took time during their conventions to pay respect to noted leaders who had died within the past year. At the 1916 convention the group retired early in memory of the late Dr. Booker T. Washington of Tuskegee Institute in Alabama. Martha York, first Vice President of the NACGN, read a glowing tribute to his life followed by a eulogy by the Honorable James W. Johnson of New York.[6]

On the Wednesday at 7:30 P.M., Thoms and the New York Local Association of the NACGN escorted the entire group down to the Lower East Side of New York City to the Henry Street Settlement House. They were graciously welcomed and entertained by their hostess, May M. Ammerman, R.N. The evening was well planned with splendid musical entertainment, refreshments, and a tour of the Henry Street Settlement. In addition, they toured Grand Street House, which had a playground on the roof where the nurses danced for a while. On a more serious note, the nurses were impressed and amazed at the good work being done in such small quarters in a big city like New York. In particular, the group thought that the settlement house work was well planned and organized. Special thanks were given to May Ammerman and her corps of workers at the Henry Street Settlement for their cooperation with the local association of New York City and for making it so pleasant for the visiting nurses who were attending the NACGN Convention. After the business of the Ninth Annual Convention on Thursday, the NACGN was given a reception and dance at the Music School Settlement. On Friday, the group gave Thoms a day of pleasure at Coney Island, which was said to be a day that would long be remembered by all. On Saturday at 4 P.M., the association was entertained with a musical program, a folk dance, and refreshments at the Lincoln Settlement House in New York City. On Sunday afternoon, as the weekend pleasure came to an end, the group was given what was said to be a most delightful sightseeing trip around Manhattan Island.

Thoms's first year as president of the NACGN revealed her extensive work toward organizational building at the grassroots level and a well-planned annual convention of business, professional presentations, socialization, and networking. However, Thoms's first year as president was the calm before the storm.

When Congress declared war on Germany the next year on April 6, 1917, Thoms immediately communicated with Black nurses, alerting and encouraging them to enroll in the American Red Cross nursing service, the only avenue into the U.S. Army Nurse Corps. The Army Reorganization Bill passed by Congress in 1901 established the Army Nurse Corps as a division of the Army Medical Service. Jane A. Delano organized the American Red Cross Nursing Service, which in addition to nurses included the surgeon generals of the Army and Navy. Although organized by Jane Delano, the surgeon generals held the administrative clout. This group developed a system by which a reservoir of nurses could be called upon as reserves for military service and emergency service with the American Red Cross. Membership in the ANA, the Army Nurse Corps, and the American Red Cross was required to join this reserve group. This was a dilemma for Black nurses, most of whom were barred from their states' nurses' associations because of their race.

On December 5, 1911, the National Committee on Red Cross Nursing Service met and discussed at length the question of the Black nurse. Prior meetings were held with the surgeon general in regard to the appointment of Black nurses to the Army Nurse Corps. They contended that it was impossible to secure proper (separate) quarters for them; therefore, the surgeon general's office never considered within its policies the appointment of Black nurses. Thus it was decided that Black nurses should not be enrolled for service under the Red Cross (Thoms 1929, pp. 155–156). When Black nurses applied to the American Red Cross, they were constantly rejected because of their race. Neither Thoms nor the NACGN accepted this rejection. It was tantamount to an expulsion and it made Thoms all the more adamant and resolute in her interest to eradicate any barriers precluding their enrollment. They organized a campaign to get the American Red Cross to accept Black nurses.

One can only speculate analytically why Thoms and members of the NACGN wanted so desperately to belong to this reserve group of nurses and serve during the war:

- Soldiers who had sustained injuries were ill, and race did not make a difference to those in pain, trying to repair an injury, or convalesce.
- They believed it was an opportunity to serve their country, change their low status, demonstrate their abilities, and for White American nurses to develop a trust in this group of nurses as colleagues and competent practitioners.
- Even though this group of Black nurses knew they were considered second-class citizens, they felt this was still their country and they would like to come together with White Americans in time of war.

On June 16, 1917, the National Red Cross met and a plan was approved for the "utilization of colored nurses in connection with base hospitals if such were organized for colored troops alone." Ironically, four days later, the plan was modified by the same body. It was then decided there would be no general enrollment of Black nurses, unless the surgeon general could find a way to use them, in which case they would be enrolled for that special service only (Thoms 1929, p. 156).

According to Staupers, by the autumn 1917, a great deal of correspondence had transpired between Thoms and Delano, chairman of the American National Red Cross Nursing Service. By a letter dated September 3, 1917, Delano responded to one of Thoms's letters stating her willingness to accept Black nurses at home and abroad. However, Delano further clarified the matter by stating that their acceptance and assignment actually rested with the surgeon general of the Army. His acceptance seemed far from realization. He staunchly refused to agree with their enrollment and would not authorize their services. His refusal was persistent even though their services were accepted by Delano. Nevertheless, some faint hope remained that Black nurses would be assigned to the training camp for Black officers at Des Moines, Iowa. However, this aspiration eventually faded and by December 1917, Thoms was informed that there would be finite enrollment of Black nurses, although there was no current indication that they would be assigned to duty. Even in light of this dubious prognosis, a few Black nurses did enroll (Thoms 1929, pp. 157–161).

Black doctors were also struggling with the U.S. Army regarding discrimination and segregation. They were in the midst of a national campaign to combat their grievances in which they also included discrimination against nurses. The NMA was informed by letter that Black nurses who were registered were eligible for enrollment in the Red Cross Service. In support of Thoms's struggle, on August 28, 1918, the NMA made the following declaration:

We heartily approve the decision of the War Department to enlist the negro trained nurses in the Red Cross Service. However, the service is limited to base hospitals at home. The negro trained nurse is loyal and true, and we appeal to the War Department to reward her loyalty and devotion, by giving her the opportunity to serve the brave black soldiers in the battlefields of Europe (Of Interest to Nurses 1918, p. 139).

In addition, on December 12, 1918, after the Armistice was signed, the NMA sent a memorandum addressed to the Honorable Secretary of War. The subject of the memorandum was "The Treatment of Negro Physicians, Dentists and Nurses by the United States Government, in the World War." Accompanied by a cadre of supporting letters, they stated that limitations based on race were still too evident in this branch of the Service.

However, while the war was still in progress, and at the Tenth Annual Convention of the NACGN, held in August 1917 in Louisville, Kentucky, Thoms was introduced as our honored president, charter member of the NACGN, and superintendent of Lincoln Hospital. What personnel crisis occurred to put Thoms in the position of superintendent of Lincoln Hospital during the war was not recorded. Thoms's presidential address encompassed many topics and/or issues, including her relentless philosophy about the American Red Cross and the NACGN's readiness:

> I feel as if we are in the midst of a great political campaign. It is true the government has not yet found it convenient to accept us in the American Red Cross Nursing Association as the individual or in the group, yet I know that this body of well trained women is ready to stand as a unit in answer to the nation's call to contribute this 'bit' towards alleviating the suffering of humanity.
>
> Let us keep within us the spirit of preparedness—nursing preparedness which means nothing more than doing our full duty along the lines assigned to us in church, society, and state—being ready to meet every emergency and give the very best that within us lies.
>
> It is a fact that we cannot at this time serve at the front with our more fortunate sisters by profession. Perhaps there remains for us a greater work at home. The spirit we show, the methods we adopt and the results accomplished will best determine our future throughout the world with all races. It is for us to outline our course. Let us find our place in our own way, along some special line, then hold to our purpose. If we cannot serve in a base hospital or be nurses on the battlefield, the service we render in our own communities will count for just as much, if wisely directed (Of Interest to Nurses 1917, pp. 209–210).

Thoms ended her national address to the NACGN with a critical analogy of Black and White women (nurses) and an indication of her forthcoming resolution for Black nurses to work at home. Thoms speaks of "our more fortunate sisters by profession," meaning White nurses who were serving their country during World War I. This experience, which Thoms crystallizes in her address, heightens and demonstrates the premise that gender equality without racial equality still leaves the Black woman outside the door of equal opportunity.

Unable to join the Red Cross Nursing Service, Thoms sought a mechanism to put Black nurses to work for the war at home. Thoms organized the Blue Cross Circle of Nurses who would work with the Circle of Negro Relief toward war efforts in the United States. The goals of the Blue Circle of Nurses were similar to the Red Cross Nursing Service: to promote the interest and improve the conditions of Black soldiers and sailors at home. These nurses were then recruited by the Circle for Negro Relief and were paid to work in local communities, to teach proper nutrition, sanitation, and appropriate dress and make home visits as community health nurses. The Blue Circle of Nurses worked with county and state agencies advising them of potential health problems.

Thoms sought to affiliate the Blue Cross Circle of Nurses with the American Red Cross Nursing Service. Thoms's interest to affiliate with the Red Cross Nursing Service was not reciprocated and never came to fruition. The Blue Cross Circle of Nurses dissolved due to a lack of funding and unsuccessful attempts to acquire philanthropic donations for this worthy cause.

By the winter of 1917–1918, there was a critical shortage of civilian R.N.s due to the war. Only graduate nurses were eligible for military service in the United States, the question regarding the use of Red Cross Nurses Aides versus trained nurses for the military was full of emotion and controversy. The Surgeon General William C. Gorges, initially against the proposition, later agreed to use nurses aides in a notice to the American Red Cross on February 9, 1918, to help defray the shortage of nurses in the Army Nurse Corps. These aides were trained in a four-week course in elementary hygiene and home care of the sick, supplemented by a short practical course of one month (Kalisch & Kalisch 1978, pp. 304–306). This controversy of trained nurses versus untrained nurses aides obviously excluded the use of trained Black nurses. Nevertheless, Thoms and members of the NACGN waited ready and prepared.

Meanwhile, a massive influenza epidemic with a morbidity far greater than the war casualties was in progress. On November 11, 1918, the Armistice was signed and troops and medical units began to return home. By the time news of the Armistice came, the influenza epidemic in America had taken its toll. In an analysis put forth by Kalisch and Kalisch, the continued movement of the troops created avenues of travel for the disease, and the mingling of people from the United States and abroad was probably the facilitating element in the development of the highly virulent strain of influenza that emerged.

The chief dangers of influenza were the complications, especially pneumonia, meningitis, neuroses, mental aberrations, destruction of mental equilibrium, sinus and ear infection. However, pneumonia was the most widespread and most disastrous. The large number of deaths from the influenza epidemic was due to a particularly virulent type of pneumonia complication which did not exist as a separate epidemic, but co-existed as a complication (Atkinson 1919, pp. 39–40; 1921, pp. 20–21).

Doctors and nurses in military and civilian hospitals also became ill with the influenza, causing a severe depletion among health care personnel. An additional analysis put forth by Kalisch and Kalisch provides further insight into this epidemic. Nurses were expected to perform the more everyday chores of caring for influenza patients and dealing with situations of life and death. Other physicians were unavailable, and in the final analysis the nurses were the heroines of the fight of hundreds of thousands of human bodies against the epidemic. Often the nurses worked until they themselves became patients, sometimes with fatal results. During this great epidemic, from September 1918 to August 1919, the United States experienced the highest death rate in its history.

With so many nurses ill, the Army was in serious need of replacements. This critical nurse shortage resulting from the epidemic finally impelled the surgeon general to authorize the use of Black nurses. Although the first Black nurse to enroll was in July 1918, it was not until December 1918, after the war was over, when eighteen qualified Black nurses were appointed to the Army Nurse Corps. They were stationed at Camp Grant in Illinois and at Camp Sherman in Ohio with full rank and pay.

According to Staupers, at neither camp were the patients segregated, and the Black nurses were assigned to all services. Marian Brown Seymor, R.N., assigned to Camp Sherman reported their acceptance by the patients, Chief Nurse, and medical and nursing staff. There was the same acceptance at Camp Grant. They were, however, forced to live in separate facilities on the base and to utilize separate recreational facilities. The Black nurses served until the crisis ended and displayed evidence that they could meet this challenge. "The war department reported that the services of the colored nurses were satisfactory in every respect" (Thoms 1929, p. 164).

Mary M. Roberts, chief nurse of Camp Sherman, wrote:

> I do not mind saying that I was quite sure when orders came for the colored group, that I was about to meet my waterloo. My feeling now is that it was a valuable experience for them and for me. They really were a credit to their race, did valuable service for our patients and it was a service that patients appreciated. I now find myself deeply interested in the problems of all colored nurses and believe in giving them such opportunities as they can grasp for advancement (Thoms 1929, p. 164).

Chief Nurse Sayres L. Millken, who was at Camp Sevier in South Carolina, wrote that the idea of securing the services of colored nurses "did not immediately meet with enthusiasm as fully 75 percent of the nurses were women of Southern birth and had very positive objections to working with colored nurses." The need was so imperative that it was decided to employ them, furnishing them with quarters separate from white nurses. Nurse Sayres stated that about twelve colored nurses reported for duty and were placed in subordinate positions. They were found to be well trained, quiet and dignified. Nurse Sayres continued her assessment by stating that, although these nurses had no opportunity to display executive ability, they did and can fill a valuable place in the nursing profession (Thoms 1929, pp. 166–167).

Thoms proudly stated that Black nurses met the influenza emergency "with a zest that proved their worth beyond a doubt." However, she realistically made a post-war analysis of the entire prolonged experience. "For many years," she said, "the Black nurse was considered inefficient, and in many branches of the profession, she has been called to serve only when absolute necessity demanded it." Thoms expressed that the Black nurse was put through the acid test, and was found skilled and efficient in the practice of her calling. She felt as if she was in the midst of a great political war, and that Black nurses were not accepted in the Red Cross Nursing Service until the eleventh hour. In addition, Black nurses were not sent overseas. However, they served in various camps and "acquitted themselves with dignity and credit." Thoms's use of the word acquitted is interesting and requires analysis. This term is often applied in a legal sense when someone or a group successfully proves itself innocent of wrongful charges. The word suggests that Black nurses had profound feelings about how they were viewed by other nurses, organizations (i.e., American Red Cross, U.S. Army), and society in general. Thoms asked the nurses in the NACGN not to give up the idea of affiliating with the American Red Cross, "Now that the war is over," she said, "this is what they expect us to do. We must become members and remain members." Thoms also thought that the NACGN should be firm, and "when the American Red Cross needs us, they must find us" (Of Interest to Nurses 1920, pp. 48–49; Thoms's Presidential Address 1919; Nurses Section: Presidential Address 1920, pp. 73–75).

The Secretary of War, Newton D. Baker, stated in a response letter dated December 19, 1918, that he had gone very thoroughly into the question of the alleged discrimination against Negro physicians, dentists, and nurses. Mr. Baker explicated that:

> . . . when hospitals at the camps were constructed, provisions were not made for the proper accommodation of both colored and white nurses. It was not known to which camps colored troops would be sent in numbers, sufficient to warrant provision for colored nurses, and in practically all camps, the numbers of colored troops has been a variable factor. Colored nurses were not called into service, because it was believed to be unwise to do so, owing to the lack of suitable accommodations. The commanding General in France was asked if colored nurses could be satisfactorily used and provided for in France, and the answer was that they could not be properly handled. This office began to take steps to provide accommodations for colored nurses when it appeared that a constant number of colored troops were expected at six camps. These quarters were nearing completion when the Armistice was signed, etc. (Baker 1919, pp. 27–28).

Clearly, the perceived need to provide segregated housing for Black nurses was a major factor in denying their entrance to the military and subsequent utilization.

Thoms's position was that the signing of the Armistice had not in the slightest degree lessened the activities of the nursing forces; the character of the work had been changed to meet the period of reconstruction. The Thoms continued her involvement with the American Red Cross regarding membership of Black nurses and in 1920, she met with Clara Noyes, head of Red Cross Nursing Service in Washington, D.C.

In April 1921, Thoms attended a Conference of the American Red Cross and was assured that the Red Cross would like every nurse to enroll in order to be prepared for duty should the need arise. However, the American Red Cross maintained that enrollment does not mean one will be called for duty (Of Interest to Nurses 1920, p. 48; Thomas 1920, p. 72; Nurses Section: Nurses Notes, *JNMA* 1921, p. 218).

By 1921, Thoms's leadership began to take on further national prominence. Thoms was appointed by Dr. C. C. Pierce, assistant surgeon general of the U.S. Army to the Woman's Advisory Council of Venereal Diseases of the U.S. Public Health Service. She was recommended to this appointment by Dr. Rosco C. Brown, director of colored work (Nurses Section: Nurses Notes, *JNMA* 1921, p. 63).

Venereal disease among the Black population was a prevalent health problem, as well as among other races, particularly in relation to World War I. Captain Arthur B. Springarn of the U.S. Sanitary Corps explicated in a 1919 article that "at the outset, we are hampered by our ignorance of the prevalence and distribution of venereal disease among negroes, and by the absence of reliable statistics." The problem, he said, was further complicated by many factors such as race discrimination, indifference of the White community and civil authorities to Negro health, morals, and general lack of education. He stated that there were bad sanitary and worse housing conditions under which negroes are obliged to live, often in dark alleys and usually in the most morally hazardous sections of the community. In addition, there were differences in the machinery available for the use of the Black races for diagnosis and treatment of venereal diseases. He further explained that the subject of venereal diseases among negroes has never been scientifically studied,[7] and the statistics available are either colored by prejudice or are generalizations predicated on the most meager facts (Springer 1919, p. 48).

The 1921 NACGN National Convention was held in Washington, D.C., as a guest of the Freedman's Hospital Alumnae Association. The NACGN was received at the White House by President Warren G. Harding. Thoms and the nurses carried a large basket of American Beauty roses, which they presented to President and Mrs. Harding. They requested that the NACGN be placed on record as the organized body of 2,000 trained women ready when needed for world service. Thoms never lost sight of her goal for Black nurses to be accepted into the military service and to serve their country.

Thoms believed that World War I taught "us" the greatest lessons of their times (Nurses Section, Presidential Address 1920, p. 73):

First, It has taught us the lesson of self-reliance. It has aroused the cooperative spirit in all welfare organizations. It has taught us to realize our material needs and inspired us to launch a campaign to remedy them.

Second, It has taught us the lesson of unselfishness and of greater love for humanity. It has brought us to a full realization of our social, moral, and economic condition, and has given us a definite understanding of reconstruction even in our day.

Third, and greatest of all, it has taught us the lesson of service.

Throughout the war, the business of the NACGN continued on as usual. The architects again, as in so many times over the years, were centerstage. The architects had quite an influence on the NACGN membership. It was now 1919, August 19–21, at the Annual Convention, in which Thoms as president was presiding. An account of officers being installed by one of the newly elected officers conveys their majestic effect and influence upon the membership:

Miss Mahoney was installing officers, assisted by Miss Franklin. Miss Mahoney in her delicate manner interestingly and instructionally told each officer of their duty before her. Miss Mahoney considered us duly installed as we took our seats with an inspiration to make more and better the coming year than before (*Minutes of the NACGN* 1919, p. 76).

ILLUSTRATION 4–2.
1921 NACGN Delegate Annual Meeting held in Washington, D.C. Mahoney is fourth from right; Franklin and Thoms are fifth and sixth from the right. Courtesy of Schomburg Center for Research in Black Culture, the New York Public Library, New York.

Thoms was an early believer in the professional nurse's identity. She was outspoken and an advocate against the NACGN merging with the NMA, the Black physicians association. Although Thoms and many members of the NACGN were anxious for other organizations to lend support to the NACGN's program, they did not want the organization to lose its identity. As president, Thoms opposed a merger and led the majority within the NACGN in opposition. Some members of the NACGN were in support of the merger, and believed it would strengthen their purpose. Thoms's position was that there could be an affiliation without a merger. She believed it was wiser to work as a group of nurses toward membership in the ANA and the NOPHN (Staupers 1969, pp. 22–23). Thoms's influence prevailed and it is well portrayed through this endeavor. This opposition facilitated the groundwork for Black nurses to obtain membership in the NOPHN and thereafter the ANA in 1951.[8]

The NMA had been established in 1895 in response to the exclusion and rejection Black physicians experienced. Their journal began in 1909. In 1911, the editors of the *JNMA* made a declaratory statement that doctors and nurses should be in closer relationship, since their common goal was to relieve suffering. Several Black nurses were subscribing to the *JNMA* and it was said that they enjoyed reading the journal as much as physicians. It was decided to open its columns to nurses for short, interesting articles pertaining to nursing, hospitals, training schools, and private nursing. The journal had an editorial column that often commented on nursing and related matters. One interesting article was entitled, "Our Allies the Nurses." (Of Interest to Nurses 1911, pp. 159, 169).

The NMA had earlier invited the NACGN to hold its annual meetings at the same time and place as the NMA. Thereafter, the NMA formally invited the NACGN to join its organization. On recommendation of the executive committee, the NACGN decided to remain as a separate and distinct organization apart from the NMA. The executive committee thanked the NMA for the invitation to join it (Kenny 1913, p. 223; Of Interest to Nurses 1915, p. 327). However, the NMA and the NACGN honored each other's invitations for a representative delegate at each other's conventions. Each representative generally addressed the group and reported the particulars of the meeting back to his or her respective organization.

Many members of the NACGN were concerned that the NMA would eventually want to control the NACGN and its practice. In addition, they were justifiably reluctant to merge with a profession that was predominantly male. This concern was justified in light of the status of women in American society: by and large nursing a woman's profession, medicine a man's profession, and the historic relationship of the physician to the nurse was one of control and subservience.

Although Thoms refused the merger, the NMA respected her as a nursing leader. In August 1917, Thoms was invited to address the NMA. She took the opportunity to discuss four important issues: the newly proposed National

Nursing Registry, small hospitals, the quality of nursing schools and their product, and her polished stance on merger of the NACGN with this medical association:

> The National Association of Colored Graduate Nurses proposes to establish a national registry which will be open to graduate, registered nurses only. This registry will be the means of aiding doctors and the public in securing the best nurses with the least exertion, and will likewise be a means of helping the nurses to secure desirable positions. Our object in establishing this registry is to raise the standard of nursing, for if doctors will employ only the best nurses, then only those who are determined to be the very best will enter the profession.
>
> Throughout the country there are many small hospitals and sanatoria trying to conduct training schools for nurses. In many instances the nurse in charge of these institutions has but little more knowledge than the pupils she is endeavoring to instruct. These hospitals and all hospitals should have as superintendents and head nurses only those who are graduates of large training schools and hold the title of "R.N." Such women are the only ones properly fitted for such work and are a benefit and a credit to any institution. If the doctors who have charge of these small hospitals would see that they employed only graduate registered nurses, it would be an incentive to those in training to pursue their courses until they became proficient. Thus we would eliminate the incompetent nurse.
>
> Many times it has been suggested that the doctors' and nurses' associations become affiliated. I take this opportunity of saying that there can be no closer affiliation between any two individuals or bodies of individuals than when they are working to accomplish a worthwhile objective. All who are working for progress and uplift are affiliated whether knowingly or unknowingly. To speak of becoming affiliated suggests that a separateness or difference exists. The very nature of our work makes it impossible for us to work apart. From the humblest nurse just beginning to take temperatures to the most renowned specialist we are one in purpose. We are all contributing our bit toward making the world a happier and healthier place in which to live and to develop.
>
> As we look back over the years and see the progress that has been made by our race in the medical and nursing professions we are filled with pride to know that, despite the handicaps that beset us on every side, we are moving steadily forward. Recently our President said in his wonderful masterpiece that the world must be made safe for democracy. Whether he meant to include us or not makes no difference; we are included and there is no power outside of ourselves that can keep us from sharing with the rest of mankind the liberty and freedom for which democracy stands (Thoms 1929, pp. 214–216).

It was 1917 and there was much debate as to whether nursing was a profession. All of Thoms's ideas were progressive and her address to the NMA clearly identified most of the factors that describe how an association can control a profession through four main functions (Monnig 1983, pp. 40–41):

1. *To set boundary lines, including lines of demarcation between qualified and unqualified persons.*

   "Only those nurses who are graduates of large training schools and hold the title of R.N. should be superintendents and head nurses."

Although in a very truthful, polished manner she informed the group that they were working together for a common cause, she maintained her position of no merger with the NMA. Therefore, she maintained nursing boundaries. According to Chaska, boundary demarcation has been achieved by a profession in three ways: professional association, legislation, and education.

2. *To define the scope of practice and maintain high standards of professional practice.*

   "If only these R.N.s were employed in small hospitals and in all hospitals it would be an incentive to those in training to pursue their course until they become proficient. Thus we would eliminate the incompetent nurse."

3. *To raise the status of the professional group.*

   "Our object in establishing this registry is to raise the standard of nursing. By raising the standard of nursing, the status of the professional group is ultimately raised."

4. *To promote recognition by society of its practitioners as the only one fully competent to practice its particular skills.*

   "This registry will be the means of aiding the doctors and the public in securing the best nurses."

Thoms's position against a merger was not taken lightly. During Thoms's presidency, the NMA continued to urge the NACGN to merge organizations, and hold its national conventions at the same time and place as the NMA. In 1920, the president of the NMA appointed Dr. John Kenny of Tuskegee Institute, Alabama, to be its representative to the August 1920 National Convention of the NACGN held in Alabama at the Tuskegee Institute.

Dr. Kenny brought warm greetings to the NACGN from the NMA and proceeded to expand upon his interesting and socially spiced perception of how the joint national conventions could be arranged. He began his address by stating:

The relationship between the nurse and the physician is very close. We regard you as our sisters and wonder why you are so selfish as to hold all your meetings apart from us? Four-day sessions properly managed gives lots of time for business and some for social intercourse, and should some of our doctors get a little close to the nurses it would not always be a bad idea, for I know some doctors and nurses who have formed a lifetime partnership that had proved very acceptable to the individuals and to society (Kenny 1920, pp. 78–79).

Dr. Kenny's address appealed to the professional nurses as a group of women, hoping to spark Cupid's interest by suggesting that marriages could grow out of the two organizations merging and holding annual conventions at the same time. Historical perceptions would have it that after hearing such an appeal, these nurses would have run to the hairdresser, polished their nails, perfumed down, and dressed up. While some of the nurses may have done some of these things anyway, the majority of the NACGN chose not to merge with the NMA.

Dr. Kenny continued by restating the NMA's position that the journal of the NMA was open to the NACGN—"make it your own." Dr. Kenny suggested that every issue should contain a full nurses' section, and if not, it is because the nurses are not contributing. In addition, he asked for group subscription to the journal of the NMA to afford the nurses' reduced rates of $1.50 per nurse per year; $45 was given to the NMA at this meeting in subscriptions from the NACGN.[9]

Review of the journal of the NMA from its inception, throughout Thoms's presidency, and through 1930 reveals that it was exceptionally interesting. The journal encompassed varied topics on clinical discourse, modes of treatment, nursing news and issues, letters of protest and support, editorials, lawsuits against doctors, appointments, promotions in small hospitals, local and national health care news, health fairs in which free health care was given, notices of births, deaths, and marriages, etc. The journal of the NMA provided insight into the image Black doctors had of the nurse as reflected in their publications. The nurses' image was low and one of servitude at its inception. It reached its peak of respect during Thoms's presidency and continued so throughout 1930. As the nurses' image improved, articles appeared stating that nurses are our allies, that we cannot do without the nurses, that nurses' work is as important as the doctors, etc. In addition, articles included such statements as, when needed, the Black nurse should share her knowledge with Black doctors because many were denied the privilege of an internship at a large hospital due to racial discrimination and segregation.

During Thoms's years as president of the NACGN, the journal of the NMA contained a full section on nursing. Although the NACGN had a journalist, Thoms at times contributed directly to the journal, making full use of the visibility this national journal could provide. In addition, the journal published interesting news about Thoms and the NACGN, always hot off the press. The organization was kept alive through national communication and a sense of sisterhood.

By the first quarter of the twentieth century, small Black hospitals had been established in many cities of the South and in strategic points throughout the North. These small hospitals were generally owned and directed by Black doctors. This movement became necessary as a result of professional segregation and racial discrimination. Thoms's concern was about the schools of nursing established by these small hospitals. She said that these hospitals should only employ nurses as superintendents who have finished their literary training, and have well-rounded theoretical and practical training in a regulated hospital. Moreover, Thoms expressed that "unless your hospital is standardized, you have no standards from which to work." Thoms told the Black doctors that "You cannot expect to secure the best type of applicants because you have little to offer the ambitious girl in return." Thoms thought that such problems demanded solutions and the attention of the NACGN and the NMA. In recognizing these problems, Thoms chose an important objective in which the NACGN and the NMA could work toward solving collaboratively. And Thoms believed that unless this was accomplished, "we have failed in doing our duty" (*The Small Hospital: Some Observations and Conclusions* 1924, pp. 20–22; Nurses Section, *JNMA* 1920, p. 77).

Despite the denial of a merger, Thoms and members of the NACGN used a viable common objective as an olive branch for the two organizations to work together and maintain an alliance.

After much talk and exchange of ideas and opinions at each other's conventions, including two proposals of marriage from members of the NMA, the NACGN put the topic of merging with the NMA to final rest and the matter was not discussed again, having maintained their identity as nurses and later gaining membership in the Nurses Association and the NOPHN. The NACGN gained this access to membership eight years after Thoms's death, proving that those who believed as Thoms did were justified in refusing the merger. According to Staupers, these women knew what they wanted and continued to pursue a course that eventually brought its reward.

An analysis of the NMA's interest to merge the NACGN into its organization can be seen through a comparison of the historic relationship among the doctor/wife/nurse and what the AMA (which excluded Black doctors) was advocating.

Physicians required their wives and nurses to perform similar duties. The nurse was the hospital and office wife and the wife he married, the nurse at home. Ehrenreich and English reaffirmed the link between nurses and wives and concluded: "The oppression of nurses is inextricably linked to their oppression as women. Nursing, the predominant role of female health workers, is a workplace extension of their roles as wives and mothers" (Lovell 1981, p. 30).

By 1913, the medical profession heightened its efforts to control the nursing profession. In 1913, the journal of the AMA announced that nurses were commodities and that physicians were the rightful controllers of these commodities, and that physicians and ultimately the only competent judge of the fitness of the nurse. The sudden interest in establishing control over nursing was sparked by its realization that nursing would ultimately be as important to the health of society as physicians. In an attempt to lure nursing over entirely to medicine and to gain control, the medical profession offered to help with nursing education reform and that the physicians were the natural allies of nursing.

The historic relationship between the physician and the nurse is a subservient partnership that ties nursing to medicine. Stern suggested a harmonious relationship in which the physician and nurse respect each other. However, he stipulated that this harmonious relationship can only be achieved with the nurse working in harness with the physician's guidance. Stern continued by stating: "Just as married couples stay together for the sake of the children, nurses should accept the bondage of their marriage, because the children (patients) need and expect it" (Lovell 1981, p. 37). Soon realizing that the physician's success was directly attributed to nursing, the medical profession intensified its efforts to control nursing. Nursing was devalued and diminished and nurses were advised that they needed a physician's strong male assistance. Offered in the form of a partnership, physicians emphasized the woman's qualities in nursing. They advised nurses to keep their mouths shut—in other words, be seen and not heard.

Major aspects of what the AMA was advocating for nursing were reflected in Dr. Kenny's August 17th, 1920 NMA speech to the NACGN. While Thoms and members of the NACGN may not have had all the above analyses and correlations, they came to the same conclusions. The NMA and NACGN suffered the same exclusionary racist segregation in American society and shared a common bond and experience. However, to merge the NACGN with the NMA, whose interest was to control, would have been the dissolution of its autonomy and direction as a group of professional nurses.

By 1919, Thoms believed that a high school diploma and college were imminent criteria for public work. She expressed that there were not enough nursing leaders and nurse educators and that training schools for nurses would soon prefer the superior influence of college-educated women. Thoms encouraged Black nurses to follow her example and continue their education. Thoms was a product of the Southern post–Civil War slave movement for education and leadership. She had a progressive philosophy that encompassed views on self-satisfaction, professional introspection, nursing for women in college, and nursing education. In 1919, Thoms addressed the NACGN and stated:

> Although I am proud of your achievements, I am not content with them. We must not become too self satisfied. Do not allow the small degrees of success to cause you to feel self improvement is unnecessary. We must stimulate ourselves to improve every moment of our spare time to prepare ourselves to cope with all other progressive organizations. Read the best journals, attend lectures, avail ourselves

of summer courses in added experiences in any of the best schools and colleges (Of Interest to Nurses, Thoms's Presidential Address 1920, pp. 48–49).

In 1920, during Thoms's presidency, the NACGN was further strengthened by its incorporation in New York State (see Appendix D). The registry was established by the NACGN because of prevalent discrimination resulting in the widespread unemployment of many Black nurses. During the latter part of her presidency, Thoms conducted a vigorous campaign for strengthening the registry and for the establishment of a permanent headquarters for the NACGN. Along with the registry program, a campaign was instituted to focus attention on the need for better opportunities for qualified Black nurses in hospitals and public health agencies. Thoms's interest paralleled the efforts of nursing leaders to raise the admission standards in schools of nursing. In 1920, the NACGN conducted a campaign in cooperation with local groups to urge that graduation from high school be required as a qualification for admission to nursing schools.

While Thoms continued to encourage Black nurses to seek a high school diploma prior to admission to a nursing program and to continue their education thereafter, racial opinions varied. At the 1920 NACGN Annual Meeting at Tuskegee Institute, held August 17–21, Petra Pinn (NACGN member who succeeded Thoms as president) reported that she attended the ANA Convention in April 1920 in Atlanta, Georgia. At the ANA Convention, a discussion was held on a questionnaire entitled "How the Problem of Nurses Training Can Be Met in the South." Pinn reported that Miss Krissler, superintendent of nurses at the University of Georgia, expressed that there was no need for one standard for nurses of both races. Krissler thought that Black nurses need only have an elementary education prior to entering nursing school, whereas the White nurse should have a high school course.[10] Pinn also added that other nurses present did not have this attitude toward the Black nurse (Nurses Section: NACGN 1920, p. 71).

In March 1919, the League of Women Voters was founded. At the final meeting of the National American Women's Suffrage, Carrie Chapman Catt proposed a new organization. She urged delegates to raise a League of Women Voters that would be nonpartisan and nonsectarian in nature. With certainty that the Federal Suffrage Amendment would pass, the group began planning for their voices to be continually heard through the strength of an organization.

The Nineteenth Amendment giving women the right to vote was ratified on August 18, 1920. Thoms believed that women in every walk of life had been awakened to the full realization of their responsibilities. She stated that "Women in trades and professions have come into the sun in public services as never before." Thoms initially was not wholly in sympathy with the suffrage movement because she was not familiar with its platform. Although acknowledging her lack of familiarity, Thoms asked that nurses residing in states where enfranchisement had become a right to accept the opportunity for women who have had to make it through life naturally. Thoms advised members of the NACGN to look upon the ballot as a practical power as much as they do the privilege to work; "Surely no one can blame them," she said. She urged the members of the NACGN to make a study of suffrage, stating, "As your humble leader, I must advise or rather insist that you make a very careful study of suffrage." She advised them to be nonpartisan and vote a clean ticket for a worthy candidate. This early nonpartisan philosophy is parallel to the present-day philosophy of the National Organization for Women (NOW), and the National Coalition for Nurses in Politics. Thoms advised the NACGN to carry on the motto of Susan B. Anthony, Dr. Anna Shaw, and others who have labored to give all women equal rights (Of Interest to Women 1920, pp. 48–49).

After becoming familiar with the suffrage movement, Thoms and members of the NACGN were quite concerned with voting rights. They decided it was important for Black nurses to vote and conducted a campaign to this end. "Nurses had a unique opportunity, through their contacts with many patients and families, to encourage other Black Americans to value their right to suffrage" (Staupers 1961, p. 23).

In addition to specific goals, involvement in legislation, education, and social injustice were major concerns of the NACGN from its inception and throughout its existence. Staupers analyzed that this involvement gave the organization a voice to be heard, thus providing an influence regarding health care and nursing legislation. In addition, other progressive legislative and civic issues were addressed that would benefit all Americans. During Thoms's years as president of the NACGN, the association was politically active, sending letters of protest and telegrams on varied issues. In 1919, the NACGN sent a letter of protest to Congress and Senator Lodge of Massachusetts against race rioting and mob violence. In addition, a plea was made regarding justice for the colored race. In 1921, a telegram was sent to Senator L. W. H. Gibbs, chairman of the New York State Senate Committee on Public Health from the NACGN, and the Lincoln Hospital Alumnae Association. The purpose of the telegram was to "kill the bill" to amend the Nurse Practice Act, for the correspondence and short-term school of nursing (Of Interest to Nurses 1919, p. 283; Nurses Section: Nurses Notes, *JNMA* 1921, p. 218).

Thoms, who loved nursing, surmised that the nursing profession has been a long drawn-out struggle, particularly for the Black nurse. Thoms expressed that the art of nursing had developed both educationally and professionally, "yet colored nurses have worked under difficulties that have beset few. Every inch of our progress has been contested, our curriculum opposed, our morals and methods questioned." Nevertheless, Thoms believed that the true nurse never lost sight of that "inherent dignity and full comprehension of her moral task." In Thoms's 1919 address to the NACGN in Boston, she stated:

> I wish I could find words to picture nursing to you as I see it and nurses as I see them. There is no art to me as beautiful as that of nursing. It is hard work, of course, and has its disadvantages. Music is

also hard work, but the nurse has the great satisfaction after all in knowing that to her is given the peculiar privilege of ministering to the living body, the temple of God's spirit (Of Interest to Nurses 1920, p. 48).

Thoms was concerned with ethics in nursing. She asked the older nurses of the NACGN to cultivate the society of younger nurses, using their "aged influence to keep them close to the ideals of the profession." She believed that financial prosperity might cause a mercenary element to creep into nursing and "once we lose sight of the vision we rob ourselves of all the joy in doing the work to which we have dedicated ourselves."

Throughout her career Thoms was an active member of many professional organizations. Through these organizations, she worked in many ways to increase educational and employment opportunities for Black nurses, then restricted almost entirely to hospitals and services for the care of Black patients. Thoms was active in numerous community organizations in New York City. She served the city that had fascinated her on her arrival, the city she always believed held great promise for the advancement of Black nurses. In Harlem where Thoms made her home, she was an active board member of the Harlem Branch of the Young Women's Christian Association (137th Street Branch in New York City), the Harlem Committee of New York Tuberculosis and Health Association, the New York Urban League, the National Health Circle for Colored People, St. Mark's Methodist Episcopal Church, the Hope Day Nursery—the only facility at that time offering care to the Black children of working mothers; and the Urban League Center of Henry Street Nursing Committee.

Lillian D. Wald described Thoms as an asset to the nursing profession, and stated further that:

> Outside of her professional work, none of the Civic Movements of Harlem remained unknown to her, and her interest reaches all good social aims. Mrs. Thoms's leadership is significant, not only for her own race, but for those socially minded persons of every race, who cherish high purposes and unselfish accomplishments that bring promise of better relationships between people (Thoms 1929, Preface).

Thoms retired from Lincoln Hospital in 1923. She subsequently married Henry Smith who died within a year on August 5, 1923. After her retirement, she continued to be active in the NACGN, the ANA, of which she had been an early member, and the NOPHN. Like an architect, Thoms laid the groundwork and the foundation for the membership of the NACGN into these organizations.

In 1926, the national headquarters for the nurses' registry was established in the Office of the National Health Circle for Colored People at 370 Seventh Avenue in New York City. The National Registry was established by the NACGN because of racial discrimination resulting in the unemployment of many Black nurses. While president, Thoms had conducted a campaign for a permanent headquarters for the registry, focusing attention on the need for better opportunities for qualified Black nurses. According to Staupers, during the first year the registry was responsible for placing 321 nurses in positions of private duty, staff nursing, and in a few instances, in the smaller Black schools, as directors of nursing. Thus, three years after her presidency, her goal of a permanent headquarters for the registry was achieved. Thoms was also a board member of the National Health Circle for Colored People, and this community organization concerned with health care was a likely permanent place for the registry. After retirement from Lincoln Hospital, Thoms directed and operated the nurses registry as a separate entity. Although she had formally retired from Lincoln Hospital, Thoms kept busy providing nurses to deliver quality nursing care.

In 1929, the first account of the Black nurse, *Pathfinders,* by Thoms was in progress. Prior to completion, her proposed book was advertised in the *American Journal of Nursing* in May, 1929. She was depicted as one of the best known "colored" nurses in this country, and in the advertisement Thoms asked Black nurses to "send letters, records, reports, newspaper clippings or other material that will help make the work comprehensive and authentic."

An author and historian, Thoms wrote songs such as the one she dedicated to the NACGN at the beginning of her presidency, that became the association's national hymn. She was a charismatic leader who loved poetry. Thoms often began her national addresses by calling the body "sister nurses," appealing to their sisterhood and common experiences, and ended her national speech with a poem reflecting her philosophy. Thoms ended her August 18, 1920 address to the NACGN at Tuskegee Institute by reading a poem entitled *The Builders* by Longfellow, which states we are all architects, great and small.

In 1929, *Pathfinders* was published. It is considered a classic literary work, a rare book, and it is indeed a primary historical source of the unique experiences of Black nurses. Her book is a chronology of the many early pathfinders who created a way for the future Black nurse (see Illustration 4–3).

> To many nurses all over the country, Adah was known as "Ma
> Thoms." Every nurses' library, no matter how small, should contain a
> copy of *Pathfinders*. It is the only story we have of our attempts—may
> it truly serve as a pathfinder and inspire other nurses to write of negro
> nursing (Hernandez 1930, p. 5).

In addition to a major publication, 1929 was a busy year for Thoms. For the second time, she attended the ICN, this time in Canada. At this conference, she received many affectionate greetings from members of the ICN.

Since 1879, Black women had been a part of the nursing profession. It is interesting to note that just twenty-one years after the NACGN was organized, Thoms realized the importance of recording the efforts of Black nurses to achieve their goals of integration and equality although hampered by prejudice. In 1936, Thoms became the first nurse to receive the Mary Mahoney Medal developed by the NACGN for her contribution to nursing and for her efforts

ILLUSTRATION 4–3.
Portrait of Adah Belle Samuels Thoms, published in the **American Journal of Nursing** *in 1929, advertising her then-forthcoming book,* Pathfinders. *A request was mde for Black women to write to Thomas about their experiences.* **Courtesy of American Journal of Nursing** *Archives,* **Lippincott, Williams, and Wilkins.**

in 1917 to have Black nurses accepted into the Army Nurse Corps. The Mary Mahoney Medal is named in honor of the first Black woman to become a professional nurse. The criteria established by the NACGN were that the recipient be a nurse who has made outstanding contributions to the nursing profession and to the community, and also has worked to improve the professional status of the Black nurse, thereby helping improve intergroup and interpersonal relations within the nursing profession. By 1928, the NACGN had developed its own journal entitled *The National News Bulletin*. In 1936, the journal published an article stating its reasons for granting the Mary Mahoney Medal to Thoms (see Appendices E and F). Thoms thereafter in a Christmas newsletter responded to having received the award (see Appendix G). In addition to earning tremendous respect, an additional honor was the Adah Belle Samuels Thoms Graduate Nurse Club formed in Tulsa, Oklahoma, named in her honor. In June 1936, *The National News Bulletin* reported the excellent work being done by this graduate nurse organization.

Thoms resided at 317 West 138th Street in Harlem from the time she came to New York until her death. Her niece Nannie Samuels resided with her.

ILLUSTRATION 4–4.
Gravesite of Adah Belle Samuels Thoms-Smith
Woodlawn Cemetery, Bronx, New York, Lot Honeysuckle, Range #19,
Grave #293.
Picture taken by Author.

Toward the end of her life, Thoms's sight began to fail as a result of diabetes. On January 15, 1943, Thoms entered Lincoln Hospital, where she had served faithfully in various leadership capacities for so many years, and died thirty-seven days later on February 21. She died from arteriosclerotic heart disease, with a right cerebral thrombosis and diabetes mellitus as major contributing factors (Death Certificate #2098). Thoms was posthumously admitted to nursing's prestigious Hall of Fame along with Mahoney and Franklin in 1976. She is buried along with her husband in Woodlawn Cemetery, Bronx, New York, under the surname of Thoms-Smith (see Illustration 4–4). The grave site is marked by an open-faced, Bible-shaped stone, indicative of Thoms's faith in God. The surname Smith is inscribed in the center of the stone, and the left side has her husband's first name (Henry) inscribed. The right side of the stone for Adah Thoms Smith, unfortunately, remains uninscribed, and thus does not conspicuously mark this great nursing leader's place of rest.

Notes

1. A thorough personal search by the author of the Richmond State Archives, at the Virginia State Library, which includes various census records, land tax records, address directories, marriage and birth records, and so on, provided no data on Thoms or her family. One explanation provided by librarians, who were exceptionally helpful and courteous, is that a serious fire destroyed many records. Thoms's death certificate states she was living with a niece, Nannie Samuels. Thoms's nee surname is Samuels; thus she had at least one sibling.

2. Neither this course nor school is listed in the Seventh Annual Report of R.N. Training Schools for Nurses, compiled by the NLN in 1900. Thus it was not an accredited nursing program (Phone conversation with NLN on November 25, 1985).

3. Lincoln was founded in 1839, thus the 100th anniversary was in 1939. The school of nursing opened in 1898, thus it was in existence 41 years by 1939.

4. In 1908, the nursing program was extended to three years.

5. At the 1918 Annual Convention, Dr. Daniel Hale Williams, a noted surgeon from Chicago, Illinois, addressed the NACGN. Dr. Williams performed the first successful heart operation on record in 1893. Dr. Williams was one of the founders of Provident Hospital in Chicago, which was the first hospital to allow Black doctors to perform surgery. He also organized a training center for Black nurses. Throughout his career, he worked with others to organize hospitals and training centers for Black Americans in various cities. This was his second documented encounter with the NACGN; his first was in 1908, in which he came to give support and his well wishes.

6. At a later convention in 1920, held at Tuskegee Institute, Thoms and the group made a pilgrimage to Booker T. Washington's grave where a short religious service was held. There, Thoms placed a wreath of white roses on his grave. The service at his gravesite closed with the singing of the hymn "God Be With You Till We Meet Again." That evening the NACGN was entertained by Mrs. Booker T. Washington at her beautiful home and given a tour of Booker T. Washington's library. It was said that the tour of his personal library left many lingering sacred memories of this great man (*JNMA* 1920, pp. 72–73).

7. In subsequent years, research studies done on venereal disease in the Black population were done without full disclosure or consent and to the patients' detriment.

8. Thoms's goal was achieved eight years after her death.

9. The NACGN developed their own journal entitled *The National News Bulletin* in 1928.

10. This attitude would facilitate the continual subordinate position of Black nurses to White nurses.

Chapter 5

The Architects:
Seen Through a Prism

If there's no struggle, there's no progress.

Frederick Douglass

The National Association of Colored Graduate Nurses (NACGN) attained membership in the American Nurses Association (ANA) and the National Organization of Public Health Nursing (NOPHN). Mary Mahoney, the first Black professional nurse in America, was one of Martha Franklin's and the organization's continuing inspirations. Franklin, whose light and life enriched the nursing profession, was the Bernadette who envisioned and founded this remarkable unit. Adah Belle Samuels Thoms, one of the early leaders of the NACGN, wrote a valuable history of Black nurses' experience (*A Salute to Democracy* 1951). Mahoney, Franklin, and Thoms individually and together worked toward increasing the membership of the NACGN, building and strengthening the organization. They worked to improve the educational qualities of Black nursing schools, increase educational opportunities for Black nurses, and improve health care and the status of women.

Mahoney, Franklin, and Thoms used female solidarity to achieve social and professional justice. They sought equality as Black Americans, as women, and as professional nurses. What similarities and factors predisposed them to this professional bond? Mary Mahoney was born in 1845, prior to the Civil War, and like all other Black Americans, she experienced varying degrees of race domination, violence, prejudice, and segregation within American society. Franklin and Thoms were both born in 1870, the post–Civil War era. Thus, they were both subject to the era of Black Codes, Jim Crow laws, violence, persistent racial discrimination, and segregation. A specific review of race relations in their respective home states revealed that each of the architects was subject to racial problems, discriminating laws, practices, and conflicting climates. Thus, they naturally shared a common bond through life experiences.

Mahoney graduated from the New England Hospital for Women and Children (NEHWC), a hospital organized by women seeking professional justice for women in medicine. In a male-dominated profession, they were discriminated against because of their sex. This hospital in particular recognized varied forms of discrimination and included a no-discrimination clause in its philosophy. In addition, this hospital took special pride in its varied racial patient population. Franklin graduated from the Women and Children's Hospital of Philadelphia, which was also organized by a group of women seeking professional justice in the male-dominated medical profession. Thoms graduated from the Lincoln Hospital and Home School of Nursing, again organized by a group of women to care for the indigent Black population of New York. The common thread in the history of all three hospital schools of nursing was that they were organized using female solidarity. In addition, Mahoney, Franklin, and Thoms were exposed to philosophies aimed at eradicating social, professional, and racial injustice. "It can be instructive to look at one pervasive form of prejudice through the prism of another" (Beck 1986, p. 44).

Mahoney, Franklin, and Thoms had different personalities, yet they got along well and supported each other. All three were persuasive leaders who earned and retained enormous support and respect from their Black colleagues. Mabel Staupers, an executive director and the last president of the NACGN, knew all three women very well (see Illustration 5–1). She stated:

> Mary Mahoney was a nice little old lady, she was such a nice old lady, she was charming. Martha Franklin was a little bossy, but all right, I got along well with her. Adah Thoms believed in younger-older. She felt that if she was older than you, she knew best. She was all right, I got along well with her also (Interview with Mabel Staupers, April 28, 1986).

The characterization of Mahoney as charming seems appropriate because her personality appears to have had an aura. Adah Thoms also characterized Mahoney as charming, with an unusual personality. Mahoney was clearly a symbol to Black nurses. With respect to Franklin, what was in that time frame considered bossy, today may be characterized as assertive. Franklin had to be assertive, as well as persistent and patient in order to have individually conducted a handwritten, two-year

ILLUSTRATION 5–1.
Mabel Keaton Staupers, first executive director and last president of the
NACGN. Staupers knew Mahoney, Franklin, and Thoms.
Reprinted from J. Franklin and A. Meier (Eds.), **Black Leaders of the**
Twentieth Century. *Chicago: University of Illinois Press, 1982. Courtesy of*
Schomburg Center for Research in Black Culture, the New York Public
Library, New York.

national survey followed by the organization of the NACGN. Thoms did indeed rely on age as a guiding factor. In one of her national addresses, she asked the older members of the NACGN to use their age-old influence and knowledge to keep the younger nurses close to the ideals of the nursing profession (Interview with Reverend Edwin R. Edmonds, June 13, 1986; Of Interest to Nurses 1919, p. 48).

> The foundations for black professional organizations were laid after the Civil War when a separate black world began to emerge. Before that time, although a number of free blacks and a few slaves had managed to move out of the labor and agricultural worker category, and pursued careers in the ministry, law, teaching, dentistry, and architecture, sometimes practicing in violation of the law. They were too few in number, working under too many constraints, and were geographically too thinly disguised to permit the forming of professional groups.
>
> With the evolution of the black community, whether in the North, South, East, or West, mores and housing patterns consistently fostered a segregated existence for the majority of whites and non-whites. This laid the groundwork for the formation of separate professional organizations. The isolated black community needed its own preachers, teachers, pharmacists, nurses, physicians, dentists, lawyers, social workers, and others to perform a variety of professional services. The first to form associations were teachers and social workers in the late 19th century when black physicians also organized the National Medical Association. More significant growth among black professional groups occurred after World War I. Barred from membership in white organizations, blacks in almost every profession formed their own associations for protection and mutual assistance (Smythe, Allport, Baker, & Beale 1976, p. 469).

Elliot Friedson, a sociologist, views professional associations as having roles and functions that are a part of the fabric of the total social system. Each part operates to control the problem faced within its domain. The dominant professional associations gain support by official and quasi-official means, exercising great influence in all matters related to that profession. If such an association has rising dissident factions, its power structure may attempt to contain them by devaluing them, discrediting their behavior, and labeling them as deviants. The deviant faction may be viewed as trying to redefine the values and norms of that professional association. The competing deviant, if successful, can produce the new dominant ethic of that professional association, and thus become the determiner, the pacesetter for the new values of the profession (Branch & Paxton 1976, pp. 23–25). Mahoney, Franklin, and Thoms were among the few early Black members of the ANA. They may be viewed historically along with the NACGN as early deviant factions trying to set new values and norms.

Several historians have suggested that efforts to unite women engendered and were sustained by "social feminism." Stanley Lemons and William O'Neill focused on what social feminists did and offered insight into what they believed.

O'Neill found social feminism exemplified in organizations that emphasized female solidarity and sought social justice. The work of Mahoney, Franklin, and Thoms along with the NACGN appears to reflect the values of social feminism. A more explicit analysis is put forth by Ellen Condliffe Lagemann (1969) in *A Generation of Women*, a study of five women reformers active at the turn of the century. They believed women's maternal instinct gave them a special "sensitivity to basic human needs" and obligated them to unite in efforts to make American life kinder and more harmonious. All three historians, Lagemann, O'Neill, and Lemons, identified social feminism as women having a distinctive nature, nurturing and altruistic. Therefore, women should band together to harmonize and humanize American society, remaking it on the model of an idealized home (Lagemann 1978, pp. 275–277; O'Neill 1969). Dr. C. V. Roman, M.D., a noted Black physician and writer for the NMA, expressed that "Women's work is to increase the goodness and diminish the meanness of the world" (Roman 1909, p. 4).

Viewed through a prism, our architects all displayed evidence of the four areas of self-expression defined by Lowenberg and Bogin as characteristic of Black women. These four areas are social reform, education, religion, and family.

Social reform was displayed by Mahoney, Franklin, and Thoms in their efforts to improve the status of the Black nurse, the quality of education in Black schools of nursing, and to produce leaders within the ranks of Black nurses. The architects sought social reform and justice by speaking out against racial injustices in American society and by improving the quality of and access to health care for the Black population. In addition, they sought social reform and justice by fostering feminism, decision-making, and choices for women. The architects supported the suffrage movement and took an active stand to seek equality for women in American society.

Education was a very important endeavor. They all entered and completed a formal program in nursing, and became trained professional nurses. The importance of their education as trained professional nurses is that, unlike the untrained nurse, they had a different body of knowledge, organized theory, and clinical practice. Having crossed that historic bridge—the advent of training schools for nursing and nursing organizations—they were exposed to the notion of female solidarity in relation to a profession as nurses. The solidarity was also an important factor in race, sex, and alumnae associations. They all took continuing education courses or enrolled in a formal college program. The architects encouraged women to finish high school, to enter nursing programs, and to continue their education thereafter. Education and the quality of education were priorities for the women and the NACGN.

Religion was important for all three nursing leaders and they displayed self-expression through religion. Mahoney, Franklin, and Thoms were dedicated Christians and active women members of the church. Mahoney was a member of the People's Baptist Church in Boston (Massachusetts); Franklin was a member of the Dixwell Avenue Congregational United Church of Christ in

New Haven (Connecticut); Thoms was a member of St. Mark's Methodist Episcopal Church in New York (New York).

Family life was important and all three nursing leaders demonstrated self-expression through close family relations. Mahoney never married; however, she was very close to her family of orientation. An interview with Mahoney's great-nephew, Frederick Saunders, reveals very close family ties. At the time of her death, Mahoney lived a half block from her sister's home. Franklin never married either; however, like Mahoney, she had very strong family ties with her family of orientation. Franklin was like a grandmother to Dr. Ernest Saunders and this was comparable to a family tie. These strong family ties are revealed in three interviews with people who knew Franklin personally: Dr. William Massie, Mrs. Georgie Saunders, and Mr. Leroy Pierce. Franklin lived with her sister during their aging years until death. Thoms, unlike Mahoney and Franklin, was married twice. Her first marriage was brief, and her second husband died within one year of their marriage. She had no children; however, like Mahoney and Franklin, Thoms was close to her family of orientation. Thoms's death certificate revealed that her niece Nannie Samuels was living with her up until the time of her death.

It was forty-two years after the Emancipation Proclamation that Black nurses, many without work or equal education, and for certain without recognition or respect, were brought together by a rare fusion of insight and energy. Franklin was that unique fusion; her sights were set far and wide. No less far reaching were her energies. In her two-year survey of Black graduate nurses, Franklin asked their opinion about the formation of a national organization to combat physical, moral, and professional illnesses (*A Salute to Democracy* 1951). It must have been quite a task to determine who the Black graduates were. She would have had to contact Black schools of nursing as well as those very few White schools of nursing that accepted Black students. Perhaps she also contacted local alumni associations of Black nurses. This can certainly be described as a monumental task.

The NACGN came together for the first time on August 25, 1908, in New York City. Franklin pointed out three reasons for its existence, which became the goals of the organization:

- To achieve higher professional standards of nursing
- To break down discrimination in the nursing profession
- To develop leadership within the ranks of Negro nurses

Mahoney was a role model for the Black nurse and for nurses of all races. In addition to her obvious role as an architect of integration and equality, Mahoney was an inspiration and a symbol for Black nurses and the NACGN. Richards was also a symbol, and her presence at meetings was revered as the first nurse to earn an American training school diploma (Armeny, in Lagemann 1983, p. 22). Minutes of meetings reflected, "We have in our presence Mary Mahoney, the first trained colored nurse in America" (Of Interest to Nurses 1913, p. 271). She was revered and respected as a model, an example for the Black nurse.

Mahoney held membership in the ANA. But although she was a member of that association, she committed herself completely to assisting other Black nurses who could not enter good schools of nursing or the ANA. Mahoney was bothered by this problem. Although she said her school of nursing was not so selfish, she knew other schools of nursing were. In addition, she knew that most Black nurses were not able to join the ANA.[1] Thus, Mahoney became an integral part of the NACGN working individually and in concert with Franklin and Thoms toward the goals of the organization.

Thoms was concerned about the plight and status of Black nurses and thus began working for equal opportunity immediately after graduating in 1905 from the Lincoln Hospital and Home School of Nursing. Thoms, as president of the Lincoln Alumni Association, responded to Franklin's survey and was the resource person who provided the accommodations for the first meeting of the NACGN in New York City. In light of Thoms's operative interest, Franklin's communication indeed provided new momentum, and perhaps a sense of urgency to unite; Thoms was committed. She was indeed an architect of integration and equality.

Thoms was elected the first treasurer of the NACGN, a key position of trust. She was also appointed by Franklin to serve on various committees to develop organizational structure. In addition, Thoms already had a following, a captive audience, and a support base as president of the Lincoln Nurses Alumni Association. She was in a crucial position to foster and strengthen the goals of the NACGN. Thoms provided the NACGN with a national organization hymn. As president, she addressed the body of nurses as sisters, fostering unity, collegiality, and comradeship. Her charismatic leadership of Black nurses lent energy, enthusiasm, heightened awareness, and self-esteem in general, and specifically in moments of low spirits and rejection. Thoms was one of the best known Black nurses in America. Her community involvement and historical account of the Black nurses' plight (*Pathfinders*) earned her further acclaim and praise. Thoms's early endeavors, like Mahoney's and Franklin's, can most accurately be measured through analyzing the goals of the NACGN. Thoms was "an inspiration to many nurses throughout the country." Her leadership in the early days of the NACGN left a record that set a standard for nurses who followed her as president of the NACGN (Hernandez 1930, p. 5).

In addition to being architects of integration and equality, Mahoney, Franklin, and Thoms are conceptualized as a prism through which illumination of the Black American nurses' struggle for integration and equality is viewed. The light that shines through this particular prism has provided an individual, collective, and continuous spectrum for analysis. The collective significance of Mahoney, Franklin, and Thoms's contributions to the nursing profession and toward improving the status of the Black professional nurse can be analyzed through the goals accomplished by the NACGN. In addition, the collective significance of their early endeavors created a legacy that provides modern nursing with direction for the future.

To Develop Leadership
Within the Ranks of Negro Nurses

Fostering leadership among "Negro" nurses began with the NACGN's membership, which provided many leaders whose achievements have been exemplary (Dolan 1963, p. 299). Leadership is defined by Henry Fairchild as: (1) A situation process in which a person (or persons) because of an actual or supposed ability to articulate some problems in the field of current group interest, is followed by others in the group and influences their behavior. In a leadership situation, the character of followership is equally important. Leadership may be based upon spontaneous personal ascendancy (physical, courageous, congenial) or upon prestige of skill, knowledge, age, alleged supernatural endowment, or position or a combination. (2) The act of organizing and directing the interest and activities of a group of persons, as associated in some project or enterprise, by a person who develops their cooperation, through securing and maintaining their more or less voluntary approval of the ends and methods proposed and adopted in their association. Leadership should be distinguished from domination, in which the group perforce accepts a dictator or through fear or strategic disadvantage submits reluctantly; and the underlying motives of the domineerer are egotistic rather than altruistic or collective. In essence, as defined by Thomas Hoult (1977), "Leadership accrues to those who take account of others in ways that facilitate group life and group cohesion."

Fairchild (1984) continues his definition stating that the two most socially significant types of leadership present in all communities are the conservative and the progressive. The conservative leader develops interest in maintaining the social order or situation in status quo, generally so far as these concern the distribution of its values and rewards, to its main beneficiaries, with some maintenance or increase of technical efficiency. The progressive leader, on the other hand, develops an interest in changing the social order or situation to distribute its benefits more widely to those who have been stinted or excluded, also with some interest in increasing technical efficiency. Mahoney, Franklin, and Thoms were progressive leaders.

A leader in the broadest sense, according to Fairchild, is one who leads by initiating social behavior; by directing, organizing, or controlling the efforts of others; or by prestige, power, or position. The effective stimulus is found in social behavior. In a restricted sense, one who leads by means of persuasive qualities and voluntary acceptance on the part of followers.

A synopsis of several studies of leadership styles by Stogdill found that the most common recurring factors (traits and behaviors) used to characterize the skills of a leader were as follows:

(1) Social and interpersonal skills, (2) technical skills, (3) administrative skills, (4) intellectual skills, (5) effectiveness and achievement, (6) social nearness, friendliness, (7) supportiveness of group tasks, and (8) task motivation and application.

In addition, Stogdill's research findings of two sets of behaviors and their effects on group productivity, cohesion, and satisfaction lend further insight into the leadership styles of Mahoney, Franklin, and Thoms. *Person-oriented behaviors* were described by Stogdill as democratic, permissive, follower oriented, participative, and considerate. The *work-oriented style* was autocratic, restrictive, task-oriented, socially distant, directive, and structured. Stogdill found that no one set of behaviors was best at all times, and he regarded structuring expectations as "perhaps the central factor in leadership."

Indeed, applying these leadership research findings to Mahoney, Franklin, and Thoms, it is clear that all three leaders possessed Stogdill's eight frequently occurring traits. Their leadership styles were person-oriented behaviors. The architects structured expectations when the NACGN adopted its goals, which provided group direction and membership participation.

In a tool developed by Kruse and Stogdill, four sets of leadership behaviors were measured: tolerance, sensitivity, role assumption, and structure. Mahoney, Franklin, and Thoms were very tolerant and patient, yet they were not submissive; they opted to seek a remedy to the problems experienced by Black nurses. They were sensitive to the problems experienced by Black nurses, patients, women, health care, and society in general. They did indeed assume a role as early Black American leaders in nursing and the architects of integration and equality. Structure was accomplished through organizing and building the NACGN as a movement to bring about change.

The following summary by Stogdill captures the essence of diversity in leadership styles:

> A leader is characterized by a strong drive for responsibility and task completion, vigor and persistence in pursuit of goals, venturesomeness and originality in problem solving, drive to exercise initiative in social situations, self confidence and sense of personal identity, willingness to accept consequence of decision and action, readiness to absorb interpersonal stress, willingness to tolerate frustration and delay, ability to influence other persons' behaviors, and capacity to structure social interaction systems to the purpose at hand (Stogdill 1974, p. 81).

In addition, all three women possessed charisma. Defined by Fairchild, charisma is possessing extraordinary merit, grace, generosity, or power in personality. Fairchild's definition continues by stating that "Ultimately, charisma is at the root of all mass movement by virtue of attraction exerted by a creative personality" (p. 81). The minutes of the NACGN placed the architects individually and jointly centerstage many times with excellent group dynamics and interaction.

The NACGN developed many leaders who traveled all over the United States, conferring, teaching, advising, counteracting bias, opening schools of nursing, inspiring young nursing students, and reassuring the nurses in outreach rural communities of their presence and support. There were presidents and officers of this national movement, in addition to presidents and officers of local and/or state Black nurses organizations. Black nurses became involved in local affiliations of the ANA and NOPHN. For example, Estelle Massey Osborne was president of the NACGN for seven years (1934–1939). She also served on the board of directors of the ANA. Through the assistance of the Rosenwald scholarship fund, she was the first Black nurse to complete a master's degree in nursing. Osborne graduated from Teachers College, Columbia University, in 1931 and subsequently taught on the nursing faculty of New York University. Among many others, there was Alma Vessels Johns, a former secretary of the NACGN who became a radio celebrity, as well as Mabel Staupers, a first executive secretary, last president of the NACGN, and author of *No Time for Prejudice*. During World War II, Staupers continued the fight that Thoms began with the U.S. Army and Navy, insisting that Black nurses be accepted. Dr. Mary Elizabeth Carnegie developed a nursing program in Florida, was elected president of Florida State NACGN, and served on the Florida State Nurses Association. Thereafter, Carnegie served as editor of *Nursing Research*, *American Journal of Nursing*, *Nursing Outlook*, and in 1986 she authored *The Path We Tread* and two more books on Black nurses.[2]

When the ANA opened its doors to all graduate nurses, they inherited a wealth of capable and industrious women from the NACGN. These talented women brought inspiration from many areas, including supervisors of small hospitals, membership on the board of directors of the ANA, directors of public health nursing, members of university staffs in departments of health, nursing instructors of county hospitals, members of various national, state, regional, city committees, with various health interests. In addition, there were many recipients of national and foreign fellowships, all of whom were developed and inspired by membership in the NACGN (A Salute to Democracy 1951).

TO ACHIEVE PROFESSIONAL STANDARDS IN NURSING

When the NACGN was organized, superstition, herbal and root cures, innocence, and general lack of knowledge adversely affected the health of the Black population and the large rural areas of the United States. There was hazardous midwifery, little knowledge of hygiene, and the transmission of communicable disease was still in the research phase. These circumstances were, in fact, an unknowing and involuntary aid to local and rural community morticians. The Black professional nurse had to conquer the notion that these unhealthy conditions were due to environmental conditions and not due to race. The Black professional nurse was the replacement for the untrained nurse and/or the poorly prepared nurse, who had created further health problems.[3] However, it must be recognized that many untrained nurses were good nurses, using their knowledge and practice of herbal medicine that was successful and handed down by tradition, family member to family member.

Black professional nurses faced tremendous odds, including inadequate hospitalization, unequal application of educational and remedial measures, and little respect, culminating in varied personal indignities suffered because of race. The Black professional nurse was not only a nurse but also teacher, psychologist, mother, confessor, policewoman, and often a maid (NACGN Testimonial Dinner 1951).

Through Mahoney, Franklin, Thoms, and the NACGN, the Black nurse faced the revolutionary fact that any nurse whose education was inferior to another's rendered that nurse less valuable in terms of salary and should not be hired. They stated that the poorly prepared nurse delays her own advancement for employment and endangers the lives of patients she cares for by her lack of adequate education. Through the endeavors of the NACGN, the Black nurse aided, encouraged, and taught the poorly trained nurse. The NACGN organized local, state, and later regional associations; held open clinics; and disseminated material containing the latest trends among its membership. In addition, the NACGN presented new research findings and insights into the work of public health nurses. The NACGN meetings at all levels had eminent health and medical authorities who presented current topics providing continuing education. The NACGN instituted and maintained contact with the communities to which they brought professional service through citizens' committees.

The NACGN had a major interest in improving the quality of Black nursing schools; however, the climate for segregation was set. In 1896, the Supreme Court sanctioned segregation in a landmark decision in *Plessy vs. Ferguson,* which legalized Jim Crow laws. The essential point of the court's decision, one that was to become a precedent for segregated schools, was that the segregation law was reasonable. Reasonable laws are those that are in accord with established ways, customs, and traditions of the people. Therefore, American customs, traditions, and established ways rendered this decision reasonable, and this decision sanctioned these customs, traditions, and established ways. This legal edict permeated all aspects of American life, and of particular note, educational facilities and hospitals. The segregation laws were built on the principle that separate accommodations were constitutional if they were equal. Equal protection of the laws was guaranteed by the Fourteenth Amendment; however, it was obvious to the Black community that in all segregated endeavors, there was no equality. In 1880, the expression "Jim Crow" meant laws that segregated and discriminated against Black Americans. They replaced the Black codes of the post-war South, but were far more numerous and formal.

From its inception in 1908, the NACGN investigated the possibility of closing schools of nursing that did not meet adequate educational standards. It was difficult to improve the quality of Black hospitals and these training schools for Black nurses. Black hospitals were generally under the control of Black doctors and the National Hospital Association (NHA). Thoms as president of the NACGN expressed concern about the quality of small Black hospitals, patient care, and quality of nursing instructors, whom Thoms described as not knowing much more than the student, and the subsequent product—the graduate nurse.

In 1916, the NACGN worked in cooperation with the National Association for the Advancement of Colored People (NAACP) and the National Urban League toward improving the conditions of Black schools of nursing and Black hospitals. Black schools of nursing were predominantly in Black hospitals. The NACGN's position was that by raising the admission standards in Black schools of nursing, it would inevitably improve the quality of the graduating nurses. This was an advanced educational concept based on raising admission criteria as a predictor of success. By 1920, Thoms, as president of the NACGN, encouraged schools of nursing and applicants that a high school diploma be a prerequisite for admission and she campaigned toward this goal. During the early years of the NACGN and throughout its existence, the Julius Rosenwald Fund was established to assist Black nurses in pursuing their education, by providing a yearly grant of $1,250.

Surveys conducted during the 1920s by Ethel Johns of the Hospital Library and Service Bureau, which were financed by the Rockefeller Foundation and the American Medical Association (AMA), found that conditions of Black hospitals were disgraceful and nursing curricula were inadequate. Black patients were predominantly hospitalized in all Black hospitals. Black patients and Black students had no alternative but to utilize these facilities and were subjected to these inadequacies.

An obvious alternative to these disgraceful conditions was integration with institutions already functioning as health care facilities. The NACGN's position was that sickness was a personal problem affecting the human race, not a racial problem. Pain, healing, and convalescence are human experiences whether the individual is White or Black. However, nursing administrators had an inveterate image of the Black nurse. Staupers analyzed that White nursing administrators thought that Black nursing students could only adequately care for Black patients, and that they were in fact happier and/or more comfortable in Black schools of nursing. This rationalization was indeed self-serving and aimed at preserving segregation as the status quo.

Relative to community health and communicable disease, "Disease knows no color line. A diphtheria germ or tubercular bacillus is blind to race destruction." This issue sparked an interesting editorial sermonette in the *Atlanta Constitution* entitled "No White or Negro Germs: They All Spell Disease." An excerpt from the editorial stated:

> The Constitution has many times set forth that there is no race line in disease; that the infected Negro hovel menaces the immaculate white homes; that the one protection is one sanitary law for white and black, high and humble, Peace Tree and Peters Street (*JNMA* 1914, Vol. 6, No. 2, pp. 131–132).

Thus, the essence of the *Constitution*'s sermon was that the South must save the Black population in order to save itself. The races have common interests, common dangers, and a common future. This principle applies to the whole race question as well as to health conditions. Common sense, the author said, should dictate a policy of mutual helpfulness and cooperation. Surprisingly, forty-eight hours after reading this editorial in the *Constitution*, the mayor of Atlanta took steps to raise the $10,000 necessary to establish a Black hospital.

Thoms had a major interest in public health nursing. She incorporated public health nursing into the curriculum at Lincoln Hospital, and encouraged members of the NACGN to seek specialized preparation as public health nurses and in other areas of interest. Although few had special preparation, the public health nurse as a community educator, Black or White, facilitated the difficult transition toward adequate health care. By 1921, Jane van de Vrede, director, Department of Nursing, Southern Division of the American Red Cross, summarized:

> It was a short time from a racial standpoint since the majority of negroes believed implicitly in voodoo charms, and banked more largely on the efficacy of a snakeskin, or the tooth of an alligator, to cure or protect from disease than the preventative measures we employ today (p. 56).

However, she cautioned not to be too discouraged at this. She continued stating that "Many white people believe things just as far from the truth, and maybe everyone in the world believes in something today that a hundred years from now will appear as absurd and false as some of these things do to us."

Most small Black hospitals were under the aegis of the NHA, which provided standards of practice for these hospitals. The NHA was integrally aligned with the NMA and members of the NACGN were involved in the NHA. The aim of this Black association was to perfect the stronger hospitals and help the weaker ones meet set standards. In 1926, the association acknowledged that nurses who were graduates of these hospitals found they were barred from entrance to practice in various states. The association summarized that this problem would be eradicated by a uniform program of training for nurses that would standardize the curriculum in such a way to prevent this from recurring (Green 1926, p. 230).

Relevant to health care, the NHA tried to bring health care to the community, and in 1926, the NHA adopted October 10–17 as National Negro Hospital Week. The purpose of this week was to bring the Black hospitals in every community in closer touch with the people they serve. A plan that encompassed the entire week was adopted, and of special note was the community day. On this day, nurses and others engaged in activities at the hospital and visited the sick in the community, especially those in destitute circumstances. The purpose of these visits was to carry sunshine and the helpfulness of the hospital to the sufferers of the community.

The goals of the NACGN also relied heavily on the smooth functioning and communication with its membership. Hampered by communication in 1928, the NACGN developed the *National News Bulletin* as a means of improving communications. The NACGN *National News Bulletin* was distributed to nurses (both Black and White) nursing and health care organizations, various professional organizations, religious and fraternal organizations, civic and social clubs, sororities, fraternities, local and state public officials, interested lay individuals, and especially individuals serving on community boards of hospitals and public health agencies. In addition to varied interests related to the Black nurse and health care, the *National News Bulletin* had a major focus on nursing education. This, of course, reflected one of the major focuses of the NACGN. However, the NACGN was plagued with financial problems. It was a volunteer organization with no permanent headquarters, staff, or budget, and membership dues alone could not sustain the organization. From the 1920s to the 1930s, the average annual R.N. salary was approximately $1,200 (Staupers 1961, pp. 28, 43; NACGN Collection, *National News Bulletin*). Thus, nurses were not in a financial position to make large contributions.

In 1934, the NACGN was revitalized and there was new inspiration toward meeting its goals and objectives. At a regional NACGN conference held in 1934, officials from the ANA, the NOPHN, the Julius Rosenwald Fund, and the NMA; the editor of *Opportunity* magazine; directors of Black schools of nursing in the Northeast; local Black nurses' associations; and the National Health Circle for Colored People were all present. These were support systems that aided the revitalization process. During this regional conference, the need was voiced by members of the NACGN for a program that would gain full recognition for Black nurses. Respect and dignity were an unwritten goal, yet it was equally important for the Black nurses' professional growth. Discussion at this regional meeting focused on economic problems affecting the Black nurse, improving existing Black schools, creating a liaison with other national nursing organizations, and allowing acceptance into all state nurses' associations.

In 1934, the NACGN established a national headquarters and appointed Staupers as nurse executive secretary. America was in the midst of the Depression, and the national headquarters came to fruition though contributions. The Julius Rosenwald Fund provided a grant of $1,250 and pledged yearly funding thereafter on a matching basis. In addition, the NACGN also received funding from Frances Payne Bolton, a Congresswoman from Ohio and the General Education Board. The office was established at 50 West 50th Street in the RCA building in New York City. This location was considered beneficial because other national nursing and health organizations were located in the same building. However, there were many policies and practices that continued to prohibit and retard the growth of Black nurses, thus preventing them from achieving professional standards in nursing.

Among the pressing old problems awaiting the revitalized NACGN were the poor quality of training schools for Black nurses and subsequent employment. Although there were a few good Black schools of nursing, in general, the conditions of Black hospitals and training schools made no progress or very little since the studies during the 1920s. However, the NACGN was now more organized, politically astute, and involved to bring about change. The appointment of Staupers in 1934 as nurse executive secretary played a major role politically in the progress of the NACGN. In addition, lack of formal recognition by the ANA—evidenced by racial barriers in some states—continued to preclude state membership into the ANA. Achieving professional standards in nursing clearly rested on removing segregation and racial barriers that impeded the progress of Black nurses.

TO BREAK DOWN DISCRIMINATION IN THE NURSING PROFESSION

This objective was the most difficult one. In fact, the success of the other two objectives depended wholly or in most part on the success of this objective. Therefore, this objective has been integrally woven throughout the other two objectives (leadership and improving nursing standards). Through intractable persistence and with assistance from influential people and places, Black professional nurses began to collapse the barriers that separated Black and White nurses as a group of professional colleagues. There was no time for Black nurses to succumb to prejudice, no time for bitterness, and less time for inert self-pity. Carol Stack summarized that the view of Black women as represented in their own words and life histories coincides with that presented by Joyce Ladner (1971):

> One of the chief characteristics defining the Black woman is her (realistic approach) to her (own) resources. Instead of becoming resigned to her fate, she has always sought creative solutions to her problems. The ability to utilize her existing resources and yet maintain a forthright determination to struggle against the racist society in whatever overt and subtle ways necessary is one of her major attributes (Ladner 1971, pp. 276–277).

In 1935, the Social Security Act, Title VI, was passed. This provided funds for training public health nurses. This act was an initial step toward addressing the training and employment problems affecting Black nurses. In addition, the U.S. Public Health Service provided a public health nursing program for Black graduates of St. Philips School in Virginia. Thoms had a major interest in public health nursing. Realizing its importance for the nursing curriculum and the community, she made early efforts in 1917 to include public health in the Lincoln Nursing Program. Black nurses were needed to go into Black communities.

Jane van de Vrede, who was director of nursing of the American Red Cross in Atlanta, stressed the need for Black public health nurses; however, she felt that better training schools and better trained nurses was the first priority. She acknowledged that the NACGN was seriously considering how to improve and expand the training schools. She thought that this could be accomplished by larger Southern hospitals providing wings, buildings, or wards where well-established hospitals and nursing facilities existed. Van de Vrede (1921) thought that this would provide the advantage of the best lecturers, nursing instructors, and superintendents (pp. 55–57). This, of course, still condoned separate facilities under one roof.

Van de Vrede further expressed that "since White nurses cannot be the best agent in the Negro home, we needed Negro public health nurses for the Negro home" (Van de Vrede, *JNMA* 1921, p. 56). Van de Vrede's analysis that White nurses could not be the best agent in the Negro home was a reflection of rejecting cases in Black homes. In order to do this work well, van de Vrede surmised that special training was required, either by working in a well-organized VNA under supervision or by taking special courses after graduating from a nursing program. Although Thoms was a pioneer in this field for Black nurses as early as 1917, few Black nurses had taken such courses.

In 1935, the NACGN formed a liaison committee with the New York Citizen's Committee for Nursing Education and Service. The major focus of this committee was to eradicate racial barriers that existed in the employment of Black nurses. As the committee attempted to meet its goal, it sought the support of the news media. It also sought and gained the cooperation of Elma Carter, then chairperson of the New York State Commission Against Discrimination. In addition, the editor of *Opportunity* magazine devoted the entire November 1937 issue to this cause, carefully describing in detail the conditions affecting the Black nurse, particularly racial barriers in employment. This edition stimulated vast interest in the conditions of employment affecting the Black nurse: nurses and citizens, Black and White, became interested in the Black nurses' plight. There was a widespread written response to the magazine articles, many of whom expressed disenchantment with the status of the Black nurse. This was indeed a consciousness-raising endeavor.

The NACGN decided to organize a National Advisory Council to promote active participation and support for the goals of the NACGN and in 1939 a biracial council was organized. The objectives of this council were to improve both the quality and quantity of educational nursing facilities available to Black students, as well as the employment of qualified Black professional nurses in all health services and programs. In addition, this council would encourage and promote professional health legislation that would include Black nurses.

At the ANA convention in 1940, the NACGN raised the issue before the House of Delegates of excluding Black nurses from membership in various states. Prior to the discussion, many well-meaning supporters of the NACGN thought this discussion would impede progress and advised the NACGN not to raise the discussion. However, the NACGN believed that failure to communicate its position and to seek understanding was a greater barrier to its progress. The NACGN believed that the convention was the ideal forum to bring the injustice before the ANA convention for discussion. This issue was fully supported by the New York State delegation and by other delegates from states with Black members.

Many delegates voiced their opinions stating that Black nurses were seeking social equality, while others reminded the membership that a professional organization should serve all nurses regardless of race. Some felt that the

NACGN should be strengthened since Black nurses would be happier in an organization of their own. Still another opinion was that the potential for leadership of Black nurses should be channeled through the ANA and in time should serve the entire profession. Additional arguments for admission were that nursing standards of practice were set by the ANA and Black nurses were required to meet these standards; thus, exclusion of Black nurses from any state or aspect of the ANA was discriminatory. The question of membership in all states, of course, was not resolved at this convention; however, the issue was now openly voiced at the convention and brought into clear focus (Staupers 1961, pp. 127–128). A conclusion drawn from this convention is that opinions were still clearly divided on this issue of accepting Black nurses.

During World War II, the Black nurse again faced racial discrimination and segregation. This problem was prevalent in the U.S. Army and the Navy. Thoms had begun this political fight during World War I. After World War I, at the eleventh hour and in light of a critical nurse shortage, the surgeon general was finally convinced to utilize the services of Black nurses. During World War II, the armed services initially tenaciously held to the strict policy of quotas—few or no Black nurses. In 1940, the surgeon general initially accepted a quota of fifty-six Black nurses, assigning them to provide nursing care exclusively for Black soldiers (Staupers 1961, p. 102). Again, as in World War I, the War Department maintained that segregation was not discriminatory if equal facilities were provided. This, of course, had been condoned and sanctioned by the Supreme Court decision of *Plessy vs. Ferguson* since 1896 as the American way of life. However, Black Americans considered segregation perforce was discriminatory, that it precluded free movement, that facilities were not equal and, in fact, segregation perpetuated inequality.

The Black nurses' prolonged struggle for respect, dignity, professional recognition, and integration into the mainstream of American nursing was rekindled with new enthusiasm. Staupers strategically seized upon the critical nurse shortage created by the war in order to heighten public awareness of the Black nurses' plight. Staupers, executive secretary of the NACGN, personally knew Mahoney, Franklin, and Thoms. Thus, she was indeed cognizant of Thoms's plight during World War I, as well as the discrimination and exclusionary tactics that the Black nurses faced. Staupers vowed that the history of World War I would not be repeated.

By the time Japan attacked Pearl Harbor on December 7, 1941, Staupers had developed a strategic sense of political savvy. In addition, Estelle Massey Riddle, former president of the NACGN, and first Black nurse to complete a master's degree in nursing, was on the National Defense Council.

Staupers, a very assertive woman, picked up the NACGN's fight and the Black nurses' military plight—rejection. The NACGN, with the support of the National Advisory Council, brought this racial problem to the attention of the National Nursing Defense Committee, which later became the National Nursing Council for War Service. Julia C. Stimson, who was the chairperson of the National Nursing Council on Defense and president of the ANA, brought this problem to the attention of the surgeon general, who failed to respond to this matter. Meanwhile, there was a shortage of nurses in the armed services. Early in 1944, the Army had an overwhelming need for 60,000 nurses; however, the quota system was in effect for Black nurses.

Meanwhile, Dr. Charles Drew, a Black physician, scientist, and scholar, made one of the most remarkable single contributions to the allied victory during World War II. Dr. Drew developed the process for extracting plasma from blood, thus providing the volume expander required to treat hemorrhage and hypovolemic shock. Black Americans were very proud of Dr. Drew's discovery and many lives were saved during World War II and thereafter.

However, subsequent to Dr. Drew's important discovery, Black doctors vociferously criticized the American Red Cross, stating: "Perhaps no single incident has done more damage to Negro morale than the gratuitous insult to the race by the Red Cross in first refusing to accept the blood of Negro donors and then in segregating it for no scientific reasons whatsoever" (Smith 1943, pp. 176–177). This was devastating and Black Americans were angry. In addition, the American Red Cross was described as:

> the culprit of the greatest national discriminatory blows that the Negro race has ever received. It is a stab in the back by our great foster mother, a stab that is so unjustifiable, unwarranted, unmerited and unscientific. It is a stab . . . which really stands out above all others because it is national and even international in its scope (Editorial by J. A. K. 1943, pp. 172–173).

In order to counter the shortages of nurses in civilian/armed forces/military hospitals and war industries, the Honorable Frances Payne Bolton, a Congresswoman from Ohio, sponsored a bill in Congress. The Bolton Act was passed by Congress in June 1943, creating the United States Cadet Nurse Corps. During this time, the Bolton Act, also known as the Nurse Training Act, subsidized the complete education of nursing students. This act provided the nursing student with a monthly stipend, tuition, fees, books, and uniforms. Recipients were obligated to serve in military or civilian nursing until the war ended. In June 1943, Bolton introduced a new amendment to the Nurse Training Act that prohibited racial discrimination. It was passed. Bolton was an advocate for equality of Black nurses, and she had a close working relationship with the NACGN and supported its goals.

More than 2,000 Black nursing students enrolled in the U.S. Cadet Corps. The U.S. Cadet Nurse Corps would only fund a student who was attending a program accredited by the then National League of Nursing Education. Thus, Black schools of nursing were stimulated to improve the quality of their curricula. The National Council for War Service assisted Black schools of nursing to improve and meet the standards of the provisions in the Bolton Act. Relevant to education it appeared progress was in the making. However, employment continued to be a problem for Black nurses.

During the last six months of training for the Cadet Nurse Corps, a nursing student could enter a military or veterans hospital with the expectation of joining the Army or Navy Nurse Corps. However, Black nurse cadets were not accepted in these hospitals. Sanctioned and endorsed by the Surgeon General, the Army Nurse Corps stated that the applications of Black nurse cadets were rejected because there were no facilities for Black nurses in Army hospitals. This was indeed déjà vu—the same experience Thoms had had during World War I. The National Council for War Service worked closely with the NACGN to remove the barrier of racial segregation.

Through the persistence of Staupers, the NACGN, and an executive order issued by President Roosevelt, the Army opened its doors to all nurses in July 1944. Staupers and members of the NACGN continued their fight to break down discrimination in nursing. Franklin formulated this goal and Thoms began this fight with the armed services during World War I. President Roosevelt wrote another executive order in October 1944 that allowed Black nurses to enter the Waves.

By the time the Cadet Nurse Corps terminated in 1945, approximately 400 Black nursing students had been admitted to thirty-eight nursing schools without regard to race. This was an improvement from the beginning of World War II, in which only fourteen schools admitted Black students. Black specialists were appointed to the Public Health Service, the Children's Bureau of the Department of Labor, and the Federal Security Agency as consultants, advisors, and staff members. By September 1945, the Navy promoted a Black nurse, Phyllis MacDaley, to Lieutenant.

After World War II, the NACGN again channeled its attention and energy toward membership into the ANA. Thoms's significance as a leader is clearly understood in this endeavor. Thoms led the majority, a dominant group that opposed a merger with the NMA, the Black doctors' association. This opposition allowed the NACGN to maintain its identity as a group of nurses, thus providing the groundwork to facilitate membership in the ANA. The decision to maintain the organization as a group of nurses was politically astute and correct. The NACGN was organized as a unified movement around a specific profession—nursing, the Black race, and Black women. If the NACGN had merged with the NMA, the nurses would have lost their identity and the control of their organization. The history of the health profession supports its decision as politically wise. In addition, the membership of the NMA was male and the membership of the NACGN was female. The history of American society again supports that its decision not to merge and be controlled by a male-dominated profession was indeed correct and politically wise.

Black nurses not only wanted recognition from American society, but specifically from their colleagues from whom they were separated by the color of their skin. The NACGN hoped that membership in the ANA would solve the educational and employment problems affecting Black nurses. Their cornerstone was the support of a large, noted, and influential organization that would fight in support of Black nurses toward their goal of equality in the nursing profession. The NACGN's goal was to incorporate its goals within the ANA. Staupers explained that although the NACGN focused on membership in the ANA, similar membership problems existed with all three professional organizations: the ANA, the NLNE, and the NOPHN. Membership in the NOPHN was individual rather than through the state association and the problem was less pronounced.

Early steps toward membership into the ANA and the NLNE were slow and fragmented. In 1921, the NLNE appointed van de Vrede as chairperson of a committee to consider the possibility of an affiliation with the NACGN (van de Vrede 1922, pp. 29–30). However, this committee never came to fruition. In 1926, the ANA met with the NACGN to consider ways in which Black nurses could acquire membership in the ANA since they were precluded from membership in many state associations because of their race (Staupers 1961, p. 24). This issue lay dormant for thirteen years. In 1939, the president of the ANA, Julia C. Stimson, stated, "A letter would be sent to the state nurses' associations requesting opinions in reference to the question of membership of colored graduate nurses in the American Nurses' Association" (Membership of Colored Graduate Nurses in the ANA 1940, p. 122). This survey appeared fruitless, since the position of many states was already well documented by their long-standing refusal to admit Black nurses. In 1940, the ANA House of Delegates made a proposal to extend the privilege of membership to qualified Black nurses. However, this matter was tabled and no final action on this proposal was taken by the delegates (House of Delegates 1940, p. 672). Thereafter, this proposal lay dormant for six more years.

Meanwhile, in 1940, the NLNE authorized a joint endeavor—the formation of a committee of the NLNE, the ANA, and the NOPHN to work with the NACGN. This committee, like the preceding NLNE committee in 1921, was inert and never met. However, In 1942, however, the NLNE set a historic precedent by granting individual membership to Black nurses. "Membership in the NACGN was accepted in lieu of membership in the ANA" (Haupt 1941, pp. 78–79; Dennhart 1944, p. 100; Forty-Sixth Annual Report of NLNE 1940, pp. 103–104).

In 1946, the ANA House of Delegates voted to adopt a platform that advocated membership for Black nurses at the state level, removal of all racial barriers, and a commitment by the ANA to find a way to grant membership to Black nurses in the ANA (House of Delegates 1940, p. 672). The NACGN pondered its future direction (see Appendix H). Two years passed, and in 1948, this platform was presented and accepted at the biennial ANA convention in Chicago. At this juncture, the ANA began to offer individual membership to Black nurses who were precluded from their state nurses' association. A committee was formed to focus on individual membership designated as the *Individual Membership Project* to ensure the ANA's commitment to this endeavor. In 1950, the Individual Membership Project was enlarged, and became the *Intergroup Relations Program*. Finally, in 1949, the ANA suggested that the NACGN absorb its functions and responsibility into the ANA.

The actual dissolution of the NACGN and membership into the ANA occurred over a two-year period. In 1949, Staupers, former nurse executive secretary of the NACGN, was elected president. She remained president for two years, during which time the main goal of the NACGN was its dissolution. At this time, the NACGN had developed financial problems because some Black nurses were now paying state and national membership dues to the ANA.

The Intergroup Relations Program was to function as the primary vehicle for full integration of Black nurses into the ANA. The program developed the following objectives:

1. Clarification in the minds of nurses about the nature and implications of racial and cultural discrimination in nursing, and about the profession's responsibility for the quality of racial and cultural relations existing among and between nurses, their parents, and their colleagues.
2. Establishment of long-term and current goals in intergroup relations by the ANA, and adoption of its policies to guide and support nurses in their actions on racial and cultural issues.
3. Inspiration and psychological support given by the ANA along with technical guidance and assistance to nurses, as they have sought to understand and act in accord with the human relations philosophy of their profession.
4. Development of a climate throughout nursing that encourages nurses to discuss racial and cultural relationships, and to seek the assistance they need to improve intergroup relations.
5. Adoption by governmental, religious, and other civic bodies of unequivocal policies in support of "liberty and justice for all" in America. (Staupers 1961, pp. 146–147)

The ANA divided the Intergroup Relations Program into five units: (1) the *Public Relations Unit* encompassed a nationwide effort to educate the public about integration and the elimination of discrimination; (2) the *Research and Statistical Unit* studied the problems of discrimination and integration; (3) the *Economic Security Unit* studied the economic differences in salaries and working conditions due to racial discrimination; (4) the *Intergroup Relations Unit* focused on problems affecting minorities and to work with state and local levels to achieve integration; and (5) the *Legislative Unit* interpreted intergroup relations and presented intergroup problems in legislation (Hastie 1951, pp. 154–155).

The Intergroup Relations Program appeared to be all-encompassing and would meet the needs of Black nurses. However, there was a time lapse before all nurses were informed about the program. Subsequent to being informed, prejudice, discrimination, and notions of group superiority and group inferiority continued to exist and prevail in a select group of nurses. In reality, the NACGN did not anticipate that segregation and discrimination would disappear immediately. However, the NACGN interests and goals were to break down the barriers of exclusion. Staupers, who was president in 1950, convinced the Black nurses that the purpose for which the organization had been established had now been achieved and that it was time to dissolve the NACGN (Staupers 1961, p. 148; Franklin & Meier 1982, pp. 255–256).

As the organization dissolved, there were many meetings, tributes, and acclamations of praise for its forty-two years of existence. Special praise was given to its many leaders, of whom the first three mentioned were Mahoney, Martha Franklin, and Thoms. The final meeting where the dissolution was voted upon by the membership took place at St. Mark's Methodist Church where the first meeting began in 1908. It was 1951. Mahoney had died in 1926; however, she had left a legendary effect on Black nurses, the NACGN, and on American history. Thoms had died in 1943 in the midst of World War II, yet her name was etched in the minds and hearts of the NACGN membership as it dissolved. Through her efforts and professional endeavors, she gained exceptional recognition. Martha Franklin, the only one of the three architects alive, was now eighty-one. Franklin received glowing tribute and accolades were given to her as its organizer, first president, and honorary president for life. Franklin was thus able to realize and assess her goals. The goals Mahoney, Franklin, and Thoms had jointly worked toward had been accomplished, and/ or had reached a level of acceptance for dissolution with continuation of goal achievement through the ANA. The day had come, forty-two years from the time Franklin's ingenuity and know-how organized the NACGN. Through membership, Black nurses were to become an integral part of the ANA. The decision to dissolve was by design, a decision that the NACGN believed would be professionally beneficial for Black nurses. It was thought that membership in the ANA would assist Black nurses to achieve professional standards in nursing. The NACGN had produced many leaders and had achieved this goal; however, it was believed that the Black nurse could promote real change by seeking leadership positions in the ANA in addition to involvement of the state and district levels of the ANA.

When the NACGN attained membership in the ANA and NOPHN in 1951, there were only five states that continued to exclude Black nurses from state nurses' associations, one of which was Washington, D.C. White schools of nursing continued to practice discriminatory tactics well into the mid-twentieth century (Troupin 1969, p. 8788). However, at the time of dissolution, there were 345 schools in the United States that admitted Black students. In keeping with this new membership status into the ANA and the NOPHN, public health nurses joined in support of this endeavor. Perhaps human needs and health care finally took precedence over racial lines.

Mabel Staupers believed that dissolution was advisable, necessary, and beneficial for Black nurses. She believed that World War II helped bring about their membership in these national organizations. She stated when people are sick they do not know prejudice and want to get well. She also believed "That the ANA grew up." In Mabel Staupers's (1961) farewell speech, she stated, "We are now a part of the great organization of nurses, the ANA. We have not lost our identity, we shall enrich this organization by our contributions to the profession of nursing with a pattern of desegregation that will serve the common good of all Americans" (p. 145) (see Appendix I). However, only time would actually tell if dissolution of the NACGN was in the best interest of Black nurses.

Notes

1. The Nurses Association Alumnae of the United States and Canada became the ANA in 1911.
2. Dr. Mary Elizabeth Carnegie developed a scholarship to facilitate Black nurses' acquiring their doctorate.
3. And, these untrained nurses provided an effective rudimentary form of birth control and choices for Black women; when enslaved, they were being bred like cattle for profit.

Chapter 6

Implications for the Future

> Our lives, hopes, and dreams depend on our ability to be heard.
>
> *James Bernard, 1965*

What can nursing leaders and nurses of today learn from the endeavors of Mary Mahoney, Martha Franklin, and Adah Bell Samuels Thoms—and the formation and history of the NACGN? Knowledge of the past provides constructive guidance, direction, and a strategy for the future.

Black nurses were in transition, and the 1950s were a new and different era in American society. Without an association of their own, they placed their hopes of integration in the ANA. On May 17, 1954, the justices of the Supreme Court, three of whom were Southerners, unanimously ruled that segregated schools were not equal and thus unconstitutional. This decision overturned the 1896 *Plessy vs. Ferguson* decision that sanctioned segregation in the school system. The Brown decision set a precedent within American society. Although the decision only addressed elementary and high schools, it was soon used as a yardstick to eliminate segregation in universities, colleges, schools, libraries, parks, beaches, and most aspects of American society. Reaction to *Brown vs. the Board of Education* varied in different regions of the United States. However, in the South resistance developed within White supremacy groups, which often included threats and violence. One incident occurred in Little Rock, Arkansas, when President Eisenhower had to call upon federal troops to stop a riot at Central High School. President Kennedy later ordered Army troops to Oxford, Mississippi, to stop a riot when James Meredith, a Black student, tried to enroll at the University of Mississippi. These two incidents reflected the height of antagonism toward desegregation.

Black nurses had neither an identified leader nor a formal network for communication or organization. The influence and control of Black nurses relied on good faith in the ANA. Providing individual membership represented the ANA's commitment to include Black nurses in all aspects of the ANA's program as well as to ensure that the program would contribute toward improving the status of Black nurses. However, some states were resistant to change, and it was not until 1964 that all state and district associations removed racial barriers to membership (Branch & Paxton 1976, p. 23).

Meanwhile, American society embarked upon yet another era, the tumultuous 1960s of race riots, peace marches, counter sit-ins in Selma, Alabama, demonstrations, civil disobedience, mass arrest, Rosa Parks who refused to sit in the back of the bus, and a national spokesman and leader, Dr. Martin Luther King Jr. Black Americans had a new dream, and had redefined some of their old dreams.

Hugh H. Smith summarized that the 1960s brought about the creation of national organizations in new fields of endeavor. This included various associations such as the National Association of Black Psychologists, the National Association of Black Political Scientists, the National Association of Black Social Workers, the Nation of African-American Education, the National Committee of Black Churchmen, the National Black Nuns, the Caucus of Black Economists, the African

Heritage Studies Association, the Society of Black Music Composers, the Black Academy of Arts and Letters, the National Conference of Black Lawyers, the National Association of Minority Consultants and Urbanologists, and the National Black Planning Network. It is estimated that there are more than 1,000,000 members affiliated with these various Black professional groups. Smythe states that although no master list of current professional organizations exists, there are organizations on some level for almost every major professional occupation. In addition to these, older established organizations such as the National Bar Association, the National Medical Association (established in the 1800s), the National Dental Association, the National Pharmaceutical Association, the Association of Social Scientists, the American Teachers' Association, and the Association of Black Foundation Executives continue to exist (Smythe, Allport, Baker, & Beale 1976, pp. 469–470). Retrospectively, it may have been unwise for the NACGN to dissolve. A better choice would have been to maintain the NACGN and simultaneously acquire membership in the ANA and the NOPHN.

Smythe expressed an opinion that Black professionals share common traditional values of the nation with fellow White Americans and thus represent an element of strength in the attempt to develop a truly interracial society. As a group, Black professionals are basically oriented toward the larger society of Americans in general and do not seek racial segregation. However, like other Black Americans, they are capable of discontent and frustration with the failure of the White community to accept their full participation.

Although the national body had been dismantled, local clubs of Black nurses continued in a few cities, functioning predominantly as social organizations that provided scholarships to nursing students. The Mary Mahoney Club of Seattle, Washington, established in the 1940s, remained in existence. This demonstrated a need (beyond integration) for Black nurses to relate to one another and to their distinct cultural orientation. Chi Eta Phi, a national sorority of professional nurses organized in 1932, was the only group in existence with a large Black membership. This sorority encouraged its members to participate fully in the ANA (Branch & Paxton, p. 23).

According to Betty Williams:

> The emergence of new ethnic nurses' associations was due to the fact that the ANA did not keep pace with the core needs of ethnic nurses of color in a time when more participation and power were needed. The current generation of nurses, many highly prepared educationally and aware of themselves as competent people, are in tune with the times, ready to be definers of their destiny and ready to strike out on their own for institutional change. (Branch & Paxton, p. 25)

Networking with colleagues in one's profession is a common phenomenon. Black nurses sought one another for identity and in unity in order to meet the new challenges they faced. Revolutionary momentum had inspired new hope; goals were reclaimed, reset, and reprogrammed for a different era.

In 1967, the Council of Black Nurses was organized in Los Angeles. This was followed by a statewide conference planned by the Los Angeles and San Francisco Bay Area and Black Nurses Association in 1970. This conference attracted national attendance and within a year, Miami, New York, and other cities formed Black nurses associations. Their major goals were to improve the health care of Black people and to safeguard the professional status of the Black nurse. This momentum was heightened by the failure of the ANA to act upon the resolution and commitments made in 1951 when the NACGN dissolved. Staupers later expressed that the ANA failed to give full attention to the problems of minority nurses and had only shown tokenism. This failure was comparable to a breach of contract.

Similarly various Filipino nurses' associations were organized in Southern California (established in 1960), San Francisco, Seattle, and other major U.S. population centers. The Chicano nurses organization was established in Los Angeles in 1969. The Korean Nurses Association of Southern California was organized in 1970, followed by the Northern California Korean Nurses Association and several other local associations throughout the United States. In 1972, the Latin American Nurses Association was organized in northern California, followed by state organizations in Colorado, various other states, and a National Latino Nurses Association. The American Indian Nurses Association began to organize in 1971 (Branch & Paxton, pp. 26–27).

Twenty years after the NACGN dissolved, a group of Black nurses came together and formed the National Association of Black Nurses to focus more attention on the development of Black professional nurses. The following objectives were identified:

1. Define and determine nursing care for Black consumers for optimum quality of care by acting as their advocates.
2. Act as change agents in restructuring existing institutions and/or helping to establish institutions to suit our needs.
3. Serve as the national nursing body to influence legislation and policies that affect Black people, and work cooperatively and collaboratively with other health workers to this end.
4. Conduct, analyze, and publicize research to increase the body of knowledge about health care and health needs of Blacks.
5. Compile and maintain a National Directory of Black Nurses to assist with the dissemination of information regarding Black nurses and nursing on national and local levels by the use of all media.
6. Set standards and guidelines for quality education of Black nurses on all levels by providing consultation to nursing faculties, and by monitoring for proper utilization and placement of Black nurses.
7. Recruit, counsel, and assist Black persons interested in nursing to ensure a constant progression of Blacks into the field.
8. Act as the vehicle for unification of Black nurses of varied age groups, educational levels, and geographic locations to ensure continuity and flow of our common heritage.

9. Collaborate with other Black groups to compile archives relevant to the historic, current, and future activities of Black nurses.
10. Provide the impetus and means for Black nurses to write and publish on an individual or collaborative basis. (Branch & Paxton, p. 28)

The impetus to organize a special association for Black nurses stems from the recognition that the ANA lacked focus for Black and other ethnic concerns. The need for a Black Nurses Association was emphasized at the 1971 National Conference on the Status of Health called by the Congressional Black Caucus at Meharry Medical College, Nashville, Tennessee. Leaders of Black health and welfare professional associations throughout the nation were gathered to assess and strategize to improve health care for Black people. Black nurses lacking an association were not formally included. The explanation set forth was that: "Black nurses have no organization, no agreed upon leaders for us to include." Although other Black health professionals, physicians, dentists, pharmacists have gained entrance to the dominant professional organizations, they still maintained their national associations through the years (Branch & Paxton, pp. 27–28). The decision to organize the National Black Nurses Association, Inc. was the vehicle for Black nurses to recapture their voices, communication, and national networking.

In 1968, the ANA called upon its membership and all nurses in the United States to fulfill their professional responsibilities by engaging in meaningful and positive action in civil rights activities. In separate messages to the state and district constituent associations and to all individual members, Jo Eleanor Elliott, then ANA president, urged that nurses, as responsible citizens, communicate immediately with representatives in state and federal government, urging prompt action on pending civil rights measures. The ANA also communicated directly with leadership in the Senate and House of Representatives, urging responsible action in the broad area of support of social programs. ANA asked Congress to place this nation's priorities where they rightfully belong, and to move swiftly to further guarantee all citizens their rights (*ANA Calls Upon All Nurses* 1968, p. 331).

In 1972, the following resolution on the Affirmative Action Program was submitted by the ANA Commission on Nursing Research:

WHEREAS, In 1951 a merger of the National Association of Colored Graduate Nurses and the American Nurses' Association was effected which resulted in the dissolution of the National Association of Colored Graduate Nurses with a subsequent commitment by the American Nurses' Association that the participation of black nurses in the American Nurses' Association would receive major promotional efforts, and

WHEREAS, It was recognized that if Negro nurses were to receive complete and adequate services within the American Nurses' Association, provision must be made by the ANA for staff and facilities which would enable Negro nurse members to participate effectively in the total program of the organization and ensure that the program would contribute to the welfare of all Negro nurses, and

WHEREAS, The Committee on Intergroup Relations, which was established as the vehicle to implement the Intergroup Relations Program, was dissolved by the ANA in 1962 before the objectives of the program were achieved, and

WHEREAS, In the 21 years since the merger of the National Association of Colored Graduate Nurses and the American Nurses' Association, black nurses have noticeably been excluded from elected office and appointed positions on committees, commission and boards within the organization and the inclusion of black nurses on policy and decision-making bodies in nursing and related health care groups has remained limited, and

WHEREAS, Increasing numbers of black nurses are finding it necessary to organize in caucus groups and associations to meet the needs created by the failure of the American Nurses' Association to discharge its obligation; therefore be it

RESOLVED, That the American Nurses' Association honor its commitment by taking immediate steps to establish an Affirmative Action Program at the National level which will rectify this failure; and be it further

RESOLVED, That such steps shall include:

1. Appointment of a Task Force composed of nurses representative of minority groups (which shall also include white nurses) to develop and implement such a program, and
2. Appointment of a black nurse to the ANA staff to work with the Task Force developing and implementing the program, and
3. ANA shall actively seek greater numbers of minority group members in elected, appointed and staff positions within ANA and urge states and districts to do likewise; and be it further

RESOLVED, That the ANA encourage and promote Affirmative Action Programs on the state and local levels; and be it further

RESOLVED, That an ombudsman be appointed to the ANA staff.

In what manner might today's leaders of nursing and nurses apply those lessons learned from a study of the lives and careers of Mahoney, Franklin, and Thoms to some selected contemporary professional problems? The individual and collective legacy of Mahoney, Franklin, and Thoms provides modern nursing with an agenda for the future as well as role models for emulation by nurses of all races.

Relevant to providing safe nursing and/or health care for the Black population, regrettably, equality of health care and equal access remain a problem. For instance, in July 1986, the New York State Nursing Home Task Force found that "many New York nursing homes refuse to accept poor black and hispanic patients." There was apparent discrimination in nursing homes; what was clear was if one were over-65, poor, a minority, or a woman, there was a problem. Among many recommendations, the report requested that the Assembly pass Bill 7516 that would specifically outlaw Medicaid discrimination (Keer 1986, p. 8).

Nurses need to be aware of the barriers to obtaining health care that exist.

> The disparity in the health of Black Americans is due, in part, to racial genocide, prejudice, institutional discrimination, system bureaucracies, socioeconomic inequalities, social and political injustice and governmental policies. Moreover, social ills such as poverty, lack of affordable health insurance and universal access to high quality, affordable health services that are comprehensive, coordinated and continuous are formidable problems in the Black community. (Fowler 1991, p. 22; James & Williams 1989)

Health care agencies that are insensitive and unresponsive to Black Americans need cultural sensitivity training and administrative leadership with an organizational philosophy that is consumer-friendly, welcoming all races.

Dr. Tucker-Allan, having recently observed a community in Texas, stated,

> There are Black communities in America today without any means of health care. No health care providers are available to render *any* care. There is a denial of health care to certain patients who are then blamed (family irresponsibility) for not getting the care which they have systematically been denied. It's an old game called blaming the victim. (Tucker-Allen 1994, p. 3)

Despite major advances in modern medicine and health care, the morbidity and mortality rates of Black Americans are significantly higher than for other minorities and the White population (DDHS 1990). An important leadership role for nursing is influencing health policy reform that is responsive to the health needs of Black Americans.

Seize the moment and the opportunity—a must for Black nursing leaders and nurses to participate in public policy debate and decision making.

Lift every voice and sing . . .

Let your voices be heard, and present at policy discussions and lobby for improved health care for Black Americans. Otherwise, emerging policies may bear little resemblance to the needs of Black Americans. We should not watch and wait for legislators to propose health care policies. Be assertive at the local, state, and national level. Be a policy maker, not a policy wait(er).

Dr. Herbert I. Walker, M.D. (psychiatrist), observed a phenomenon in colleagues, residents, social workers, interns, and medical students dealing with Black patients and human rights. For the most part, the White population revealed a complete lack of knowledge of important Black historical figures, the African past of the American Black, the history of slavery, and the contemporary scene with its varied militant and nonviolent groups and philosophies, yet they were "treating" Black patients (Walker 1968, p. 397). Regrettably, most existing nursing histories ignore or pay fleeting attention to the contributions of early Black American leaders in nursing.

Mahoney, Franklin, and Thoms had major concerns regarding the education for Black nursing students, in addition to the end product of a nursing program—specifically, lack of equal opportunity and the quality of their educational process. An agenda for the future advanced to present day would be nursing curricula that recruit and provide retention programs for Black students and for students of all races. Black students in associate degree programs need to be encouraged to enter baccalaureate programs or continue their education. In addition, nursing faculty should assign and/or encourage clinical assignments within course goals and objectives that provide all student nurses with patients/clients of various ethnic groups. According to Branch and Paxton, the curriculum should provide for a nurse who:

- Recognizes the existence of racial and cultural diversity in American society.
- Is knowledgeable of how culture influences the health beliefs and health practices of people of color.
- Recognizes the influence of the culturally determined values and behaviors of the nurse and the patient on the nursing process.
- Maintains and fosters the ethnic identity and cultural practices of patients.
- Is able to make nursing assessments and interventions appropriate to the culture.

Philosophically, issues in contemporary nursing are often better understood if one knows the history of nursing. Knowledge of the past renders a professional nurse sensitive to current issues in nursing and intergroup relations. Nursing history was once a required course in order to complete a bachelor of science degree in nursing. As an agenda, the history of nursing should be an integral part of every nursing curriculum, particularly the professional curriculum. The reassessment posed here is not only that the history of nursing be a required course but to include the Black nurses' historical experience, which is too often ignored or suppressed. This historical knowledge would provide a basic premise to facilitate intergroup relations in nursing within the curriculum. In addition, this history intricately provides the bridgework toward understanding cultural diversity within the profession and toward providing safe nursing care for ethnic people of color by a nurse of any race.

Cultural diversity within the Black race is rarely, if ever, distinguished by the American mainstream. Within the White race, culture is noted and may be reflected in ethnicity—Irish, Italian, Polish, and so on. Dr. Sybil Lassiter analyzed the similarities and differences among African Americans and African West Indians (from the English-speaking islands) with cultural implications regarding health beliefs and care. Another largely undetectable group within the Black race is the first-generation American born of West Indian parentage. These offspring as adults sound like Americans by accent and are American by birthright. However, their cultural beliefs, well-ingrained through rearing, custom, tradition, and family values, may be identical to their parents. Some first-generation and second-generation Americans may exhibit varying degrees of both cultures.

> Awareness of the diversity among the Black population, socioeconomic status as well as generational level is essential to understand their behavior and responses. Knowledge and understanding of intraracial human responses should enhance the health professional's ability to interact successfully and intervene effectively with culturally diverse clients. (Lassiter 1994, pp. 4–9)

It is vital for all health professionals to identify the patient's culture and to develop new and creative approaches in delivering culturally sensitive and relevant health care in the Black population.

In July 1986, a federal government study reported that "Cancer Hits Blacks Harder." White patients had diagnosis of cancer while it was still localized and thus had better survival rates. In contrast, Black patients were diagnosed after metastasis, thereby decreasing their survival rates (American Cancer Society 1989). Chronic illnesses that may coexist with cancer and that are prevalent in the Black population are hypertension, glaucoma, kidney disease, and diabetes. In addition, lack of health education and primary prevention has led to a higher incidence of sexually transmitted disease, AIDS, and HIV infections in comparison to other minorities and the White population.

As an agenda, it is incumbent upon the nurse educator of any race to share in a common responsibility with other health professionals to convey within the nursing curriculum that a historical problem related to health care has persisted throughout the years. Thus, select groups of a population continue to be at risk. Similarly, nursing theory textbooks historically omitted or ignored specifics of nursing care related to the Black patient. Equality of nursing care today is part of a nursing school curriculum that includes ethnic diversity and specific theory related to care of the Black patient. For instance, how to detect pallor in the Black-skinned patient, the varied appearance of particular skin diseases in Black patients, hair care for the Black patient, and particular health problems prevalent in the Black population such as hypertension, glaucoma, sickle cell anemia, and HIV. And, for Black females, Lupus.

A study by Barger and Rosenfeld (1993) substantiated that nurse practitioners are managing nursing centers and caring for an exceptionally high proportion of minority clients who are very young, very old, economically indigent, and among the groups that are disadvantaged in terms of health care.

Healthy People 2000 Report has made a national agenda to reduce the cost of health care and achieve healthier, productive lives for all Americans. This national report addressed specific population objectives for minorities and Americans with low income.

Two major categories of nursing centers are presently in existence in the United States: (1) community-based primary care centers operated by public or private organizations, and (2) academic nursing centers associated with schools of nursing (Gray 1993; Starks 1996, p. 144). One such school of nursing is at Columbia-Presbyterian Hospital and its services are nationally televised. Nursing centers can provide the quality care needed in underserved populations, located in inner cities, rural areas, and shelters, and for the homeless.

Nurse practitioners have met with approval and patients appreciate the personal attention nurse practitioners are known to provide. Nurse practitioners in nursing centers and in traveling mobile health vans can provide at-risk populations with primary care that is lower cost, high quality, accessible, and culturally sensitive.

Analogies set forth by Wayson and Hine (in Verma 1975) provide insight into race relations and perceptions, Black history, and nursing history: "The American atmosphere of racism may be understood only through an analysis of our history and economy, lending an examination of the process through which unrecognized attitudes subtly influence everyday decisions and actions. Racial attitudes and behaviors in the United States are profoundly influenced by our history of Black slavery" (pp. 78–79).

"Black nursing history mirrors the unending quest of all Black Americans for social recognition of their contributions, open access to equal educational opportunities, and acceptance as competent professionals. The history of Black nursing is therefore a microcosm of the history of Afro-Americans" (Clark-Hine 1989, p. xxii). Likewise, the status of discrimination and race relations in the United States today emerges from our history and is the macrocosm for the microcosm in any profession.

On August 9, 1996, the Glass Ceiling Report was discussed on Channel 13, national television. The findings were that 30 to 50 percent of minorities encounter discrimination in society today and that discrimination is often subtle. Gatewood (in Salzman & Smith 1996) analyzed that research has continued to substantiate that within the Black race, one's complexion can be the determinant of racial experiences, employment opportunities or exclusion, and fair-skinned Blacks were favored in employment. "Sociological studies of the color question as related to Blacks clearly suggested that in the early 1990s skin color remained one of the mechanisms that determined 'who gets what' in Black America" (p. 2,449). Research in *JAMA* reported that racial discrimination or differences in patient preferences may influence the types of treatment received by patients with ischimic heart disease (Alexander 1995, p. 1,037).

An agenda for the future would be involvement in professional women's organizations that seek to foster and perpetuate racial equality and improve the status of women. In addition, women should become involved in organizations that seek to foster leadership and higher levels of educational achievement for minority women.

The significance of Mahoney, Franklin, and Thoms as nursing leaders is not only what they accomplished individually and in concert with one another, but the legacy they have given to modern nursing. Their leadership and commitment to equality demonstrated through organization of the National Association of Colored Graduate Nurses, organizational building and involvement, acquiring jobs for Black nurses, leadership development, educational and nursing standards, concerns for the status of women, and eradicating discrimination has a rich and proud history. Indeed, the Black nurses' experience is an integral and significant aspect of American nursing history. Mary Mahoney, Martha Franklin, and Adah Bell Samuels Thoms, the architects of integration and equality, were an inspiration and continue to be role models for the Black professional nurse. An agenda for the future is that their leadership continue to provide role models for emulation by nurses of all races.

Bibliography

MONOGRAPHS AND GENERAL WORKS

Andermahr, S., T. Lovell, C. Wollowitz. (1987). *A Glossary of Feminist Theory.* London, New York: Arnold.

Anderson, J. (1988). *The Education of Blacks in the South, 1860–1935.* Chapel Hill, NC: The University of North Carolina Press.

Archer, J. (1991). *Breaking Barriers: The Feminist Revolution.* New York: Puffin Books.

Barzun, J., & C. Graff. (1977). *The Modern Researchers.* 2d ed. New York: Harcourt, Brace, Jovanovich, Inc.

Belenky, M., B. Clinchy, & N. Goldberger. (1986). *Women's Way of Knowing: The Development of Self, Voice and Mind.* New York: Basic Books, Inc.

Bennett, L. (1987). *Before the Mayflower, a History of Black America.* 6th ed. New York: Penguin Books.

Blassingame, J. (1972). *The Slave Community: Plantation Life in the Antebellum South.* New York: Oxford University Press, 1972.

Blassingame, J. (1982). *Long Memory: The Black Experience in America.* New York: Oxford University Press.

Blum, J., et al. (1981). *The National Experience.* 5th ed. New York: Harcourt, Brace, Jovanovich, Inc., 1981.

Boyd, J. (1993). *In Company of My Sisters: Black Women and Self-Esteem.* New York: Dutton Publishers.

Branch, M., & P. Paxton. (1976). *Providing Safe Care for Ethnic People of Color.* New York: Appleton-Century-Crofts.

Brent, L. (1973). *Incidents in the Life of a Slave Girl.* New York: Harcourt Brace Jovanovich.

Brewster, R. (1993). "Black Feminist." In Andermahr et al. (1997), *Glossary of Feminist Theory.* London and New York: Arnold.

Carnegie, M. E. (1986). *The Path We Tread: Blacks in Nursing, 1854–1984.* Philadelphia: J. B. Lippincott Co.

———. (1991). *The Path We Tread: Blacks in Nursing, 1854–1990.* 2d. ed. New York: National League for Nursing Press.

———. (1995). *The Path We Tread: Blacks in Nursing, 1854–1994.* 3d. ed. New York: National League for Nursing Press.

Chaska, N. L., ed. (1983). *The Nursing Profession: A Time to Speak.* New York: McGraw-Hill Book Co.

Chunn, J., D. Dunstan, & F. Ross-Sheriff. (1983). *Mental Health and People of Color.* Washington, DC: Howard University Press.

Cole, J., ed. (1986). *All American Women: Lines That Divide, Ties That Bind.* New York: Free Press.

Dannett, S. G. (1966). *Profiles of Negro Womanhood.* 1st ed. New York: Educational Heritage, Inc. (Vol. II, 20th century).

Davis, A. Y. (1983)C 1981, "Racism, Birth Control and Reproductive Rights." *Women, Race and Class.* New York: Vintage Books, pp. 202–221.

Dietz, L., and A. Lehozky. (1967). *History and Modern Nursing.* Philadelphia: F. A. Davis Co.

Dolan, J. ([1958]1963). *Goodnow's History of Nursing.* Philadelphia: W. B. Saunders Co.

DuBois, E. (1980). *Feminism and Suffrage: The Emergence of an Independent Women's Movement in America, 1848–1869.* Ithaca, NY: Cornell University Press.

Ehrenreich, B., & D. English. (1973a). *Complaints and Disorders: The Sexual Politics of Sickness.* New York: The Feminist Press.

———. (1973b). *Witches, Midwives, and Nurses: A History of Women Healers.* New York: The Feminist Press.

Exley, H. (1996). *In Celebration of Women.* New York: Exley Publications.

Fairchild, H. P., ed. (1984). *Dictionary of Sociology and Related Sciences.* Totowa, NJ: Rowman E. Allenheld.

Farlow, J. W. (1918). *The History of the Boston Medical Library.* Norwood, MA: The Pimpton Press.

Fishel, L., & B. Quarles. (1970). *The Black American.* New York: William Morrow & Company, Inc.

Fitzpatrick, M. L., ed. (1978). *Historical Studies in Nursing.* New York: Teachers College Press.

Flexner, E. (1973). *Century of Struggle: The Women's Rights Movement in the United States.* New York: Atheneum.

Franklin, J., & A. Meir., eds. (1982). *Black Leaders of the Twentieth Century.* Chicago: University of Illinois Press.

Giddings, P. (1985). *When and Where I Enter: The Impact of Black Women on Race and Sex in America.* New York: Bantam Books.

Goodnow, M. (1982). *Outlines of Nursing History.* 4th ed. Philadelphia: W. B. Saunders Co.

———. (1938). *Nursing History in Brief.* Philadelphia: W. B. Saunders.

Gray, W. (1964). *Historians Handbook.* Boston: Houghton Mifflin.

Gripando, G. (1983). *Nursing Perspectives and Issues.* 2d ed. New York: Delmar Publishers, Inc.

Gunnar, M., et al. (1944). *An American Dilemma: The Negro Problem and Modern Democracy.* New York: Harper and Brothers.

Gutman, H. (1976). *The Black Family in Slavery and Freedom 1750–1925.* New York: Vintage Books.

Harris, M., & M. Levitt et al. (1974). *The Black Book.* New York: Random House.

Highlights in the History of the Army Nurse Corps. (1995). Washington, DC: U. S. Army Center of Military History.

Hine-Clark, D. (1989). *Black Women in White: Racial Conflict and Cooperation in the Nursing Profession: 1890–1950.* Bloomington: University of Indiana Press.

———. (1993*). Black Women in America: An Historical Encyclopedia.* New York: Carlson Publishers.

Hodges, G., ed. (1994). *Studies in African American History and Culture.* New York: Garland Publishing Co.

Hoult, T. F. (1977). *Dictionary of Modern Sociology.* Totowa, NJ: Littlefield, Adams, & Co.

Hughes, L., M. Meltzer, & E. Lincoln. (1983). *A Pictorial History of Black Americans.* New York: Crown, Inc.

Hull, G. T., P. B. Scott, & B. Smith, eds. (1982). *But Some of Us Are Brave.* New York: The Feminist Press.

Humm, M. (1989). *The Dictionary of Feminist Theory* (2d ed.). Ohio: Ohio State University Press.

Staupers, M., "Adah B. Samuels Thoms." In E. James, ed., *Notable American Women 1607–1950.* Vol. 3. Cambridge, MA: The Belknap Press of Harvard University.

Jordan, W. (1974). *The White Man's Burden: Historical Origins of Racism in the United States.* New York: Oxford University Press.

Joyner, C. (1984). *Down by the Riverside.* Urbana and Chicago: University of Illinois Press.

Kalisch, P., & B. Kalisch. (1978). *The Advance of American Nursing.* Boston: Little, Brown & Co.

Katz, P., & D. Taylor, eds. (1988). *Eliminating Racism.* New York: Plenum Press.

Kruse, L., & R. Stogdill. (1973). *The Leadership Role of the Nurse.* Columbus: Ohio State University Research Foundation.

Lagemann, E. C., ed. (1983). *Nursing History: New Perspectives, New Possibilities.* New York: Teachers College Press.

Lerner, G. (1973). *Black Women in White America.* New York: Vintage Books.

Levesque, G. (1994). *Black Boston: African American Life and Culture in Urban America, 1750–1860.* New York: Garland Publishing Inc.

Levine, L. W. (1977). *Black Culture and Black Consciousness: Afro American Folk Thought from Slavery to Freedom.* New York: Oxford University.

Litwack, L. (1961). *North of Slavery: the Negro in the Free States, 1790–1860.* Chicago: The University of Chicago Press.

Logan, R., & M. Winston. (1982). *Dictionary of American Negro Biography.* New York: Norton.

Low, A., & V. Cliff. (1981). *Encyclopedia of Black Americans.* New York: McGraw-Hill.

Lowenberg, R., & R. Bogin et al., eds. (1976). *Black Women in the Nineteenth Century in American Life: Their Words, Their Thoughts, Their Feelings.* University Park, PA: Pennsylvania State University Press.

Lunardini, C. (1994). *What Every American Should Know about Women's History.* Boston: Bob Adams Co., Inc.

McManus, E. (1973). *Black Bondage in the North.* Syracuse, NY: Syracuse University Press.

McPherson, J. (1982). *The Negro's Civil War.* New York: Ballantine Books.

Melosh, B., & J. Leavitt, eds. *Women and Health in America.* Madison, WI: University of Wisconsin Press.

Morton-Neverdon, C. (1989). *Afro-American Women of the South and the Advancement of the Race 1895–1925.* Knoxville: University of Tennessee Press.

O'Neil, W. (1969). *Everyone Was Brave: A History of Feminism in America.* Chicago: Quadrangle Books.

Osteweis, R. (1953). *Three Centuries of New Haven.* New Haven, CT: Yale University Press.

Painter, N. I. (1996). *Sojourner Truth, a Life a Symbol.* New York: W. W. Norton & Co.

Pleck, E. (1979). *Black Migration and Poverty, Boston 1865–1900.* New York: Academic Press.

Ploski, H., & W. Marr, eds. (1976). *The Negro Almanac, a Reference Work on the Afro American.* New York: Bellwether Publishing Co.

Roberts, M. (1955). *American Nursing: History and Interpretation.* New York: MacMillan Co.

Rothman, S. M. (1978). *Woman's Proper Place: A History of Changing Ideals And Practices, 1870 to the Present.* New York: Basic Books.

Ryan, W. (1972). *Blaming the Victim.* New York: Vintage Books.

Salzman, J., D. Smith, & C. West, eds. (1966). *Encyclopedia of African American Culture and History.* New York: Simon & Schuster/Macmillan.

Sanford, E. (1887). *A History of Connecticut.* Hartford, CT: S. S. Scranton and Co.

Smythe, M., Allport, G., et al. (1976). *The Black American Reference Book: A Brief History.* Englewood Cliffs, NJ: Prentice-Hall.

Staupers, M. (1961). *No Time for Prejudice.* New York: MacMillan Co.

Steady, F. (1981). *The Black Woman Cross-Culturally.* Cambridge, MA: Schenkman Publishing Co.

Steinhorn, L., Diggs-Brown, B. (1999). *The Color of Our Skin*, New York: Dutton Penguin Group.

Stephens, A. (1992). *Wild Woman.* Berkeley, CA: Conari Press.

Sterling, E., ed. (1984). *We Are Your Sisters: Black Women in the Nineteenth Century.* New York: W. W. Norton and Co.

Stewart, I., & A. Austin. (1962). *A History of Nursing.* New York: Putnam's Sons.

Stogdill, R. (1974). *Handbook of Leadership: Survey of Theory and Research.* New York: Free Press.

Strapp, C. (1993). *Afro-Americans in Antebellum Boston: An Analysis of Probate Records.* New York: Garland Publishing Inc.

Tatum, D. B. (1997). *Why Are All the Black Kids Sitting Together in the Cafeteria?* New York: Basic Books.

Thoms, A. (1929). *Pathfinders.* New York: Kay Printing House Inc.

Tilly, L. (1993). *Industrialization and Gender Inequality.* Washington, DC: American Historical Association.

VanDeburg, W. L. (1984). *Slavery and Race in American Popular Culture.* Madison, WI: University of Wisconsin Press.

Verma, G., and Bagley, C. (1975). *Race and Education Across Cultures.* London: Heinemann Educational Books.

Wayson, W. (1975). "White Racist in America." In Vermar, G., & C. Bagley, *Race and Education Across Cultures.* London: Heinemann Educational Books.

Webber, T. L. (1978). *Deep Like the Rivers: Education in the Slave Quarter Community, 1831–1865.* New York: Norton.

Wesley, C., et al., eds. (1968). *International Library of Negro Life and History: I Too Am America* (Vol. 6). New York: Publishers Co., Inc.

Wesley, C., et al., eds. (1968). *International Library of Negro Life and History: In Freedom's Footsteps* (Vol. 7). New York: Publishers Co., Inc.

Winthrop, J. (1968). *White Over Black: American Attitudes Toward the Negro 1550–1812.* New York: W. W. Norton & Co.

Woodson, C. G. (1969). *The Mis-education of the Negro.* Washington, DC: Associated Publishers.

Woody, T. (1966). *History of Women's Education in the United States: 1891–1960.* New York: Octagon Books.

JOURNALS

American Journal of Nursing. (1929). A History in the Making. Vol. 29, No. 5, p. 560.

American Journal of Nursing. (1940). House of Delegates. Vol. 40, No. 6, p. 672.

American Journal of Nursing. (1944). Negro Nurses. Vol. 44, No. 5, p. 477.

American Journal of Nursing. (1950). This Is the Joint Board. Vol. 50, No. 4, p. 206.

American Journal of Nursing. (1950). A Two Organization Structure. Vol. 50, No. 11, p. 741.

American Journal of Nursing. (1951). The Two Organizations in the New Structure. Vol. 51, No. 5, pp. 288–289.

American Journal of Nursing. (1954). Intergroup Relations. Vol. 54, No. 11, pp. 1341–1343.

Atkinson, N. J. (1921). Influenza. *Journal of the National Medical Association, 13*, 20–21.

———. (1919). Historical Notes on Influenza. *Journal of the National Medical Association, 11*, 39–40.

Carnegie, E. (1984, October). Black Nurses at the Front. *American Journal of Nursing.*

Carnegie, E. (1951). . . . but Integration Is Empty Talk. *Modern Hospital, 76,* 55–56.

Chayer, M. (1954). Mary Eliza Mahoney. *American Journal of Nursing, 54,* 429–431.

Davis, A. T. (1999). Martha Minerva Franklin. In J. Garraty & M. Carnes (eds.), *American National Biography,* Vol 8 (pp. 400–401). New York: Oxford University Press.

———. (1999). Petra Pinn. In J. Garraty & M. Carnes (eds.), *American National Biography,* Vol. 7 (pp. 549–550). New York: Oxford University Press.

———. (1996, Spring). Historical Roots of Cultural Diversity in Nursing: The New England Hospital for Women and Children. *Journal of Cultural Diversity, 3,* 16–19.

———. (1995, Spring). Sojourner Truth and Harriet Tubman: Sources of Inspiration. *The ABNF Newsletter, 9,* 1–2.

———. (1992). Mary Eliza Mahoney. In J. Carney-Smith, ed., *Notable Black American Women* (pp. 370–371). Detroit: Gale Research Inc.

———. (1992). Martha Miverva Franklin. In J. Carney-Smith, ed., *Notable Black American Women* (pp. 720–721). Detroit: Gale Research Inc.

———. (1992). Adah Belle Samuels Thoms. In J. Carney-Smith, ed., *Notable Black American Women* (pp. 1137–1138). Detroit: Gale Research Inc.

———. (1992). Ethel Incledon Johns. In V. Bullough, ed., *American Nursing: A Biographical Dictionary* (pp. 164–166). New York: Garland Publishing Co.

———. (1991, April). America's First School of Nursing: The New England Hospital for Women and Children. *Journal of Nursing Education, 30,* 158–161.

———. (1988). Mary Eliza Mahoney. In V. Bullough, ed., *American Nursing: A Biographical Dictionary* (pp. 226–228). New York: Garland Publishing Co.

———. (1988). Martha Minerva Franklin. In V. Bullough, ed., *American Nursing: A Biographical Dictionary* (pp. 120–123). New York: Garland Publishing Co.

———. (1998). Adah Belle Samuels Thoms. In V. Bullough, ed., *American Nursing: A Biographical Dictionary* (pp. 313–316). New York: Garland Publishing Co.

Dondson, D. (1953). No Place for Race Prejudice. *American Journal of Nursing, 53,* 165–166.

Editorials. (1951). *American Journal of Nursing, 51,* 153.

Educational Facilities for Colored Nurses and Their Employment. (1925). *Public Health Nursing, 17,* 203–204.

Elmore, J. (1976). Black Nurses: Their Service and Their Struggle. *American Journal of Nursing, 76,* 435–437.

Grace, M. (1956). Discrimination Is on Its Way Out: The Nursing Profession Keeps Pace. *American Journal of Nursing, 56,* 166–168.

Green, H. M. (1926). National Negro Hospital Week. *Journal of the National Medical Association, 18,* 230.

Harter, C. (1958). But We Have No Problem. *American Journal of Nursing, 58,* 687–688.

Hastie, W. (1951). A Fairwell to NACGN. *American Journal of Nursing, 51,* 154–155.

Heisler, A. (1956). Promoting the Intergroup Relations Program. *American Journal of Nursing, 56,* 588–589.

Hernandez, M. (1930, June). Adah Belle Thoms, R. N. *National News Bulletin, 3,* 5.

Hoekstra, F. (1949). Human Rights and Nursing. *American Journal of Nursing, 49,* 8.

Jack, H. (1951). Is Segregation Really Necessary? *The Modern Hospital, 76,* 52–54.

Journal of the American Medical Association. (1929). Investigation of Negro Hospitals. Vol. 92, No. 16, pp. 1375–1376.

Journal of the National Medical Association. (1911). Of Interest to Nurses: Nurses Notes. Vol. 3, No. 4.

Journal of the National Medical Association. (1913). Of Interest to Nurses. Report of the 6th annual meeting of the NACGN. Vol. 5, No. 4, p. 271.

Journal of the National Medical Association. (1914). Editorial. Vol. 6, No. 2, pp. 131–132.

Journal of the National Medical Association. (1915). Of Interest to Nurses. Vol. 7, No. 4, pp. 326–327.

Journal of the National Medical Association. (1916). Of Interest to Nurses. Vol. 8, No. 4, pp. 203–207.

Journal of the National Medical Association. (1917). Of Interest to Nurses. Vol. 9, No. 4, pp. 209–210.

Journal of the National Medical Association. (1918). Of Interest to Nurses. Vol. 10, No. 2, p. 139.

Journal of the National Medical Association. (1919). Letter to the Committee of the National Medical Association from Newton D. Baker, Secretary of War. Vol. 11, No. 1, pp. 27–28.

Journal of the National Medical Association. (1919). Of Interest to Nurses. Vol. 11, No. 4, p. 283.

Journal of the National Medical Association. (1920). Nurses Section. Presidential Address (Thoms). Vol. 12, No. 4, pp. 73–75.

Journal of the National Medical Association. (1921). Nurses Section: Nurses Notes. Vol. 13, No. 1, p. 63.

Journal of the National Medical Association. (1921). Nurses Section: Nurses Notes. Vol. 13, No. 3, p. 218.

Journal of the National Medical Association. (1924). The Small Hospital: Some Observations and Conclusions. Vol. 16, No. 1, pp. 20–22.

Journal of the National Medical Association. (1968). Ana Calls Upon All Nurses to Engage in Meaningful Civil Rights Activity. Vol. 60, No. 4, p. 331.

Journal of the National Medical Association. (1943). Editorial by J. A. K. Vol. 35, No. 5, pp. 172–173.

Kenny, J. (1920). Welcome Address—NACGN. *Journal of the National Medical Association, 12,* 78–79.

———. (1913). President's Address: Recommendations. *Journal of the National Medical Association, 5,* 223.

Lovell, M. (1981). Silent but Perfect Partners: Medicine's Use and Abuse of Women. *Advances in Nursing Science/Women's Health.*

Massey, E. (1933). The NACGN. *American Journal of Nursing, 33,* 534–536.

———. (1934). The Negro Nurse Student. *American Journal of Nursing, 34,* 806–810.

Membership of Colored Graduate Nurses in the ANA. *American Journal of Nursing, 39,* 922.

National News Bulletin. The Mary Mahoney Graduate Nurses Club of Detroit. Microfilm R1237, Schomburg.

———. 1928–1951. Microfilm R1237, Schomburg.

Notes, from Headquarters: ANA Board of Directors' Meeting. (1934). *American Journal of Nursing, 34,* 499.

Petry, L. (1945). The U. S. Cadet Nurse Corps: A Summing Up. *American Journal of Nursing, 45,* 1027–1028.

Richards, L. (1915). Early Days in the First American Training School for Nurses. *American Journal of Nursing, 16,* 174–176.

Roberts, S. (1983, July). Oppressed Group Behavior: Implications for Nursing. *Advances in Nursing Science.*

Roman, C. V. (1909). Woman's Work. *Journal of the National Medical Association, 2,* 4.

Romm, A. (1997, March/April). Gentle Expectations. *Herbs for Health.*

Rorem, R. (1951). No Color Line but No Alternatives. *Modern Hospital, 76,* 57.

Smith, G. (1975). From Invisibility to Blackness: The Story of the National Black Nurses Association. *Nursing Outlook, 23,* 225–229.

Smith, T. M. (1943). Cancel Radio Talk Show on Negro Blood Donors. *Journal of the National Medical Association, 35,* 176–177.

Southwest Christian Advocate. (1914). The Interlocking of the Races. *Journal of the National Medical Association, 6,* 131–132.

Springer, A. (1919). The War and Venereal Disease Among Negroes. *Journal of the National Medical Association, 11,* 48.

Staupers, M. (1970). The Black Nurse and Nursing Goals. *Journal of the National Medical Association, 62,* 304–305.

———. (1942). The Negro Nurse Advances. *Trained Nurse and Hospital Review, 108,* 112–114.

————. (1951). The Story of the NACGN. *American Journal of Nursing, 51,* 222–223.

Stewart, I. M. (1939). Next Steps in the Education of Nurses. *National News Bulletin, 9.*

Thomas, D. (1920). Nurses' Section: Report of the Thirteenth Annual Meeting. *Journal of the National Medical Association, 12,* 72.

Thoms, A. (1920). Nurses' Section: Presidents Address. *Journal of the National Medical Association, 12,* 206–207.

Troupin, J. (1969, November). School of Public Health in the United States and Canada, 1954–1960. *American Journal of Public Health, 50.*

Van de Vrede, J. (1921). Nurses' Section: The Need for Negro Public Health Nurses and the Provision Being Made to Meet It. *Journal of the National Medical Association, 13,* 55–57.

Walker, H. (1968). Some Reflections on the Death of Dr. Martin Luther King—A Commentary on White Racism. *Journal of the National Medical Association, 60,* 397.

NEWSPAPER ARTICLES

Beck, J. (1986, August 12). Change It to Black and She Still Sees Red. *New York Daily News.*

Cancer Hits Blacks Harder. (1986, July 18). News Wire Services, *New York Daily News.*

Death Notice of Martha Franklin. (1968, September 27). *New Haven Register.*

Friends, Relatives Pay Tribute to Mary E. Mahoney. (1973, September 6). *Boston Bay State Banner, 9,* 14.

Keer, K. (1986, July 1). Nursing Home Bias Charged. *New York Daily News.*

Walton, L. A. (1929, September 8). *New York World.*

DOCTORAL DISSERTATIONS

Chesson, M. (1981). *Richmond after the Civil War, 1865–1890.* Richmond: Virginia State Library.

Davis, A. T. (1987). *Architects for Integration and Equality: Early Black American Leaders in Nursing.* New York: Teacher's College, Columbia University.

Lagemann, E. C. (1978). *A Generation of Women: Education in the Lives of Progressive Reformers.* New York: Teachers College, Columbia University.

Sloan, P. (1978). *A Commitment to Equality: Early-Afro American Schools of Nursing.* New York: Teachers College, Columbia University.

ANNUAL REPORTS

Annual Report of the New England Hospital for Women and Children for the year ending November 14, 1865.

Annual Report of the New England Hospital for Women and Children for 1867.

Annual Report of the New England Hospital for Women and Children, General annual report, 1868.

Annual Report of the New England Hospital for Women and Children, 1869.

Annual Report of the New England Hospital for Women and Children, 1870.

Annual Report of the New England Hospital for Women and Children, 1872.

Annual Report of the New England Hospital for Women and Children, 1873.

Annual Report of the New England Hospital for Women and Children for the year ending September 30, 1874.

Annual Report of the New England Hospital for Women and Children, 1875.

Annual Report, 1876 report of training school for nursing, Women's Hospital, Philadelphia.

Annual Report of the New England Hospital for Women and Children, 1876.

Annual Report, Eighteen seventy-seven (1877) report of training school for nurses. Women's Hospital of Philadelphia.

Annual Report of the New England Hospital for Women and Children, 1878.

Annual Report, Eighteenth annual report of the New England Hospital for Women and Children for the year ending September 30th, 1879. Report of the committee on nurses.

Annual Report of the New England Hospital for Women and Children, 1880.

Annual Report, Seventeenth annual report of the Howard Orphan Asylum Society for the year ending September 30, 1885.

Annual Report, Fiftieth annual report of the board of managers of the Women's Hospital of Philadelphia, 1861–1911, for the year ending 1911.

Annual Report, Forty-sixth annual report of NLNE, 1940.

Annual Report of the Dimock Community Health Center, July 1984–June 1985.

Dennhart, L. (1944). Report of the joint committee to work with the National Association of Colored Graduate Nurses. *50th Annual Report of the NLNE.*

Haupt, A. (1941). Report of the committee to work with the NACGN. *47th Annual Report of the NLNE.*

Rorem, R. (1934). The field for negro nurses. *40th Annual Report of the NLNE.*

Van de Vrede, J. (1922). Report on affiliation with the colored nurses' association. *28th Annual Meeting of the NLNE.*

VITAL RECORDS

Certificate of Birth, Mary Mahoney, #1845, *17* (52), 107. The Commonwealth of Massachusetts, Boston State Archives.

Death Certificate of Mary Mahoney, 1926, *1* (148), 12. The Commonwealth of Massachusetts, Registry of Vital Records and Statistics.

Certificate of Birth, Mary E. Gauson, 1848, State of Connecticut, County of Litchfield, Town of New Milford, County Registrar.

Certificate of Birth, Florence Franklin, 1868, State of Connecticut, County of Litchfield, Town of New Milford, County Registrar.

Certificate of Birth, Martha Franklin, 1870, State of Connecticut, County of Litchfield, Town of New Milford, County Registrar.

Certificate of Marriage, Franklin's parents, 1866, Mary Gauson to Henry Franklin. State of Connecticut, County of Litchfield, Town of New Milford, County Registrar.

Death Certificate, Martha Franklin, 1968, #18466. Connecticut Department of Health, Public Health Statistics, Hartford, Connecticut.

Death Certificate, Adah Thoms Smith, 1943, #2098. New York Department of Health, Bureau of Vital Records.

CENSUS RECORDS

Census Records, Boston, Massachusetts, 1800–1900.

Census Records, Meriden, Connecticut, 1800–1900.

Census Records, Richmond, Virginia, 1850–1900.

ORAL HISTORY

Carnegie, E. (1986, June 13). Interview. Connecticut Afro-American Society, New Haven, CT.

Edmonds, E., Rev. (1986, June 13). Interview. Dixwell Avenue Congregational United Church of Christ, New Haven, CT.

Lagemann, E. (1984). Lectures, History of education. Teachers College, Columbia University, New York.

Lees, N. (1984, March, October, December). Supervisor of ANA archives. Telephone interviews. Kansas City, MO.

Lees, N. (1986, April). Supervisor of ANA archives. Telephone interview. Kansas City, MO.

Maken Keys Funeral Home (Mr. and Mrs. Williams). (1985, October 13–14). Interviews. 59 Dixwell Avenue, New Haven, CT.

Massie, W., M.D. (1985, October 12). Interview, New Haven, CT.

Pierce, L. (1986, March 27). Telephone interview. Masonic Home and Hospital, Unit Ramage Three, Wallingford, CT.

Rinsland, R., Dr. (1985, October 10). Dean, Office of the Registrar, Teachers College, Columbia University, New York.

Saunders, F. (1987, January 16). Interview. Boston, MA.

Saunders, G. (1985, October 14). Interview. New Haven, CT.

Scott, J. J. (1987, January 16). Interview. Administrator, Dimock Health Center (Previously the New England Hospital for Women and Children), Boston, MA.

Staupers, M. (Ret.), R.N. (1984, March, July, August). Telephone interviews. Distinguished Leader in Nursing, Last President of the NACGN, Author of *No Time for Prejudice*.

———. (Ret.), R.N. (1985, February). Telephone interview.

———. (Ret.), R.N. (1986, April 28, October). Telephone interviews.

Waring, L. (1984, September). *The Concept of the Calling*, presented at the American Association for the History of Nursing Conference, University of Virginia.

SITE VISITS

Dixwell Avenue Congregational United Church of Christ, New Haven, CT. June 13, 1986.

Gravesite, Martha Franklin, Walnut Grove Cemetery, Section C West, Lot 298, Old Colonial Road, Meriden, CT, October 27, 1985.

Gravesite, Adah Thoms Smith, Woodlawn Cemetery, Lot Honeysuckle, Range 19, Grave 293, Bronx, NY, November 18, 1986.

New England Hospital for Women and Children, now known as the Dimock Health Center. Accompanied by Mr. Frederick Saunders, great nephew of Mary Mahoney, January 16, 1987.

The Peoples Baptist Church, Camden Street, Boston, MA, January 16, 1987.

Roxbury, Boston Community where Mary Mahoney lived, January 16, 1987.

SURVEYS AND PROJECT REPORTS

Committee for the Study of Nursing Education, 1918–1924.

Johns, E. (1924–1925). Nursing education, Negro survey report, 200 folder, 1505.

Johns, E. (1924–1925). Nursing education, Negro survey report. Colored nurses in public health work.

Johns, E. (1925). Nursing education, Negro survey. Study of the present status of the negro woman in nursing.

National Organization for Public Health Nursing. (1914–1922).

Supplementary materials. (1922–1924).

SPECIALIZED HISTORICAL WORKS

Cremin, L., D. Shannon, et al. (1954). *History of Teachers College.* New York: Columbia University Press. Special Collections.

History and description of the New England Hospital for Women and Children. (1876). The training of nurses for the committee by Edna Cheney.

History of the Nurses Training School of the Women's Hospital of Philadelphia. (1861–1925). Nutting Collections.

History of Lincoln School for Nurses. *National News Bulletin*, Microfilm R1237, Schomburg Library for Research in Black Culture.

Sloan, I. *America's First Trained Nurse: The Story of Linda Richards, 1841–1930.* Nutting Collection.

HISTORICAL DOCUMENTS

Catalogue, Teachers College, Columbia University. (1928–1929, 1929–1930, 1930–1931). Special Collections.

Directory for Nurses (Vol. 2). Countway Medical Library, Boston, MA.

Family Bible, Martha Franklin, Births and Marriages. Connecticut Afro-American Historical Society, New Haven, CT.

The Franklin Family Folder, a collection of papers and documents pertaining to Martha Franklin and the Franklin Family.

Minutes of the National Association of Colored Graduate Nurses. (1908–1917, 1917–1937).

Student directory, Martha Franklin, Registrar's Office, Teachers College, Columbia University, New York.

PROGRAMS AND PUBLICATIONS

American Nurses Association. (1983–1984). National Awards pamphlet.

Building today for tomorrow's world. The Mary Mahoney Nurses Local of the National Association of Colored Graduate Nurses presents a conference on Nursing Problems Today and Tomorrow, Cambridge, MA, June 10, 1944.

The Dimock Story. The Dimock Health Center, previously known as the New England Hospital for Women and Children.

Doona, M. (1984, November). Mary Eliza Mahoney. *The Massachusetts Nurse*, 7–8.

Lincoln's School for Nurses on the occasion of its 100th anniversary. Lincoln Hospital, New York.

Program of the unveiling and dedication of Mary Mahoney's gravestone (shrine), Boston, MA, August 15, 1973.

Program of the national pilgrimage to Mary Mahoney's grave, Everett, MA, September 1, 1984.

Salute to Democracy at Mid-Century: National Association of Colored Graduate Nurses. Testimonial dinner honoring organizations and individuals who helped further democracy in nursing. Essex House, NY, January 21, 1951.

ARCHIVES

Academy of Medicine, New York, NY.

Afro-American Historical Society, New Haven, CT.

American Nurses' Association, Kansas City, MO.

Boston Public Library, Special Collections, Boston, MA.

Boston State Archives, Boston, MA.

Countway Medical Library, Boston, MA.

Meriden Public Library, Meriden, CT.

National League of Nursing, New York, NY.

Nutting Collection, Teachers College, Columbia University, New York, NY.

Richmond State Archives, Richmond, VA.

Rockefeller Archive Center, Pocantico Hills, NY.

Schomberg Library for Research in Black Culture, New York Public Library, New York, NY.

Special Collections, Teachers College, Columbia University, New York, NY.

Appendix A

1879 Annual Report of New England Hospital for Women and Children

REPORT OF COMMITTEE ON NURSES

During the past year we have had forty-two applications from young women who were considering the matter of becoming nurses. Ten of these were from the Western and Southern states, and the remainder from residents of New England. Several of this number were, however, deterred from entering by the conditions. Others entered, and, after a month's trial, either were found in some way unequal to their duties, or were not sufficiently in earnest to promise well for their future career and were permitted to withdraw. Others, again, having enlisted in the cause, were called home by serious illness in their families, and, in two instances, by failure of their own health. In view of these various contingencies it will seem less surprising that we can report only four nurses as having graduated with diplomas during the year, though several others have now nearly completed their course. These four graduates, Miss Edwards, Miss Mahoney, Miss Clough and Miss Tarlton, it is believed are fully entitled to confidence as efficient nurses, and will be sure not to disappoint those who may employ them.

There have been several changes in the office of superintendent. The vacancy caused by Dr. Crawford assuming the office of resident physician was filled for a time by Miss A. C. Davis, who has later taken the charge of the training school in the City Hospital, in the temporary absence of Miss Richards. Miss Clough, who had just finished her course with us as pupil nurse, was appointed her successor for three months. After a vacancy of a few weeks, Miss Tarlton, having finished her regular course of training, entered upon the duties of head nurse until we could secure the much needed services of a permanent superintendent. The committee are happy to report that they believe they have now found a competent person to fill this important office. Mrs. O'Neill, who has been two years in the department of nurses in the N. Y. Hospital, and most of that time superintendent of a ward, has engaged to come to us Nov. 1st on trial. We trust the coming year may show the good results of her efforts, and that the nurses in training may not suffer from the irregularities which we have so much regretted in the year that has closed.

M. C. E. BARNARD,
For Com. On Nurses.

Appendix B

A Letter from Pauline Lyons Williamson to Her Sister

Mary Elizabeth Pauline Lyons, a Black woman, was born in November 1850 in New York. Her first occupation was with needlework as an embroiderer. After the untimely death of her husband, and widowed at the young age of 31, she moved to Oakland, California, with her young son Harry to start a new life. There Pauline Lyons Williamson worked as a nurse. Her dream was to enter a formal training program and become a trained professional nurse. She wrote many letters to her sister Maritcha Lyons who was back East and whom she affectionately called May. In excerpt, the essence of her dreams and the Black woman's plight is captured in a long letter to her sister. Unfortunately, her dream to become a trained nurse never came to fruition.

Oakland (California), Nov. 10th, 1885

My Dear May,

    Your letter was received by me this day.... Now my dear don't
fash yourself. I am not coming home. At present what the future has
in store for me I don't know. Now to commence my story.... I shall
never leave the fields until I am thoroughly convinced that I can't get
a living here. I got along nicely with my case and got $20.00 for the
two weeks. But I have found that the one great obstacle is I have no
certificate to prove I am a trained nurse. Without one I shall have
a hard time to get established; people and doctors both require some
proof of one's proficiency. So I have been trying to get into the only
training school that there is in Frisco. I cannot enter now but I
have a promise from the Board of Directors that in the spring they will
admit me on probation. And if the term is pass satisfactory that they
will give me a chance to take the two year course. They were willing
to take me this month but the nurses of whom they are eight would not
work with a colored person. As there accommodations are small they
could not at present accommodate me under the existing unpleasantness
of the nurses. But in the spring their new building will be complete
and there will be other changes made which will render it more to my
advantage to be admitted. In the mean time the ladies interested will
try to keep me employed as best they can until the time comes for me to
be admitted. If I succeed and get in training I want Harry to return
to Plainfield and stay with his grandmother until I come out which will
be at the end of two years. Then my mind will be at rest concerning
him and I shall be better able to attend to the duties required of
me.... Now don't fash yourself.... and when I write and tell you I
am coming back it will be time enough to believe it.

                 From

                 Pauline

Appendix C

The Incorporation and Bylaws of the NACGN, Revised 1933–1939

ARTICLES OF

INCORPORATION

AND BY-LAWS

NATIONAL ASSOCIATION

OF

COLORED GRADUATE NURSES

ARTICLES OF INCORPORATION

and

By-Laws

National Association

of

Colored Graduate Nurses

Organized in New York

August, 1908

By Martha M. Franklin, R. N.

Incorporated January 10th, 1920 under
the Laws of the State of New York
Revised 1088

CERTIFICATE OF INCORPORATION

We, the undersigned, residents of the State of New York, desiring to form a membership corporation pursuant to and in conformity with the laws of the State of New York, do hereby certify as follows:

1.   The name or title by which this Society shall be known is the National Association of Colored Graduate Nurses.

2.   The term for which it is organized is perpetual.

3.   The purposes of this corporation shall be to promote the professional and education advancement of nurses in every proper way; to elevate the standard of nursing education; to establish and maintain a code of ethics among nurses; to own and control a permanent headquarters and all rights and property held by the National Association of Colored Graduate Nurses as a corporation duly incorporated under and by virtue of the laws of the State of New York.

3

4.   The territory in which the operations of said corporation are to be principally conducted is the Borough of Manhattan, City and County of N. Y., but that said Association will meet from time to time in the various cities of the United States, which may be determined upon at the annual meetings.

5.   That the annual meeting of said corporation shall be held on the third Tuesday of the month of August, in each and every year.

6.   That the number of directors of said corporation shall be sixteen.

In witness whereof the undersigned residents of the State of New York have hereunto set our hands and seals this 10th day of January, 1920.

ADAH B. THOMS
JULIA B. PHILLIPS
JESSIE F. SAMPSON
OCTAVIA WATERS
MADGE H. HAGERMAN

Personally appeared before me a Notary Public, Adah B. Thoms, Julia Phillips, Jessie Sampson, Madge Hagerman and Octavia Waters, to me personally known to be the

4

individuals who signed the foregoing and annexed certificate of incorporation and acknowledged the same to be their act and deed.

Given under my hand and notorial seal this 10th day of January, 1920.

> (Signed) PHILLIP WEINRIB,
> Notary Public

Commission expires March 30, 1920

★★★★★★★

BY-LAWS

ARTICLE I.

Membership in this Association shall consist of the members in good standing in their Alumnae Associations, such members being graduates of training schools connected with general hospitals giving a continuous training in hospital of not less than three years

5

The school must be registered in its own state. This training must include practical experience in caring for men, women, and children, together with theoretical and practical instruction in medical, surgical, obstetrical and children's nursing. In those states where nurse practical laws have been secured registration shall be an additional qualification.

All applications for membership shall be filled by the applicant, signed by the President, and Secretary of the Alumnae Association and referred to the Membership Committee. Upon favorable report of this committee, the applicant may be elected by the Association at a regular meeting, or by the Executive Board at any meeting thereof.

ARTICLE II.

The officers of the Association shall consist of a resident, First Vice President, Second Vice President, Recording Secretary, Corresponding Secretary, Financial Secretary, Treasurer, Executive Board, Chaplain and chairman of all Standing Committees.

6

ARTICLE III.

Section 1. The officers shall be elected yearly by ballot at the annual meeting, and shall hold office until the adjournment of the next annual meeting or until their successors are chosen.

Section 2. A member is eligible to office who has been a member of the Association for one year.

Section 3. Vacancies occurring in any elective office shall be filled for the unexpired term by the majority vote of the Executive Board.

Section 4. A majority vote of those present entitled to vote, and voting, shall constitute an election.

Section 5. On the first day of the convention the President shall appoint inspectors of election and tellers.

Section 6. The Secretary shall furnish to the chairman of the tellers, not less than two hours before the opening of the polls, a list of the members present.

Section 7. The teller in charge of the register shall check the names of the members voting.

7

Section 8. The teller in charge of the ballot box shall place her official mark upon the back of the ballot and the voters shall then deposit the ballot.

Section 9. Polls shall be open for such a period of time as shall be specified by the Board of Directors.

Section 10. Each officer shall hold office until the adjournment of the annual convention following that of her election.

Section 11. In case of a vacancy in any office, the Executive Board shall appoint a member to serve until her successor is elected.

ARTICLE IV.

Duties of Officers

Section 1. The President shall preside at all meetings of the Association and perform all duties incident to her office. She shall be President of the Board of Directors, and an ex-officio member of all committees. In the absence of the President, the Vice Presidents in their order, shall preside, and have the same powers and perform all the duties of the President.

8

Section 2. The Recording Secretary shall keep the minutes of all meetings of the Association and the Executive Board, preserve all papers, letters and transactions of the Association. She shall render a full report at the annual meeting.

The Corresponding Secretary shall notify members of all meetings and shall send notices to all Superintendents of Training Schools and all graduate nurses three months before the annual meeting. She shall keep a report of all letters and notices sent out during the year and present a written report at the annual meeting.

Section 3. The Financial Secretary shall receive all moneys and take account thereof; and shall then turn such moneys and a report to the treasurer of the organization.

Section 4. The Treasurer shall receive and have charge of all funds in a bank designated by the Executive Board, shall pay such bills only as shall have been approved by the President and Secretary. She shall have custody of the official seal, which shall be affixed to all bills and receipts of the Association. She shall report the financial standing of the Association, whenever requested by the Executive Board. She shall

9

give bond subject to the approval of the Board of Directors. She shall deposit all money amounting to over $25.00. The nurces' club fund shall be deposited independent of the other money of the Association. The Treasurer shall sign membership tickets upon receipt of dues and notify members when in arrears.

Section 5. The books shall be audited on the third day of the annual meeting and a report of the same shall be presented to the Association.

Section 6. All retiring officers shall on the expiration of their terms surrender all property, books and papers belonging to their office to their successors within one month after the close of the annual meeting.

ARTICLE V.

The Executive Board

Section 1. There shall be an Executive Board of fifteen members, consisting of the President, First Vice and Second Vice Presidents, Recording, Corresponding and Financial Secretaries, Treasurer, Chaplain and chairman of all standing committees and

10

three floor members, appointed by the President and elected by the National Association to serve one year.

Section 2. The President shall be ex-officio chairman of the Executive Board.

Section 3. The Executive Board shall keep a constant supervision over the affairs of the Association, devise and mature plans for its growth and prosperity, and have general control of its property and affairs.

Section 4. The Executive Board shall hold an annual meeting on the same day as the annual meeting of the Association.

Section 5. Stated meetings of the Executive Board shall be held at any time upon written application of five of the Board addressed to the President.

Section 6. Five members of the Executive Board shall constitute a quorum for the transaction of business.

Section 7. The Executive Board shall make all arrangements for the meetings of the Association, appointing such auxiliary committees from its own body, or from other members of the Association and making

11

such other provisions as shall be requisite.

Section 8.   The Executive Board   shall hold a meeting at 8.00 P. M. on the Monday night previous to the first day of the annual meeting.

ARTICLE VI.

Section 1.   Application blanks must be accompanied by $5.00 of which $3.00 is joining fee and $2.00 for first year's dues.

Section 2.   Annual dues $2.00 shall be paid in advance on or before the close of the annual meeting for the following year.

Section 3.   Nurses having forfeited their membership by non-payment of dues may be reinstated by payment of $3.00 to rejoin.

They may have the right to vote—but they cannot have the privilege of holding office until they have been in the organization one year.

ARTICLE VII.

Resignations

Members in good standing wishing to withdraw from the association shall send a written resignation to the Corresponding Secretary, to be read and acted upon at the next annual meeting.

ARTICLE VIII.

Meetings

Section 1. The annual meetings of this Association shall be held the third Tuesday in August. The time of meeting is subject to change only by decision of the Executive Board. Printed notices of the meetings shall be sent by the Corresponding Secretary to each member of the Association and to each Superintendent of training schools throughout the country at least three months previous to the date of meeting. The chairman of the Printing Committee shall have printed upon the fly leaf of the envelope the dates and place of meeting. The entire morning session of the first day (Tuesday) is to be given over to the Executive Business and Registration. The afternoon session is to be open to nurses only.

The first public meeting is to be held at 8.30 on the evening of the first day (Tuesday).

13

There shall be, during Wednesday and Thursday of the annual meeting an Institute which shall consist of lectures and group conferences on subjects of nursing and such subjects co-related to nursing as are of benefit to the organization or individuals of the organization.

The fourth day (Friday) is to be given over for unfinished business (closed meeting). All members must present their bills to the Association during Wednesday and Thursday during the session.

Section 2. Fifteen members shall constitute a quorum for the transaction of business at any regular meeting of the Association.

Section 3. The order of exercises at each annual meeting of the Association shall be in accordance with the program submitted, including:

1. Registration
2. Call to order.
3. Invocation.
4. National Anthem.
5. Roll Call.

14

6. Annual Reports.
   a—Recording Secretary, minutes.
   b—Corresponding Secretary.
   c—Financial Secretary.
   d—Treasurer.
   e—Auditor
   f—Standing Committees.

7. Miscellaneous Business.
8. Address of President.
9. Election of Officers.
10. Adjournment.

ARTICLE IX.

The Official Organ

Section 1. The official organ of the National Association of Colored Graduate Nurses shall be known as "The National News Bulletin." Subscription $1.00 a year.

ARTICLE X.

Standing and Special Committees

Section 1. The following standing committees consisting of three members each,

15

shall be appointed annually:— Membership. Printing, Auditing, and Ways and Means Committees. , The chairman of each committee shall be appointed by the President and shall choose her associates to assist in the work devolving upon each of them.

Section 2. A special committee (Publicity) shall be appointed by the President.

ARTICLE XI.

Amendments

These By-Laws may be amended by a two-thirds vote of the members present at any regular meeting, provided such proposal has been submitted in writing at a previous meeting or a due notice shall have been mailed to each member by the Corresponding Secretary.

ARTICLE XII.

All members of this Association shall be governed by Parliamentary Usage of Women's Clubs, by Mrs. Emma A. Fox.

16

Organized in New York

August, 1908

By MARTHA M. FRANKLIN, R. N.

Incorporated January 10th, 1920 under
the Laws of the State of New York
Revised 1939.

BY-LAWS

ARTICLE I

MEMBERSHIP

SECTION 1.—Classes of Memberships.

There shall be four classes of membership in this association, i. e. Nurse — Associate Nurse — Lay and Honorary.

SECTION 2.—Nurse.

Nurse members shall be those registered nurses who have graduated from an accredited school of nursing offering at least a three year course of instruction. This school shall be connected with a general hospital having a daily average of at least 50 patients. This course of instruction shall include practical experience in caring for men, women, and children together with the theoretical and practical instruction in medical, surgical, obstetrical and pediatric nursing.

SECTION 3.—Associate Nurse.

Associate nurse members shall be those graduate nurses not eligible for individual nurse membership who may be admitted as associate members upon the approval of the Membership Committee.

SECTION 4.—Lay Members.

Lay members shall be those individuals interested in the promotion and welfare of nursing and Negro nurses.

SECTION 5.—Honorary.

Honorary members shall be recommended by the Board of Directors and conferred

3

unanimously at the Bi-ennial Convention on those individuals who have rendered outstanding service to this association or to Negro nurses. Only two persons may be presented for Honorary membership at any one convention.

SECTION 6.—*Application for Membership.*

Application for membership must be made on a blank furnished by this Association, and must be accompanied by dues. All applications shall be submitted to the Chairman of the Membership Committee. On approval of this committee, the applicant shall be accepted and a record forwarded to the office of the Association.

ARTICLE II

BOARD OF DIRECTORS

SECTION 1.—*Number.*

The directors of this corporation shall be seven (7) officers to wit being; the president, first vice-president, second vice-president, recording secretary, financial secretary, treasurer, and executive secretary; all regional presidents, the chairmen of committees and four floor members.

SECTION 2.—*Terms of Office.*

Members of the Board of Directors shall be elected as follows:

The directors who are officers shall be elected at the Bi-ennial Meeting and shall hold office on the Board until their successors are elected. The Regional presidents and floor members are to be elected by their region prior to the Bi-ennial Meeting of the National Association, and they are to serve until their successors are elected.

4

SECTION 3.—*Powers.*

All powers of this corporation are vested in and shall be exercised by the Board of Directors unless otherwise prescribed by statutes or by the certificate of incorporation.

SECTION 4.—*Meetings.*

Regular meetings of the Board of Directors shall be held immediately preceding and following the Bi-ennial Convention at a time decided upon by the majority of the members of the Board.

SECTION 5.—*Special Meetings.*

Special meetings should be held in the interval between conventions either by correspondence or in person if finances permit.

SECTION 6.—*Place of Meeting.*

The Board of Directors may hold its meetings both regular and special at a place within or without the State of New York as the Board may from time to time determine.

SECTION 7.—*Notice of Meetings.*

The executive secretary shall give notice of all meetings of the Board of Directors, stating the purpose of the meeting to each member of the Board of Directors by mail at her last known address as appears on the records of this association. Notices shall be mailed not later than two weeks before each meeting.

SECTION 8.—*Quorum.*

Seven members of the Board of Directors shall constitute a Quorum at all meetings.

5

SECTION 9.—*Duties.*

The Board of Directors shall provide for the maintenance of the National Headquarters which is to be the center of all activities of the association. Shall appoint an executive secretary, fix her compensation and define her duties.

Select a place of deposit for all funds of the corporation and provide for their investment.

Give a report of the work of the association to the members at each Bi-ennial Convention.

Shall provide for the auditing of the association's books in the regular way; i. e., by a certified public accountant.

SECTION 10.—A member of the Board shall not incur any expense for this association without the approval of the majority of the Board of Directors.

ARTICLE III

OFFICERS

SECTION 1.—*Number of Officers.*

The officers of this association shall be a president, first vice-president, second vice-president, recording secretary, financial secretary, treasurer and executive secretary.

SECTION 2.—The officers shall be elected by ballot at the Bi-ennial Meeting and shall hold office for not less than two years except the Executive Secretary who shall be appointed by the Board of Directors.

SECTION 3.—No members are eligible to serve as officers who have not been a member of this association for one year.

6

SECTION 4.—Should a vacancy occur in the office of president, the first vice-president shall succeed her until the Bi-ennial election. The second vice-president succeeding the first vice-president. A vacancy occurring in any other office shall be filled by appointment by the Board of Directors.

SECTION 5.— Necessary expense incurred by the officers in the service of the association may be refunded from the general treasury by order of the Board of Directors.

SECTION 6.—All retiring officers shall on the expiration of their term surrender all property, books and papers belonging to their office, to their successors within one month after the close of the Bi-ennial meeting.

SECTION 7.—One half of the mileage of the Bi-ennial Convention shall be paid by this association for the following officers:

President, Recording Secretary, Financial Secretary, Treasurer and Executive Secretary.

ARTICLE IV

DUTIES OF OFFICERS

SECTION 1.—*President.*

The president shall preside at all meetings of the association and at all meetings of the Board of Directors. She shall be a member ex-officio of all committees. She shall exercise, subject to the control of the Board of Directors a general supervision over the officers of the organization. She shall sign or counter sign all certificates, contracts and all other instruments of the organization and shall perform such other duties as are incident to her office, or that may be assigned to her from time to time by the Board of Directors.

7

SECTION 2.—*Vice-presidents.*

The vice-presidents shall perform the duties of the president in her absence or during her inability to serve.

SECTION 3.—*Recording Secretary.*

The Recording Secretary shall keep the minutes of all meetings of this association and of the Board of Directors. She shall pass on to Headquarters for preservation all papers, letters and transactions of the association. She shall deliver to her successor within one month after the close of the Bi-ennial Meeting all association property in her possession.

SECTION 4.—*Financial Secretary.*

The Financial Secretary shall receive all moneys and take account thereof, and shall forward such moneys and a report to the treasurer of the organization. Also, make report of the financial status of the association at the Bi-ennial Convention.

SECTION 5.—*Treasurer.*

The treasurer shall collect, receive and have charge of all funds and securities of this association; shall deposit such funds in a bank designated by the Board of Directors and pay such bills only as shall have been approved by the president or her accredited representative. She shall have custody of the Corporate seal. She shall keep full and accurate account of all the association's business and shall report to the Board of Directors the financial standing of the association at each Bi-ennial Convention. She shall be bonded for the performance of her duties by the association. Her signature shall appear on all membership cards. She shall deliver to her successor within one month after the close of the Bi-ennial meeting all money

8

vouchers, books and papers of the association in her custody with a supplemental report covering all transactions to the close of the Bi-ennial meeting.

SECTION 6.—*Executive Secretary.*

The duties of the executive secretary as defined by the Board of Directors shall be:

1. Conduct an information service for the association at headquarters.
2. Release publicity for the association.
3. Assist the editorial committee in publishing the Bulletin, which is the official organ of the association.
4. She shall make field visits as the organization's time permits.
5. She shall coordinate the activities of the association.

SECTION 7.—*Regional Presidents.*

The Regional Presidents shall be expected to inform the president and headquarters of all local or state-associations in her region. She shall plan and conduct with the president of the association or her representative an Annual Conference for her region.

ARTICLE V

VOTING

SECTION 1. — All elections shall be by ballot.

SECTION 2.—The majority of those present entitled to vote, and voting shall constitute an election.

SECTION 3.—On the first day of the Convention, the president shall appoint inspectors of elections and tellers.

9

SECTION 4—The treasurer shall furnish to the chairman of the tellers not less than two hours before the opening of the polls a list of the delegates entitled to vote.

SECTION 5—All delegates not entitled to vote shall not be permitted to enter the polls.

SECTION 6. — No delegates shall be permitted to enter or leave the polls while the members are voting.

SECTION 7.—Adequate tellers shall be provided for the conduct of the polls—ratio of one teller to twenty delegates.

ARTICLE VI

MEMBERSHIP AND DUES

SECTION 1.—Membership fee in this association shall be $3.00 for nurse and associate nurse members.

ARTICLE VI

SECTION 6.—Nurses who forfeit their membership by non-payment of dues for two years may be reinstated by paying current dues. ($3.00).

They may have the privilege of voting, but may not hold office until one year after reinstatement.

ARTICLE VII

SECTIONS

SECTION 1.—The Board of Directors shall authorize the development of sections representing the different phases of nursing also

10

of the lay members interested in the welfare of and promotion of the nursing profession.

SECTION 2.—Sections shall have no legislative or administrative function but shall be discussion and recommendation groups.

SECTION 3. — The officers of the sections shall be a chairman, vice-chairman and secretary.

SECTION 4.—Each section may make rules for its conduct of business which shall in no way conflict with the by-laws of this association.

ARTICLE VIII

MEETINGS

SECTION 1.—*Bi-ennial Convention.*

This association shall hold a Bi-ennial Convention at such time and place as determined upon by the members for the purpose of electing officers and members of the Board of Directors also to conduct such other business as may be brought before the convention.

SECTION 2.—*Special Meetings.*

Special meetings of the members shall be called by the Executive Secretary upon request of the president or the majority of the Board of Directors, or upon the written request of the financial members representing one-third of the different states in our membership. No business other than that specified in the call thereof or matters relating thereto, shall be considered at a special meeting.

SECTION 3.—*Notices.*

Notices of the Bi-ennial Convention and of any special meeting or any other meeting provided for by the laws of the State of New

11

SECTION 7.—*Order of Business at Meeting*

The order of business at the Bi-ennial Convention of this association shall be registration, invocation, Nurses National Anthem (by Adah B. Thoms).

Roll Call — Reading of the minutes.

Bi-ennial reports:

Officers	Regional Presidents
Organizations	Standing Committees

Auditors report.

Address of the president.

Miscellaneous business.

Report of tellers.

Adjournment.

ARTICLE IX

OFFICIAL ORGAN

SECTION 1.—The official organ of this association shall be known as the National News Bulletin.

SECTION 2. — This Bulletin shall be published quarterly from the headquarters of this association by an editorial committee composed of members representing the various regions.

ARTICLE X

STANDING COMMITTEES

SECTION 1.—Standing Committees shall be appointed Bi-ennially at the time of or following the Convention.

13

SECTION 7.—*Order of Business at Meeting*

The order of business at the Bi-ennial Convention of this association shall be registration, invocation, Nurses National Anthem (by Adah B. Thoms).

Roll Call — Reading of the minutes.

Bi-ennial reports:

Officers	Regional Presidents
Organizations	Standing Committees

Auditors report.

Address of the president.

Miscellaneous business.

Report of tellers.

Adjournment.

ARTICLE IX

OFFICIAL ORGAN

SECTION 1.—The official organ of this association shall be known as the National News Bulletin.

SECTION 2. — This Bulletin shall be published quarterly from the headquarters of this association by an editorial committee composed of members representing the various regions.

ARTICLE X

STANDING COMMITTEES

SECTION 1.—Standing Committees shall be appointed Bi-ennially at the time of or following the Convention.

13

SECTION 2. — Standing Committees shall consist of:

Committee on Membership

Committee on Education

Committee on Finance

Committee on Nominations

SECTION 3.—The Committee on Membership shall consist of five members appointed by the president. This committee shall investigate the eligibility of all classes of members applying to this association. It shall report its findings to the Board of Directors whose decision shall be final.

' SECTION 4.—The Committee on Nominations shall consist of five members; four to be elected at the Regional Conventions and a chairman who is to be elected at the Biennial Convention. The duty of this committee is to nominate candidates for the Board of Directors and all elective offices. The report of the committee shall be filed with the secretary at least six weeks before the convention, and shall be sent to all members of the organization with notice of such convention at least one month before the convention.

SECTION 5.—The Nominating Committee shall request from member organizations the names of persons eligible to hold office. No name shall be presented to the convention unless the nominee has consented to serve if elected.

SECTION 6.—The Finance Committee shall consist of five members appointed by the president and shall plan the budget with the Board of Directors and devise ways and means of raising all finances of this association.

14

SECTION 7. — The Education Committee shall consist of five members appointed by the president and shall plan and develop educational projects for the association.

ARTICLE XI

AMENDMENTS

SECTION 1.—These by-laws may be amended by a two-thirds vote of the members present at any regular meeting, provided such proposal has been submitted in writing at a previous meeting or due notice shall have been mailed to each member by the corresponding secretary.

ARTICLE XII

Deliberations at all meetings of this association shall be governed by PARLIAMENTARY USAGES of WOMEN'S CLUBS by Emma Fox.

Excerpts from A Study of the Present Status of *The Negro Woman* in Nursing, 1925, by Ethel Johns

Factors affecting the general situation

Race Conflict. If the influence of race conflict could be eliminated from the situation the problem of the negro nurse would not differ greatly from that of the relatively inferior type of white nurse, and a common solution might possibly be found for both. At present this is far from being the case. As a matter of fact there are certain definite disabilities arising directly out of the racial conflict which bear heavily upon the negro nurse throughout her training and afterwards in the practice of her profession. The degree of disability varies greatly according to the part of the country she lives in but there is no part where she is free to practice on a basis of absolute equality. No matter how high her personal and professional qualifications may be, certain doors remain closed to her (p. 6).

In practically all of the southern states the negro public health nurse is paid a lower salary though she performs the same duties as the white nurse. The claim made that her living expenses are proportionately less is not always sustained by the facts. Furthermore the two groups are socially distinct and there is no bridging of the gaps in the north. How extraordinarily embarrassing, these social restrictions can be I did not realize until I went south. It was occasionally necessary for me to remain all day at a colored hospital. A meal would be served to me alone in a private room. I could not ask the colored superintendent of nurses in a recognized government institution to take lunch with me at the hotel. A colored public health nurse who showed me her district had to sit at the back of the street car while I "took the front." These circumstances were humiliating to me as a professional woman and yet all had unwillingly to acknowledge the heart-breaking difficulty and complexity of the social situation from which they arise (p. 8).

Professional Relationships. White physicians approve of the negro nurse in private duty, but do not take her seriously in an executive capacity either in hospitals or in the public health field. Colored physicians of the inferior type are inclined to treat the negro nurse with arrogance and discourtesy, but the more outstanding men recognize her value and are willing to help her.

The attitude of the white nurses is sympathetic so long as there is no possibility of having to accept negro nurses as superior officers. In some parts of the south the white private duty nurse feels the competition of the colored nurse to be unfair because she accepts a lower fee and assumes domestic responsibility (p. 12).

Outlook for the Future

The rapid multiplication of inferior schools seems likely to continue and will be extremely difficult to check. One of the best means of doing so would be to strengthen the existing good schools and give prominence to their activities in negro newspapers and periodicals.

If women of a superior type are forthcoming it is probably that the demand for them in public health nursing activities will gradually increase. One reason why negro nurses are not more commonly employed is that most of those already in the field are obviously inferior and are fitted only for routine duties. Competent negro nurses would be invaluable in the control and direction of midwifery, which is just being inaugurated in the South.

Any attempt to force the services of negro nurses upon people who resent them is futile. It seems probable that for some years to come the negro nurse will find her fullest measure of opportunity among her own people (p. 12–13).

Original Announcement of the Establishment of the Mary Mahoney Medal

NATIONAL NEWS BULLETIN

THE MARY MAHONEY MEDAL

At the New Orleans Convention it was decided to present annually an award to be known as the Mary Mahoney Medal. This award is to be presented to a nurse who has made an outstanding contribution to nursing. She must be a member of the National Association of Colored Graduate Nurses.

The recommendation should state accurately the nurse's name and her address. It should describe in detail her accomplishments and the reason for selecting her.

Nominations must be submitted to National Headquarters, 50 West 50th Street, not later than August 1st.

Appendix F

Announcement of Medal Awarded to Adah Belle Samuels Thoms

MEDAL AWARDED TO MRS. ADAH B. THOMS

Because of her outstanding contribution to the field of nursing and her successful years as a graduate nurse, Mrs. Adah B. Thoms, R. N., 317 West 138th Street, New York City was selected as the first person to be awarded the Mary Mahoney Medal, which the National Association of Colored Graduate Nurses plans to award every year.

The medal commemorates the life of Mary Mahoney who was the first Negro woman to be graduated from a nursing school. Miss Mahoney was a personal friend of Mrs. Thoms. She was eulogized by Mrs. Thoms in her book "Pathfinders," a history of Negro nursing.

Dr. Louis T. Wright in presenting the medal to Mrs. Thoms said, "She is an institution and a symbol." Her untiring efforts in behalf of the National Association of Colored Graduate Nurses was largely responsible for its growth and development.

The medal committee decided that Mrs. Nancy L. Kemp of Philadelphia, a charter member of the association who has attended every meeting in the past thirty years should receive the medal in 1937. Miss Carrie E. Bullock of Chicago who founded the National News Bulletin and served as a former president of the association will receive the award in 1938.

The committee decided unanimously that until these outstanding women had received the award, other nominations would not be accepted.

Appendix G

A Christmas Letter from
Adah Belle Samuels Thoms

A CHRISTMAS LETTER
From Adah B. Thoms

At this season when all the world is thinking "Peace on earth and good will to all men," we pause to count our blessings and to give thanks to Him who is ever present. As I think back over the years I cannot remember one that has been more kind to me than 1936.

To you, my dear Nurses everywhere, I am sending my sincere thanks and best wishes for a very Merry Christmas and a Happy and successful New Year.

I shall always think of you and love you even more for the very great honor and for the words of appreciation that you expressed during our convention of the N. A. C. G. N. last August, when you presented me the Mary Mahoney Award. Not until then did I realize that I meant very much to you. The few little things that I have tried to do in the past came with the opportunity that I had always prayed would be mine, the opportunity that so

to have lived to see the fulfillment of that hope with the dawn of a new and brighter day for the young graduate.

I rejoice to note the continual growth of the N. A. C. G. N. under the leadership of our young and efficient president, Mrs. Estelle Massey Riddle and her officers. Yet I am not surprised at the progress made, knowing Mrs. Riddle as I do, and her progressive mind. For in addition to training and college work, Mrs. Riddle continued her nursing education at Columbia University and received the Masters Degree.

While there is little that I can do now, I can, and do pledge my full support throughout the remaining years.

I shall never forget the tribute paid me by our own Dr. Louis T. Wright, who presented me the Mary Mahoney Award at the 1936 annual convention.

Another memory which I am pleased to cherish, is my induction into the Lambda Pi Alpha Sorority.

Appendix H

National News Bulletin—The NACGN Pondered Their Future Direction

NEWS - LETTER

Published by: NATIONAL ASSOCIATION OF COLORED GRADUATE NURSES, Inc.
1790 Broadway, New York 19, N. Y.   Circle 5-8000

VOLUME 5 No. 1   MAY 1947

JUNE 15-21   1947

WHICH WAY N. A. C. G. N. ?

STABILIZING OUR BUDGET

EFFECT ON NEGRO NURSES
of The Structure Study

Membership and Participation in Professional Organizations

CONVENTION ISSUE

Appendix I

Telegram from the NACGN— National Headquarters Closes

National Association of Colored Graduate Nurses, Inc.

1790 Broadway   New York 19, N. Y.

Executive Secretary
Mrs. Alma Vessells, R.N.

March 16, 1951

FOR IMMEDIATE RELEASE

NATIONAL HEADQUARTERS CLOSES

The headquarters office of The National Association of Colored Graduate Nurses located at 1790 Broadway, New York City, was officially closed on March 15, 1951.

Mrs. Alma Vessells John, Executive Secretary, announced that all inquiries should be sent to The American Nurses Association located at, 2 Park Avenue, New York 15, New York.

The association takes this means of expressing its sincere appreciation to the thousands of citizens throughout the nation and the world who have given both moral and financial support to the program throughout the forty-two years of its existence.

APPENDIX CREDITS

Appendix A: Courtesy of the Trustees of the Boston Public Library.

Appendix B: From the Lyons-Williamson Collection, Schomburg Center for Research in Black Culture, The New York Public Library, New York.

Appendix C: Courtesy of Schomburg Center for Research in Black Culture, The New York Public Library, New York.

Appendix D: Courtesy of Rockefeller Archive Center.

Appendix E: Originally from *The National News Bulletin,* June 1936, Vol. 8, No. 11. Courtesy of Schomburg Center for Research in Black Culture, The New York Public Library, New York.

Appendix F: From *The National News Bulletin,* October 1936, Vol. 9, No. 13. Courtesy of Schomburg Center for Research in Black Culture, The New York Public Library, New York.

Appendix G: From *The National News Bulletin,* December 1936, Vol. 9, No. 14. Courtesy of Schomburg Center for Research in Black Culture, The New York Public Library, New York.

Appendix H: From *The National News Bulletin,* 1947, Vol. 5, No. 1. Courtesy of Schomburg Center for Research in Black Culture, The New York Public Library, New York.

Appendix I: Courtesy of Schomburg Center for Research in Black Culture, The New York Public Library, New York.

Index

About the Author

Dr. Althea T. Davis holds degrees as a Practical Nurse, Wyckoff Heights School of Practical Nursing, R.N.-A.A.S., City University of New York (CUNY), New York City Technical College, B.S.N., CUNY, City College, M.A., M.Ed., Ed.D., Teachers College, Columbia University (Department of Nursing Education), C.N.P., State University of New York, Stonybrook, and George Washington University, DC.

Dr. Davis has practiced at every level of the nursing profession and has taught in both associate and baccalaureate degree nursing programs. As Associate Professor, she is an expert in nursing theory and practice and has received numerous awards as a Role Model Nursing Professor.

Dr. Davis has authored many historical articles and given professional presentations throughout the U.S. She has taught historical methodology and nursing history—making the past come alive, enlightening students to the possibilities in nursing research, and teaching inclusive nursing history about Black leaders in nursing, which so many nurses have never heard.

Dr. Davis is a Major in the US Army Corps and was called to active duty for Operation Desert Storm. She has an Affiliate Appointment as a Nurse Practitioner with Regular Practice Privileges at Fort Hamilton Army Base where she provides care for soldiers during Sick Call and appointments. In 1998, she performed a humanitarian military mission as a nurse practitioner working in the mountains of Honduras. Dr. Davis is the recipient of many military awards and also works in primary care in the Brooklyn community.

Dr. Davis is a member of several professional organizations, including the American Association for the History of Nursing, The Museum of Nursing History, and was previously Corresponding Secretary of The Society for Nursing History. Dr. Davis received the MABEL STAUPERS AWARD from CHI ETA PHI, Omicron and organizational service awards from the Association of Black Nursing Faculty. She is an Editorial Board member of the Journal of Cultural Diversity and member of the American Nurses Association and the National League for Nursing.

Dr. Davis is a Nurse Historian, Educator, Nurse Practitioner, an Officer and a Lady. The uniqueness of her broad background and experience make her eminently qualified to write this book. This excellent history of Early Black Leaders in Nursing, is a significant addition to American and women's history.